MW01442369

Contents

1.	SWAT Teams for Jesus	9
2.	Heaven Can Wait	27
3.	A Sex What?	33
4.	A Man or a Mouse?	45
5.	Mannequin Boy	55
6.	California Dreaming	69
7.	The Rapture	77
8.	Cults and Isms	85
9.	Seeing Isn't Believing	95
10.	Hollywood Harvest	101
11.	Heaven's Number One Salesman	111
12.	No Hope Street	119
13.	Exorcists and Flying Prophets	129
14.	California Adieu	139
15.	Walking Away	149

16. Undercover Capers	163
17. Jesus Doesn't Live Here Anymore	175
18. The Tupelo Ayatollah	189
19. Why Wasn't Jimmy Carter Reelected?	197
20. Meet the Media	205
21. Meet Morton Downey, Jr.	217
22. Sound Off	229
Epilogue	269
Reflections on Don Wildmon	273
Appendix A: Anatomy of a Small-town Crusader	285
Appendix B: Righteous Keating Plays the Name Game	291
Index	295

1

SWAT Teams for Jesus

During the 1980s, the failure of Pat Robertson's presidential bid, the collapse of Jerry Falwell's Moral Majority, and the downfall of several major TV evangelists caused most of us to breathe a collective sigh of relief. The radical religious right, which had been gaining momentum, finally seemed to be running out of steam. In the spring of 1990, religion writer Michael D'Antonio published a book titled *Fall From Grace—The Failed Crusade of the Christian Right*. He concluded: "With the demise of [Pat] Robertson's [presidential] campaign came the death of the Christian Right's political hopes. The born-again movement soon ceased to be a significant religious or social force as well."

But in fact, the Christian right itself has been quietly born again. It has reorganized, and is beginning to arise as a major religious and social force. These radicals have not, and will not, go away.

"By the end of the decade," exhorts Dallas evangelist Paul Cain, "the whole earth will view the church in a different light. The church will no longer be mocked and despised, but either loved or feared. . . ." Up-and-coming evangelist Roberts Liardon adds that during the 1990s, "We will be in an offensive position and no longer on the defense. . . ."

As we approach the year 2000 we can expect an unprecedented flurry of activity as Christian missionary and evangelistic groups pull out all the stops in an attempt to "bring in the harvest." These organizations have set an unusual goal for the year 2000: They aim to make one-half of the world Christian by then—as a birthday present for Jesus.

Millennial madness has its monetary value as well: according to the *New York Times,* sales of Bibles, prophecy books, and books warning of Armageddon soared after the August 1990 invasion of Kuwait. And, as we come closer to the year 2000, books purporting to predict what will happen in the coming century are selling at an increasingly brisk pace. All told, the Book Industry Study Group reports that total sales of religious books have grown from $537 million in 1985 to an estimated $784.1 million in 1990, and will likely top the $1 billion mark in 1994.

Militancy is the prevailing theme at many Christian conferences—this keeps the troops of believers in a state of alert. In August 1989, The Forceful Men organization held a "Take It by Force" conference in Phoenix, where they implored a crowd of 16,500 to "invade, conquer and possess the land" through Christian activism. One of the event's speakers, German evangelist Reinhard Bonnke, predicted that the nineties would be "the greatest soul-winning decade we've ever seen," and the organizers' call to "Prepare for war! Rouse the warriors!" stirred the huge crowd. At the "Militant Church Conference" in Tulsa the following October, believers were told to "be bold, full of authority—militant." In Florida that November, at the Orlando Christian Center near Walt Disney World, several thousand attendees were exhorted to engage in "hand-to-hand combat with the enemy."

While some of this millennial activity may appear to be almost *too* far on the fringe to warrant serious concern, closer inspection reveals three significant and disturbing trends which have taken firm hold in the new religious right. First, a broad doctrinal consensus has been reached in order to provide much-needed unity. Second, a dramatic shift in political focus has moved the new religious right's target from national politics to towns, cities, counties, and states. Third, the "troops" are now being recruited and trained. All of this is being accomplished through carefully planned organizing and networking, and carried out through a commitment to decisive action.

The goal of the radical religious right of the nineteen-eighties was to reconstruct American society according to the Bible. A term for this —Reconstructionism—has surfaced as a leading, across-the-board philosophy for the new religious right. While Reconstructionists do not agree on everything, a consensus has been reached on many social and moral issues; and many Christians, without their knowledge, are greatly influenced by Reconstructionist philosophy.

Tenets of this philosophy include: God's law, as revealed in the Bible, should govern every area of life; local government should rule; prisons could virtually be closed if serious offenders were executed, and if less serious criminals worked to make restitution for their crimes; capital offenses, requiring the death penalty, should include unrepentant homosexuality, abortion, and adultery; pornography in any form should be eliminated; schools should be run by churches, and property taxes should be abolished; husbands should be the heads of the household, and women and children should be subservient.

Pat Robertson revealed the influence of the Reconstructionist mindset on his own thinking when he predicted the time when Christians will take dominion over society. In December 1984, he told an audience at evangelist Robert Tilton's Word of Faith World Outreach Center in Dallas, what he sees down the road.

> [T]he church members have taken dominion over the forces of the world . . . there are no more abortions . . . education is going to be in the hands of the godly people . . . prisons will be virtually empty . . . pornographers no longer have any access to the public whatsoever, where there is no more of that stuff on our newsstands or any place else.

The Rev. Leonard Coppes is pastor of the Providence Church of Denver, Colorado, and his 100 member church is part of the Orthodox Presbyterian sect, a group of 180 churches spread across the country. Coppes, a soft-spoken man, is an avowed Reconstructionist. I spoke to him by phone about some of the more shocking aspects of Reconstructionism. I asked Pastor Coppes if he agreed that homosexuality and abortion should be punishable by death. Coppes replied at once:

> Both of those I would agree with. The question is who is going to set the law system? I think God should set the law system, not man. Those laws that define the seriousness of a crime, and are rooted in the moral nature of God, are still binding on us. If they [homosexuals] don't repent, the Bible says that they ought to be put to death. It's just a matter of what God says.
>
> In our humanistic society, there's no attempt to separate them

[homosexuals] so that they can't infect others. Homosexuals are given a free reign.

With reference to abortionists, if abortion is murder—and I believe it is—the penalty for murder from almost any evangelical theology is death.

Believers have to stand for what they believe is right. We're commanded in the Scripture to pray that God's kingdom would come on earth as it is in heaven. And that's my prayer. What we pray for, surely, we're commanded to work for.

He added that Christians are "not to take up arms against the state, unless they get to the point of where it's like it was in Germany. We struggle with that, many of us, because if abortion is murder, there are more people being put to death by our society than there was [sic] by the German society. It's a difficult struggle to know just what to do. To me, it's a horrendous crime."

Rousas John Rushdoony, a former Presbyterian minister, is generally considered the father of Reconstructionism. Since 1964, the seventy-four-year-old minister has quietly devoted his energies to research, writing, and promoting Christian Reconstructionism. Rushdoony's small organization, Chalcedon, has disproportionately affected American Christianity.

Born-again Christian activism has not realized its political potential because of its lack of unity and organization. While many doctrinal disputes will never be resolved, a confederation of new religious right leaders have made an important and enormous step in this direction. And it has gone almost unnoticed.

Since 1986, the California-based Coalition On Revival (COR) has labored with little or no publicity. Its elusive founder and National Director is Jay Grimstead. Grimstead, professorial in appearance, is an acccomplished, dynamic networker. COR advances its purposes within a close-knit alliance of new religious right leaders who direct geographical "regions" and "spheres" of influence. Its steering committee of 112 well-known Christian leaders (including the American Family Association's Rev. Donald Wildmon) is a virtual *Who's Who* of the born-again movement. They represent millions of American Christians, and, collectively, they wield more power than any single Christian group in the country.

All COR members sign a pledge in which they vow to work toward

Christianizing America, and ultimately the world. Their covenant with God, and with one another, binds them "to live in obedience to the Bible until they die."

COR's National Director, Jay Grimstead, carefully explained to me what COR is all about, and as he spoke, a grim, frightening outlook unfolded.

First, he explained, "COR creates documents that provide the philosophical foundation for action." He went on to say that there are ". . . a number of items that we think ought to happen. And one of them is political involvement. And one is educational involvement. And that the Founding Fathers in our Constitution said that there are supposed to be well-regulated militias locally."

Grimstead contends that Christians should be at the helm of these "spheres." My surprise may have registered with him when he mentioned "well-regulated militias locally," because he quickly added, "We don't have any dreams or plans of organizing militias. That's for the county to do, and the state to do."

However, Grimstead maintains that Christians should be at the helm of these "spheres." When I asked if that means Christians should have control over county governments, he stated: "Well, here's what we believe: We believe that God has given the Bible as a rule book for all society, Christian and non-Christian alike. And Christians who believe the Bible . . . are to influence government and get people elected, and encourage people to vote the right way—there being a right way and a wrong way, and there being right candidates and wrong candidates."

On the critical matter of Reconstructionism, Grimstead said, "I concur with most of the Reconstructionist matters; and I am trying to help rebuild the society on the Word of God, and loosely, that would be a Reconstructionist orientation in anybody's book."

And how would the Reconstructionist banner be carried into the nineteen-nineties and beyond? Grimstead replied, "There's a very definite conservative swing in the American population . . . a move back to old American traditional values. A number of us believe the Holy Spirit of God is getting active in a way that he wasn't before 1980. So, from 1980 to 1990, we saw a great proliferation of movements, and organizations, and newsletters, and activists, and so on. And that's just kind of beginning."

He continued, "We now think that the church is beginning to

awaken. I would guess that maybe as much as 5 percent of the Bible-believing body of Christ is awake. . . . The rest are pretty much asleep and content with small goals."

Excitedly, COR's director went on, "Now, a bunch of us think we're awake, and are trying to awaken the church to do the whole job, which includes not only saving souls, and keeping people pure and getting them mature personally, but to take our salt and light and be God's hands and feet; to affect with the biblical message of reality, and justice, and truth, law, government, economics, education, obedience, science, the arts, and general culture." [By "salt and light," Grimstead is referring to the biblical tenet that Christians are the "salt of the earth" and "the light of the world."]

"Is there any truth," I interrupted, "that you have targeted Orange County and Santa Clara County . . ."

"That's true," Grimstead interjected. "Those are two targets."

"They're big counties," I noted. "It doesn't seem like a group like yours, for instance—I don't know how large your group is—but, that you could have any effect in large areas like that."

Grimstead acted like it was a piece of cake.

"Well, we think it's going to be pretty easy, actually," he said. "Here's the plan that's written out for many to see. Essentially, we're saying Christians must become good Americans after they become good Christians . . . then start informing themselves, and then voting and running for office."

Grimstead continued detailing the strategy. "For example, in Santa Clara County there are about 14 cities, including San Jose, the big city. We think it's very possible, by the year 2000, to have Christians—mature, biblically literate—gain the majority of seats in all the city councils in our county. Plus, the Board of County Supervisors." He added, "That's one step, the political scene. That'll be the easiest."

"It's just organization," he continued. "And the facts are, we have enough Christians to totally, politically, by vote, overpower any other groups of minorities, if we would just do it. We have the majority vote. We are the largest minority."

"And most Christians," he continued, "like I, twelve years ago, didn't believe we should take the trouble to be the salt and light to anything other than individual hearts. We didn't know we were supposed to be salt and light to city government, and the law courts, and the educational institutions, and the *San Jose Mercury*, and Orange County, and so on. We didn't know we were supposed to do that. Now we believe we know that. And now we're going to go and do something about it, by God's grace."

"If you had that kind of authority in a county government," I asked, "there are a lot of county laws that could be changed and affected to meet your agenda."

"Exactly," he confirmed.

"Earlier," I said, "you mentioned local, or county militias. I've heard of state militias before, but I've never heard of a county militia. Is that just a figure of speech, or something that's . . .

"Well," he interrupted, "it's our understanding that both the county and the state were supposed to have that, that the state ones were organized by counties. In other words, local government with force."

"Would that be like a police force?" I asked.

"Yeah, a police force, and sheriff's department," he confirmed.

"A city in northern California," I said, "had a gay rights referendum that was defeated, and a minister got elected to the city council, because the Christians organized . . ."

"Yes, in Concord," he shot in.

"Some," I said, "have expressed concern about the Reconstructionist viewpoint of the death penalty for homosexuals and for abortionists. How do you feel about that?"

"Well, the Bible had something like eleven reasons for capital punishment. And murder was one. And homosexuality, and rape, and kidnapping were some others. Personally, where we are right now, all we can get consensus on among ourselves is the death penalty for murder.

"In general, we have great monolithic consensus on a list of them. The actual punishments we don't have agreement on, but we think that homosexuality, and abortion, and pornography should be outlawed. I noticed," he said with glee, "in China, having pornography is now a capital offense."

I interjected, "By pornography being outlawed, what do you mean? *Playboy, Penthouse,* soft-core . . ."

"Yeah, I mean that too. I mean, that's how it ought to be. Eliminated."

"If you had the kind of strength in Orange County and Santa Clara County that you want," I said, "you'd also be very strong in the whole state of California . . ."

"Yes, in fact," he replied, "California—I can tell you—it is the goal of a number of us to try to Christianize the state of California. That includes San Francisco."

I spoke, "I'm sure you're networking with other groups around the country . . . "

"We're really a networking group," he said. "In fact, we're very small. We have an impressive list of steering committee members, but we're really a very small operation. What we are is a networking, philosophical group. So, we write things that other men put into practice. We network people to come together to work on common goals."

"So," again I asked, "you must be networking across the country."

"Yes. That's right," Grimstead replied.

When I asked him about church/state separation, he fed me a line meant to deceive any non-thinker.

"Well, here's the deal," he said. "The church is not supposed to try to take over the government of San Jose. The people who take over the government of San Jose are American citizens who happen to be informed by the Bible on what is justice, and what is injustice. That's the difference; see what I mean?"

"How would you define the church then?" I asked.

"Well, the church is made up of individuals, but it is an entity, it is an organization, and it has its own task as an organizational entity which is separate of the state. The two are not to be blended."

I started to ask the obvious question, "So, in effect, the Bible acts as . . ."

"The Bible controls both church and state, yes. Now, that's what we're saying," he affirmed. "And so the Bible is the governing force," he continued, "in God's mind, over the church, and the governing force philosophically, as far as defining justice, for the state. That's what we're saying. Now, a lot of people hate that . . . [that] state officials, like our early Founding Fathers, and the people before them in the colonies, look to God and the Bible to govern their courts and legislation."

The Coalition on Revival is coordinating several Northern California groups to gear up for its grassroots political efforts. "We're just building them now. We're building the Bay Area Council of Pastors, and the different political networks in each of the 10 counties of the Bay Area." Moreover, Grimstead asserts that his organization is actively networking with other groups across the country "to come together to work on common goals."

Fred Clarkson, a Washington-based journalist, has written extensively on the Rev. Sun Myung Moon, the Unification Church, and other aspects of the religious right. He says that COR represents a serious threat:

> [They are] putting together a theological common ground—that's Reconstruction in flavor—with acceptable rhetoric . . . and detailing areas where everybody agrees to disagree, and avoid those areas—mostly areas of eschatology [the doctrines of the Second Coming, the Last Judgment, or the Resurrection of the dead]. That lets everyone agree to say, "let's do something about sin," so they can go out and fight pornography, elect candidates, and do all that kind of stuff, without having to worry about the specifics of exactly when or where Jesus is going to return. "In the meantime, we can do battle with Satan," they say.

Clarkson is also aware of the pledge that COR members sign. "It is absolutely true that everybody who is a member of COR must ascribe to these things and put their name to it," he says. And adds, "It's to the point where you can't get into COR meetings unless you sign those things. They're very closed door, very hush-hush."

I asked him, "Do you really think COR is a threat?"

"Oh, yeah!" he replied unhesitatingly. "They are what the new ideology of the religious right is; and it cuts across the Pentecostals and Fundamentalists." He was referring to the number of Falwell associates, and Robertson associates, who turn up at COR conferences and in COR literature.

Clarkson agrees that COR is a Reconstructionist front; a way of packaging theo-political ideas to do effective networking and political bridge building; to build a much more serious and permanent religious right political movement. He added:

> The numbers may not be large, as yet, but they don't have to be. Because if you develop an ideologically committed cadre of well-trained leadership, it doesn't matter what your numbers are, because you've got ministers of congregations. You have people who have a vision for the long haul.
>
> They're hot. They're hot, and absolutely serious, and I really believe they're going to be running a lot of candidates. And the extraordinary

thing is—yeah, there'll be a bunch of flakes—but they'll also have some serious contenders who will know how to package themselves to get some county council seats, local sheriffs, and that kind of stuff. I have no doubt about that; there are so few people who vote in those kinds of elections; you turn out a couple of churches full of people and away you go.

After the born-again industry scandals of the 1980s there was a temporary dip in giving. By and large, though, the money flow has remained remarkably steady.

In 1985, the National Religious Broadcasters (NRB) listed ninety-six Christian TV stations. At the end of 1989 it listed 336 Christian TV stations. From 1985 to 1989, the number of Christian radio stations rose from 1,043 to 1,485. According to the NRB, religious broadcasting is a $2 billion-a-year industry.

Evangelical and fundamentalist churches continue to grow at a rapid pace, while liberal churches decline. And money continues to pour into Christian organizations. According to the *World Christian Encyclopedia,* 54,000 people, worldwide, become Charismatic or Pentecostal each *day;* and Christian contributions, worldwide, total $693 billion annually.

Beverly LaHaye is a member of the COR's Steering Committee. She also heads the radical Concerned Women for America, a group which promotes the new religious right's agenda. Now ten years old, Concerned Women claims to have more than 600,000 members, making it the largest women's organization in America.

Like every group in the new religious right, Concerned Women has a detailed plan of action to achieve its agenda; and it, too, maintains that "This battle must be waged at the local level."

Concerned Women has developed its own "no-sex without marriage/hands off your own body" sex-education program. In a joint venture with Focus on the Family, they will work to place this curriculum in public schools.

LaHaye's group has effective chapters in every state, and additional political action groups in many metropolitan areas. Their political training seminars are sometimes referred to as "basic training/boot camps."

Local chapters conduct briefings on state issues, and hold meetings and receptions with state legislators. Colorado State Representative Kathi Williams called CWA "a powerful force at the Capitol." When I called her to verify that remark, she responded, "I don't *remember* making that quote, but I agree with it."

If the Supreme Court overturns its *Roe* v. *Wade* decision, the question of a woman's right to abortion will ultimately be decided in the various states. Concerned Women, and these other groups, intend to have a major impact on the issue. Pro-choice groups, such as the National Organization for Women, have neither the numbers, nor the infrastructure to compete with the new religious right.

"Prayer and action" serve well as the battle cry for Concerned Women and the other groups. The philosophy is that people will work for the agenda for which they pray. This is emphasized continually.

Concerned Women has four full-time attorneys. Their hands are full as they argue cases that affect their agenda across the country. Concerned Women attorney Michael Farris also serves on COR's steering committee.

LaHaye's group is hardly the only organization of the new religious right with an active legal staff. In fact, R. J. Rushdoony, the "father of Reconstructionism," is a former board member of The Rutherford Institute, a Christian legal organization he helped found. Attorney John Whitehead is the group's National Director—and a COR Steering Committee member.

In 1989 Rutherford handled some 190 cases, with several dozen currently pending. They specialize in "religious liberty" cases—that is, special privileges for Christians. Within the framework of the radical Christian right, "religious liberty" can include Sunday blue laws, prayers at public school graduations and sporting events, the teaching of creationism in public school science classes, placement of religious displays on public property, tax exemptions for churches and church-run businesses, and housing and employment discrimination against gay and unmarried couples who cohabitate. The Institute has prevailed in dozens of cases.

Focus on the Family is another highly organized, radical ministry. Headed by Christian psychologist Dr. James Dobson, this California-based organization employs 750 workers, and operates on a $60-million-a-year budget. With the aid of a $4 million private grant, Focus on the Family plans to relocate to Colorado Springs, Colorado, in the near future.

Dobson, too, is forming coalitions of radical Christian political special interest groups. Although not directly connected to COR, Focus on the Family networks with, and endorses, a number of COR-affiliates. "Once these coalitions are in place," Dobson says, "our state legislators will discover they can no longer write off the concerns of conservative Christian families."

To date, Focus on the Family has twenty state offices; each state group has its own distinctive name. In Pennsylvania, the group is called the Pennsylvania Family Institute.

I asked Michael Geer, President of the Pennsylvania Family Institute, about the notion that America's religious right had peaked in the nineteen-eighties and was now in decline. He replied, "I don't think that anybody thought that the time was up, that it was the end of an era or anything else. It is simply a logical progression."

He explained that the efforts of the religious right in the early 1980s helped elect Ronald Reagan and a Republican senate; and that they thought their goals would be accomplished as a result. Then the religious right began to realize that that was not sufficient; a lot of the policies that concerned them were policies that were made not at the federal level, but at the state and local level.

According to Geer, "People realized that the President didn't control what went on in Washington, with the separation of powers, etc." So, the new religious right is "just the logical continuation of the same idea, people being involved in their communities, people being involved in the political field, if you will, realizing that work needs to be done at the state level and local level."

The Pennsylvania Family Institute, according to Geer, helps Pennsylvanians understand the political process, presents the Christian right's agenda, and encourages citizens to take action.

Geer says that most people are well-attuned to what goes on in Washington; that is reported on their evening news and in the newspapers, but most people know very little about what goes on in their state capital. He worked for a TV station in Pittsburgh, an NBC affiliate, and says, "We very seldom reported what was going on in Harrisburg [the state capital]. And when we did report on it, it was usually an accomplished fact; you just tell people that this law was passed, or whatever." He said that doesn't get people involved in the process.

"What it basically comes down to, is that there are issues, whether it be education; whether they be obscenity issues; whether they be issues dealing with abortion; and, by and large, the laws are made at the state level.

"Our group is a service organization to other groups that exist. We provide materials and do research on issues, to try to raise public awareness, and then encourage people to get involved in groups that are local to them. We'll say, 'Get in touch with Pennsylvanians Against Pornography.' I steer people toward the groups that they can be locally involved with."

Geer's affiliate, Focus on the Family, provided born-again Miami attorney Jack Thompson with the materials he used in his losing campaign against Luther Campbell of the rap group 2 Live Crew. When Focus on the Family provided Thompson with the album's lyrics, he responded: "No one should be allowed to listen to 2 Live Crew's music. This stuff is so toxic that it shouldn't be allowed to be sold to anybody or by anybody. It's my desire that Luther Campbell go to jail." He said that he wanted to see Campbell do "a lot of time" in state prison.

Arrests on obscenity charges will likely continue as a pattern in the assault from the new religious right. The local coalitions will insist that archaic obscenity laws be enforced. And, if these laws don't already exist, groups such as the Phoenix-based Children's Legal Foundation have drafted model obscenity statutes for use in communities across America.

Tom Minnery, Executive Editor of Focus on the Family's *Citizen* magazine, boasts, "Some thirty cities are now virtually free of hardcore material, and five national organizations are carrying the fight onward community by community. Nearly half of the nation's ninety-three U.S. Attorneys have obscenity investigations or prosecutions underway, up from just a handful several years ago."

Having failed in his venture into national politics, Pat Robertson has also switched his efforts to the local arena. In the spring of 1990, he created a new organization called the Christian Coalition. While Robertson is not personally a member of COR, some of his Regent University staff are members. According to Ralph Reed, the Christian Coalition's executive director, "The Christian community got it backwards in the nineteen-eighties. We tried to charge Washington when we should have been focusing on the states. The real battles of concern to Christians are in neighborhoods, school boards, city councils and state legislatures."

Jodie Robbins, assistant to Ralph Reed, told me, "When Pat was running for President, and when Reagan was in, we saw that, even with Reagan and his very conservative views, the Christian community was still put on the back burner, so to speak."

She said that the American Civil Liberties Union works on the local level; that is where their strength is greatest; and she indicated that the Christian Coalition learned from the ACLU's savvy.

While they tried to make their voice heard in Washington, Robbins said, they were losing the battle back in their hometowns. They realized, she said, that "back home," they could "really make an impact." "We can decide who our school councils are going to be, who the board of education's going to be, who our city council's going to be, who the representatives are, etc., etc."

According to Robbins, the Christian Coalition is established in twenty states, and is "represented strongly in about twenty-seven states." Their Leadership School, a two-day intensive political training seminar, was slated to have been presented in ten states by the end of 1990.

She said participants in the Leadership School use "a nuts-and-bolts manual on how to start a coalition; how to fund raise for your candidate; how to back a candidate; how to groom a candidate; how to deal with the media for their candidate; how to be a candidate—if you feel called to do so—how to canvass your voters, that kind of stuff."

Could Robertson's coalition find itself in conflict with some of its already-entrenched brethren?

"No," replied Robbins, "Pat Robertson is in constant contact with Beverly LaHaye, with Jim Dobson, with Don Wildmon, and a lot of the national abortion groups. So it's really a hand-in-hand."

Robertson's daily "700 Club" TV broadcast is the primary vehicle used to promote the Christian Coalition. Since his return to the program—after his failed presidential bid—the "700 Club" has reached an annual income of $140 million.

Now that the Supreme Court has blessed the establishment of Bible clubs in federally funded public high schools, the recruitment and training of the troops can begin in earnest. In other words, Christian missionary groups are set to invade our schools.

Pat Robertson declared the Court's June 1990 ruling on the Equal Access Act "a tremendous victory . . . a major landmark decision!" Robertson proclaimed that high school students can now "meet together as Christians, it's opened the door wide for students to express their faith, to let students give out tracts, to carry their Bibles, to read the Bible, and to talk about Jesus and faith. It's a fabulous decision!"

After the Court's decision, Stephen Strang, editor and publisher of the popular *Charisma & Christian Life* magazine, editorialized, "We encourage Christian young people all over America to be bold when school begins this fall and to meet with their friends before and after school—not only to take advantage of this freedom that has been upheld by the Supreme Court, but to pray for a revival to sweep high schools all over this nation."

Youth Alive, the high-school ministry of the 18 million-member Assemblies of God, has developed a simulation game for teens called "Win Your Campus to Christ." An integral part of their self-described "plan of attack" is a study guide called *First Hour Bible Studies*. One section outlines "5 Ways to Use Your Classroom for Christ."

Another group, Youth Invasion Ministries, offers seminars on teen evangelism. The goal of these seminars is "to raise up Holy Ghost SWAT teams on every campus who will lead the campus to God."

Robert L. Simonds—another member of COR's steering committee—is president of the California-based Citizens for Excellence in Education (CEE) and the National Association of Christian Educators (NACE). He supports Christian Bible clubs in public schools. "Our job," according to Simonds, "is to evangelize . . . our schools are the battleground."

He explains, "The National Association of Christian Educators is a group of professional educators in our public schools." He claims that there are "over 500,000 born-again Christians working from 'inside' of the system, to change it, and return the Christian ethic of morality and excellence to education." Their goal is ". . . to bring public education back under the control of the Christian community."

The sixty-four-year-old Simonds continually rails against sex education, international relations, humanism, evolution, values clarification, and sexual/gender orientation in the public schools.

As radical as the NACE/CEE may be, a high-ranking public official has endorsed the group. Thomas G. Tancredo, Director of the U.S. Department of Education's regional office in Denver, confirmed, "Bob Simonds' organization is the most valuable thing I have ever seen in all the current talk about educational reform. While everyone else talks, NACE/CEE acts." He added, "They are certainly reflective of our own goals in the Department in many ways."

A spokesperson for the National Educational Association (NEA) in Washington admitted that Simond's groups are "effective." They do show up in a number of states," he said. "They are in about 15 states that we know of, and are involved in a number of school board fights. They've won some and lost some. They control the school board in Bennett, Colorado [just outside of Denver]."

According to the NEA, CEE's effectiveness has been helped by their U.S. Department of Education ally, Thomas Tancredo. The NEA spokesperson said, "The teachers in Bennett had a grant to attend Denver University to learn about 'global education.' The program had been in effect for about 10 years. Tancredo went up and spoke against global education and the school board cancelled the grant. About a third of the faculty left that year. Two principals and a superintendent left as well. He's done a lot of damage to public education."

CEE claims over 10,000 members with 500 well-established chapters, and a strong influence in about 1,500 school districts—out of 15,700 nation-wide. Political action training is conducted through seminars, tapes, and books. These tools are effective.

An incident in San Antonio, Texas provides a good example of prayer leading to action. It also shows how radical Christians have progressed in their political acumen.

In 1986, a fundamentalist parent, Anne Newman, expressed concern and outrage over the use of the novel *Clan of the Cave Bears* in classrooms. She organized other fundamentalists to pray about this, and then asked the Northside school board to ban the book, but the board voted five to two to keep it.

Newman decided to put prayer into action, and ran for a seat on the board. She was defeated. Then she organized a local chapter of CEE [which I refer to as CEE-cells], and in 1987 the group ran its Vice

President, Ron Johnson, as a candidate. He lost.

The CEE-cell was determined to gain control, so, as their next step, in 1988, they utilized Simond's book, *How to Elect Christians to Public Office,* to train its members in political activism.

As a result, the fundamentalist group won two seats on the board. They intend to continue their fight until they gain full control. This is only one example of their determination.

Robert Simonds boasts that in 1990, CEE-cells helped elect 450 born-again Christians to school boards across the nation. According to Kathi Simonds, his daughter and National Operations Manager, in that same year, they won thirty school-board seats in San Diego (California) County alone.

Americans who respect the Bill of Rights, and the various groups that defend these rights, will face frustration as the new religious right becomes more offensive. Instead of doing battle with a Jerry Falwell or a Pat Robertson, our fight will be on many fronts, against many groups of highly organized, and dangerous religious zealots. Various leaders and groups will come and go. Some of the people and groups I've mentioned will fall by the wayside. Be assured, others will rise up and take their place. The battle of the century looms ahead.

How do I know these things? As the national director of the Institute for First Amendment Studies, Inc., one of the groups actively engaged in battle with the radical religious right, I am called upon daily to draw from my past years of experience as a Fundamentalist Christian and Pentecostal minister. Although I wouldn't want to do it again, I'm glad I experienced what I did. Perhaps my story will help others avoid the pitfalls to which I fell prey along the way.

Come along with me as I tell my story. The best place to start is at the beginning.

2

Heaven Can Wait

Charles Edward Porteous, my grandfather, came over on a boat from England with Agnes Dodds, his bride, a teenage Scottish lass. They lived in New York City, where he found employment as a bank messenger and teller. In 1920, after they saved a small nestegg, my grandparents moved upstate to Hillsdale where they bought a hardware store. The oddball store, a cornucopia of wares, had so much merchandise that one could hardly pass through the aisles. Stuff hung from the ceiling like stalactites and rose up from the floor like stalagmites. People came from many miles because of the selection. I think the store's motto was, "If we don't have it, you don't need it."

Grampa, always the entrepreneur, also ran a taxi service. The Harlem Division of the New York Central Railroad made numerous stops in Hillsdale. Taxis were in demand at the train station—until the line closed in the 1960s and the tracks were torn up and sold for scrap.

My father, also named Charles, and his brother, George, and sister, Irene, were reared in the apartment above the C. Porteous & Son hardware store. George worked in the store, and eventually purchased it. Dad moved away and settled in Hartford, where he met my mother, Marian Guy. They married, and I was the first child to come along. That was 1944. I, too, was named Charles, but was nicknamed Skipper. Later, my two sisters, Linda and Barbara, were born.

Just before I was born, Grampa, for $8,500, purchased a large 150-year-old house next to the Hillsdale Library. George lived over the hardware store, where he reared a family. Grampa and Grandma turned the old house into a combination convalescent home/boarding house and named it The Gateway. They lived in a downstairs apartment on one side of the house and used the other parts for guests and boarders.

When I was three, I moved to The Gateway with my mother and father. My grandfather agreed to sell the house to my parents, where my mother continued to run it as a boarding house and bed and breakfast place. Dad took a job at the hardware store delivering bottled gas. My grandparents stayed in their apartment until they built a house on the edge of town.

Grampa and Grandma were devout members of the Hillsdale Methodist Church. From early on I was influenced by their religious zeal, which was strict but never approached fanaticism. They didn't smoke or swear. And while Grampa served his homemade dandelion wine on Thanksgiving, he cautioned me to never drink beer. I vowed to never touch it.

Prayer became a routine part of my life. It started with grace at meals and bedtime prayers. At three, I learned the ditty: "Now I lay me down to sleep. I pray the Lord my soul to keep. If I die before I wake, I pray the Lord my soul to take." Although short and simple, I took it seriously.

There were, from time to time, elderly boarders at The Gateway. One old lady, who had a room at the top of the stairs, died in her sleep one night. The next morning I watched in awe as the undertakers carried her shriveled body down the stairs.

After her room was cleaned out, it became mine. At night, after I said my little prayer, I wondered if I, too, would die before I woke. Sometimes nightmares haunted me while I slept.

Religion, although mostly in the background, seemed a natural part of my life. One time my sister Linda and I sat by the living room window to watch for Mom's return from shopping in Hudson. It was winter, when the sun set around five o'clock, and Dad was still at work.

As the sun set, it penetrated the clouds with broad beams of greenish light. The radiant light resembled depictions of the Second Coming found in Bible story books. Excitement overwhelmed us as we, in reverence and wonder, observed the phenomena. We had no doubt that Jesus would be back before our parents got home.

Church attendance was mandatory, although I seldom found any joy in the rituals. The hymns we sung contradicted the reality around me. For instance, the lyrics of one oft-sung hymn included: "This is my story, this is my song, praising my Savior all the day long." I didn't know of anyone in the church who praised Jesus, or even thought of him, all the day long.

One sermon, or least a part of its anatomy, impressed me, though. It was on Palm Sunday, when the small church was packed with twice-a-year Christians. The minister related the story of Jesus's triumphant ride into Jerusalem on a donkey. Before that event, he noted, the disciples tied Jesus's ass to a tree, where the Lord would find it for his use. When I heard, "The disciples tied Jesus's ass to a tree," I came out of my stupor. In my vivid imagination, I saw a bare-assed Jesus tied to a tree.

My cousin Jeff sat in the pew right next to me. He, too, picked up the double meaning of the sentence. For the remainder of the service we sat there bursting at the seams while attempting to hold back hysterical laughter.

Sunday school, as a whole, was inane. Sometimes it was a holy horror.

There were, of course, occasions on which I enjoyed Sunday school. Cheerfully, I drew camels, colored Joseph's celebrated coat, and, because of the Biblical characters in Sunday-school literature, came to believe that all Jewish men wore robes, sandals, and had long beards.

I never really knew what I was supposed to believe about Jews, for I received many conflicting messages. According to the New Testament, the Jews not only rejected Jesus as their Messiah and Savior, but they also had him killed. Wasn't it God's plan, though, for Jesus to die anyway? But, people said, the Jews hated him enough to do it. Although Jesus was Jewish, he was different from most Jews. The picture of Jesus over the altar in the Methodist church depicted him as having long, flowing blond hair. I had never seen a Jew like that before. Jews were referred to as the apple of God's eye, and, whatever that meant, it sounded favorable. They were also called the Chosen People, which couldn't be bad.

Nothing distinguished the two or three Jewish kids in my school from anyone else. One, my friend, wore dungarees, sweaters, and high-top sneakers just like mine. I imagined his father, though, as some sort of biblical character like the pictures in the Sunday-school books.

On occasions, I heard the expression, "Jew him down," which meant to bargain with someone in order to receive a better price. This, and the presence of New York Jews with summer homes, made me wonder if Jews had some sort of innate business sense to make money. Nah, that couldn't be either, because my Jewish friend came from a poor, struggling farm. They never had any money.

Later, when I was fifteen, I spent an entire summer plowing through William L. Shirer's epic, *The Rise and Fall of the Third Reich*. The book settled forever any uncertainty I had about the Jewish people. No one should suffer like they did for their religion, or race, or whatever you want to call it.

Mrs. Burch, my favorite Sunday-school teacher, tried hard to be responsive to the young children in her charge. As a good listener, she wasn't concerned about just getting through the day's lessons. I pumped her with questions, most for which she had no sure answers. And she admitted that she didn't know. While I received pitifully few answers to my queries, I respected her because of her honesty and sincerity.

Sunday school taught me military terminology. Through "sword drills" I became proficient in the ability to quickly locate Bible passages. I was taught that the Bible is the "sword of the Lord," and could be used as a weapon against Satan and unbelievers. This doesn't mean to literally wallop people over the head with the book, but to quote appropriate scriptures to unbelievers in an effort to make them feel guilty about their sinful activities. Also, when temptation came along, I learned to speak firmly, "Get thee behind me, Satan," just like Jesus did when Satan tempted him.

The Sunday-school superintendent assembled all the classes; the students stood at attention with their "swords" at their sides. She—usually a she—called out a Bible reference, such as John 3:16, and yelled "charge!" The children quickly sat, and the first child to find the verse jumped up and read it aloud.

To excel in sword drills I put colored plastic tabs on my Bible, one to mark each book of the Bible. This enabled me to quickly locate the correct book; from there it was easy to find the proper chapter and verse. After a while I realized that this method actually slowed me down. The better way was to memorize the names of all sixty-six books and familiarize myself with their location.

We were also encouraged to memorize scriptures. Prizes were

awarded each time assigned verses were committed to memory. Week after week of this caused me to soak up hundreds of Bible verses.

I learned to respect the Holy Bible. Everything about the book commanded respect. The leather cover and onion-skin pages felt good in my hand, and gave the volume a sense of credibility. The division of the Bible into books, numbered chapters, and verses lent to its authority.

The respect I had for the Bible caused me to trust it blindly, which, I learned later, was dangerous.

One Sunday, when I was about nine, we learned the story of Abraham and his young son, Isaac. I related to it because of my love and trust for my father. Dad often took me hunting and fishing in the abundant woods and fields around Hillsdale. And he took the whole family on a variety of day trips and vacations to some of New England's historical locations and to the seashore. We were a close family.

Well, in the biblical story, Abraham received instructions from God to take his son Isaac on a journey. Abraham, with a knife strapped to his side, carried wood for a fire, and hiked to the top of a mountain. I imagined the two were having a grand time. My Dad and I had hiked similar hills together. On our mountain hikes he taught me how to locate signs of various animals and how to track them. I always looked forward to our outings with enthusiasm.

Dad made sure that we were dressed properly for the environment, and he always had his sheathed hunting knife at his side. One never knew when it could be useful in the woods.

The purpose of Abraham and Isaac's mountaintop journey was to make a sacrifice to God. God told Abraham to present Isaac as a human sacrifice—a burnt offering. Had Isaac had any idea of this, he certainly would have run away from home.

After the two built an altar and placed the firewood around it, Abraham seized his son, tied him up, and placed him on the altar. Isaac, panic-stricken, fought for his life.

In complete obedience to his God, Abraham withdrew his long, razor-sharp knife to slaughter the sacrifice. As he lifted the knife to plunge it into his son's heart, Isaac experienced sheer terror.

Suddenly, according to the Bible, an angel of God appeared and ordered Abraham to stay his hand. Surprise! It was just a test—a test of Abraham's faith, to see if he loved God more than his son.

I wondered, did Isaac ever say to his father, "Dad, were you really going to kill me?" Abraham would have had to answer, "Yes, son, because God told me to kill you."

I was shaken by this horrible story. My attention fixed on the abused and terrorized Isaac. Without a doubt, his trauma lingered for the rest of his life. "What a cruel hoax for God to play," I thought. All the theology about the love of God, and the sacrifice of his only begotten Son on the cross didn't lessen the effect of this story on me.

Very soon after I learned this tale in Sunday school, something happened which intensified my trauma over the story. Dad suggested we take a hike up the mountain.

Was God going to test my father? How would he respond? Suppose the angel didn't arrive in time to stop him? Although struck with fear, I went anyway.

That hike was the most dreadful time I ever spent with Dad. He encouraged me to lead the way up the trail, which put me at a disadvantage because my back was constantly toward him. His large hunting knife was at his side. Every time I heard him get close, I turned to face him, and eyed the knife still in its sheath.

When will he jump me? Can I escape? Will someone save me? Reality evaded me. My only thought was, "This is the day I will die."

Well, Dad didn't murder me. It was, of course, the furthest thought from his mind.

3

A Sex What?

The tenacious Mormons first came to my attention through TV's "Death Valley Days." Mom and Dad didn't usually let me watch it, but not because of sex and violence, for there was little or none of that. They claimed it was on too late, but they probably just wanted to spend the evening by themselves. So, for me it was off to bed before "Death Valley Days."

This unusual Western opened each week with a shot of the 20-mule team borax wagons plodding across Death Valley. The sound track emanated a lone, somber bugle. A crony called the Old Ranger, with a Western twang, narrated each week's story. After a few lines, the Old Ranger faded away and viewers were transported to the not-so-colorful Death Valley via the magic of black and white television. The stories I was lucky enough to see almost always made an impact on me.

Remote control was unheard of in the fifties. So, before the bugle preamble, Mom or Dad had to clamber off the old sofa and turn down the volume; otherwise I'd hear the bugle from my upstairs room. Once the wall-piercing bugle faded they could turn the volume back up. But if I heard the bugle I'd bounce down the stairs and beg them to let me watch the program. Once I hid behind the couch and watched the whole show without detection.

My most memorable episode of "Death Valley Days" taught me about the Mormons. The Mormons created such discord everywhere they went that they had to keep moving. Joseph Smith, their original leader, started the movement in upstate New York. The West, as the new land of opportunity, beckoned them. In Illinois, Smith was persecuted and jailed for his teaching about divine revelation and the practice of polygamy. He incurred such wrath from the husbands, boyfriends, and fathers of local women, that, in the middle of the night, a mob dragged him from jail and killed him.

Then, Brigham Young took over, and along with Smith's women, and some men, ended up at the Great Salt Lake in Utah. I don't know if it was already named that or if the Mormons named it, but it didn't take much imagination to come up with the name. They claimed that God led them to Utah—it was their land of milk and honey—although that hardly described the locale.

This episode focused on how God saved the day for the Mormons. The year was 1848. The Mormons tilled the land by the sweat of their brow. They planted seeds for crops and kept everything well-watered. It looked like the harvest was going to be bountiful. Then, a biblical-type plague, a horde of grasshoppers—known today as Mormon crickets—descended upon their crops.

Used to hardship, the Mormons prayed. Meanwhile, the grasshoppers munched away at their crops. Suddenly, the sky filled with seagulls. It was as if the gulls flew right out of heaven. The gulls had a picnic at the expense of the grasshoppers, and the harvest was saved.

I was moved. "Does God intervene in our everyday affairs?" I asked myself.

Later, though, when I thought about it, I realized that every large body of water attracts gulls; and Salt Lake is larger than the state of Rhode Island. When word spread among the gulls about the arrival of the grasshoppers it was every grasshopper for himself. The result would have been the same whether or not the Mormons had uttered a prayer. Under the circumstances, they naturally gave God the credit.

I didn't know the Mormons were still active; I thought they went the way of the Shakers, and had become practically extinct. Of course, if I had used reason, I would have known that Mormonism would thrive when compared to the Shakers. While the Shakers practiced celibacy, the early Mormons enjoyed polygamy!

My next exposure to Mormons happened many years later, and many miles away, but I won't get ahead of myself.

If idle hands are the devil's tools, then the monotony of small town life and the devil are allies.

The long, cold northeast winters are bleak. While outdoor activities are limited because of early sunsets, I frolicked outdoors with my friends until well after dark. Because of the frequent snowfalls, our activities often centered around sleigh-riding and snowball fights. When we tired of snowball fights with one another, we sought others to ambush.

To ambush the mail train, our favorite target, we trekked about half a mile through the meadow west of the station. At that point a bluff overlooked the tracks. We scheduled our arrival to give us plenty of time to make a good quantity of snowballs, and stacked them like cannonballs.

As the train neared town, the clerk in the mail car slid open the large door and readied the mailbags for pickup at the station.

With the early darkness as our cover, we attacked the train with the furor of Jesse James and his gang. The mail clerk dove for cover behind the sacks of mail, but the few bags provided little protection from our fusillade.

Actions based upon dares were commonplace in my youth. Spring arrived, and I dared my friend Walter to walk in the street blindfolded. I covered his eyes with a red bandana tied around his head, led him to the middle of the highway, and quickly retreated to the safety of the sidewalk.

Fortunately traffic was slow. Walter looked comical as he stood in the middle of the street with outstretched arms. We both giggled over our silly prank.

A Chrysler Imperial slowly approached the blindfolded figure in the road. Before the car even stopped, I recognized the driver as Walter's dad. I disappeared in a flash.

One night at supper Dad asked me if I'd like a job. Other than mowing grass in the summer, and shoveling snow from sidewalks in winter, I never had a job before.

"Sure!" I replied. "Where?"

"The church is looking for a sexton," he said.

"A sex what?" I said with embarrassment.

"A sexton. That's another word for a janitor."

"Oh," I said, relieved. For all I knew, the word meant a ton of sex.

I accepted the job, and was given a key to the church so I could get in when no one else was there.

The church was spooky, with the sense that the Holy Ghost hid somewhere in the building. After a while I got used to being alone in the church. In fact, I became so comfortable with my surroundings that I preached from the pulpit. I imagined that all the regular members were there, and preached what I thought they should hear. Had they really been there, I would have stepped on a lot of toes.

Roman Catholicism, in my opinion, was an odd and inferior religion. Catholics worshipped idols; of that, I was sure. Weren't their churches filled with them? They also prayed to Mary and their saints; I knew that one should only pray to God. They even called Mary the Mother of God. How absurd. Catholics called their minister "Father." I read in the Bible that Jesus said not to call any man "Father." It amazed me how my Catholic friends fawned over their priests and nuns. I was appalled to learn that Catholics believe that during Holy Communion the wine (we used grape juice) and bread actually changed into the blood and body of Jesus. Then, they ate it. If that was true, to me it was tantamount to cannibalism.

Yes, Protestantism made me proud.

My mother, along with her dozen siblings, was an orphan. After her parents died, the younger children were adopted by different families. Forrest and Barbara Bassett, my mother's aunt and uncle, took her into their home.

Grampa Bassett, as we called him, hated Catholics, and imagined that they were out to get him. This was ironic, since a devout Catholic family adopted my mother's younger sister, Barbara.

When Grandma Bassett died, Grampa brought her body home from the funeral parlor and placed it in the living room, where her cat traipsed on it as it lay in state. After her burial, he purchased a second plot at a different cemetery, had her removed from the first grave, and reburied in the new grave. He never revealed the location of the new site. According to Grampa, he carried out this convoluted scheme "so the Cat-licks won't get her."

Mom's sister, Aunt Barbara, was the youngest of the thirteen children, and my favorite. She became a Franciscan nun, and, eventually, a Mother Superior. To Catholics, she was known as Sister Mary Robert. She was so loving that I pretty much overlooked her Catholicism.

Aunt Barbara liked to visit in the summer. She was a lot like my mother; when a project had to be done, she jumped right in and did the thing. Sometimes, she was sort of a home wrecker. Once, while garbed in her traditional black and white nun's habit, she took a crowbar and tore down an entire wall in The Gateway in order to enlarge a room. She emerged from the project cloaked in dust and grime, but with an exuberant smile.

Sister Mary Robert—aka Aunt Barbara—took her Catholicism seriously. When she felt her actions or deeds violated church rules, she applied self-imposed penance. One day I caught her painting the bathroom wall with a tiny camel's hair art brush.

"Aunt Barbara, what are you doing!" I asked.

"I'm painting the bathroom."

"I know that, but why are you using that tiny brush?"

"Penance," she replied.

I didn't ask what terrible deed brought on such an extreme punishment.

On one memorable summer visit, Aunt Barbara brought another nun along—Sister Carmencita. My aunt, an old hand at fishing, was determined to teach the sport to the other sister. So, on Sunday, the two attended early Mass at St. Bridget's in Copake Falls; after Mass they went fishing at Prospect Lake in nearby Massachusetts. As Sunday is observed by many Christians as the Sabbath, Aunt Barbara thought that she really shouldn't fish on that day, but she ignored her intuition.

That afternoon, Grampa Porteous drove me, my mother, and my sisters to his cottage at Prospect Lake for a swim. Enthusiastically, we piled out of his Plymouth.

"Penguins!" my sister Linda screamed.

To our utter amazement, in the middle of the lake, we saw what appeared to be two penguins bobbing in the water. The penguins turned out to be nuns—Aunt Barbara and her friend—with their black and white habits and all, in the lake. They clung to their overturned rowboat for dear life.

Grampa scurried back into his Plymouth and raced to the other side of the lake to borrow a boat. Already in my swimsuit, I dove into the lake to save the nuns. Grampa and I reached them simultaneously. Jocular by nature, the two sisters were having the time of their lives.

Not only did they fish on Sunday, they went swimming, too.

We later learned that the accident happened when Sister Carmencita, a portly woman, decided to switch seats. The moment she stood, the little boat flipped over.

When the rowboat flipped, my new rod, reel, and tackle box, which I loaned to Aunt Barbara for the day, sunk to the bottom of the lake. She assured me that if I prayed to Saint Anthony, he'd help me recover the lost fishing gear.

Pray to a saint? Disgraceful! I thought.

Nevertheless, while Aunt Barbara prayed the Rosary, I looked toward the sky and talked to St. Anthony.

I didn't know if it was because I wasn't Catholic, didn't have enough faith, or what, but I never retrieved my equipment. Perhaps St. Anthony was away fishing that day.

At eleven, I wasn't ready for adolescence, especially its sexual aspect. My parents didn't tell me a thing, until it was too late.

On warm summer nights a bunch of boys and girls played hide and seek on our front lawn. One night as we all horsed around, I wrestled with a girl on the grass. My body pinned her down, and, quite unexpectedly, I got an erection while laying on top of her. Nothing like this had happened before and I didn't know what to think. Alarmed, I jumped up, and leaving my friends, disappeared into the house.

Sex quickly became the leading topic of discussion among the neighborhood boys. We were hanging out behind a barn one day, when Chucky, who was several years older than the rest of us, pulled out his penis. Enormous, like an Italian sausage, he grabbed it with his hand and masturbated. We watched in stunned silence as the white semen spurted out. Chucky roared with laughter.

Sometimes this new-found sexuality felt good, but it also embarrassed me at times—like when I, and my friends too, got erections in class at school. When the bell rang we walked to the next class with a book held conspicuously in front of us, just below the belt.

Once, my mother and I engaged in a short talk about sex after I sought answers about things I had heard from my friends. We were both embarrassed, and it turned out to be an unproductive talk.

Along the way, I picked up the notion that sex was dirty, and not to be discussed or practiced until one was married. And even then its purpose was only to make babies. As a result, these new sexual thoughts and feelings became an almost constant source of guilt.

Our television set received only one channel, and, for a while, a Senator named Joe McCarthy hogged the airwaves, ranting and raving about Communists running around loose in America. From what I overheard of adult conversations, I assumed that Communists were just about everywhere. And everyone had to be careful, because everyone was suspect.

About that time, our family vacationed for a week at the beach in New London, Connecticut. As we passed the famous naval yard, I spotted an orange submarine in dry dock. I begged Dad to stop so I could snap a picture with my new Ansco camera. The orange primer paint wouldn't show up on my black and white film, but I didn't mind.

He stopped, and I got some good shots through the chain-link fence. As Dad attempted to drive away, our course was blocked by a military police jeep. The MPs informed us that we were in a restricted area and photography was strictly forbidden.

The two officers took Dad, and my camera, in their jeep and drove off. They thought we were spies. Over an hour later, the MPs pulled up with Dad. To my relief, he had my camera in his hand, minus the film. In spite of all the inconvenience, Dad remained a good sport. However, it wasn't the last time I'd get into trouble for taking photographs.

About six months later, the United States launched the world's first nuclear powered submarine, the Nautilus, from the naval base at New London. Perhaps that explains what all the fuss was about when we almost got arrested as suspected Russian spies.

Senator McCarthy—although disgraced when he couldn't substantiate his hysteria over Commie infiltrators in the United States—set the stage for a long cold war with the Soviet Union. Americans accepted as fact that Communists, within and without the United States, were a menace to us. Congress acted to reinforce this idea.

Daily, in school, we recited the Pledge of Allegiance. It went like this:

> I pledge allegiance to the flag, and to the Republic for which it stands.
> One nation indivisible, with liberty and justice for all.

On June 14, 1954, by an act of Congress, the words "under God" were added to the pledge—I guess they thought that anyone uttering "under God" couldn't be a Communist. Two years later, the country's motto, "In God we trust," was adopted.

Over in the Soviet Union, Nikita Khrushchev wrestled his way to power, and declared that he would bury American children. In 1958, Khrushchev became Premier, and I was scared.

My prayers at night became more sophisticated. Instead of "Now I lay me down to sleep," I recited the Lord's Prayer. In church, I learned to pray for my enemies, so, before I nodded off, I invoked the Lord:

> Our Father, who art in heaven, hallowed be thy name; thy kingdom come; thy will be done, on earth as it is in heaven. Give us this day our daily bread, and forgive us our trespasses, as we forgive those who trespass against us. And lead us not into temptation, but deliver us from evil; for thine is the kingdom, the power, and the glory, forever . . . *and God, bless Nikita Khrushchev, so he will be good, and won't bury us.* Amen.

Around this time, a "fightin' fundy" family moved into Hillsdale. Fightin' fundies are fundamentalist Christians who constantly fight to protect God and the Bible. They are easily distinguished from other Christians, if you just let them talk for a few minutes.

The Rev. John Duchardt and his wife felt led by the Lord to save the wayward youth of the village, and anyone else they could. Duchardt accepted a call to the decrepit little independent Baptist church in Martindale, about seven miles west of Hillsdale. Socially acceptable people didn't go to that church; either the Rev. Duchardt didn't know that, or else he didn't care. Probably, the latter.

The Duchardts employed two methods to build their church. First, they stole "sheep" from other churches. As a result, the Rev. Duchardt found disfavor among the other area ministers. Second, they resorted to deceptive devices, including an after school arts and crafts club which they offered without charge in their home. Unwary youngsters from the village, myself included, fell prey. We didn't realize the purpose of the club was to make converts.

Soon, those who attended the club received invitations to Billy Graham movies on Sunday nights at the Baptist church. Who could resist free movies? The nearest year-round movie theater was in Great

Barrington, Massachusetts, ten miles away.

As an adolescent, my vulnerability left me open to the church's dominant influence. At first, I didn't think of myself as a bad sinner; after all, I regularly attended Sunday school and services at Hillsdale's only church. But adolescence proved difficult, and my thoughts and deeds, obviously, were not pure.

Week after week I listened to Billy Graham's filmed sermons, which were cleverly worked into the plot of the movies. These were followed by the pastor's pleas to "invite Jesus into your heart." Soon, convinced of my vile, sinful nature, and that, without Jesus, eternity in Hell awaited me, I knew I had to make a choice. I chose Jesus.

Around the same time that I "went forward"—that is, went to the front of the church to accept Jesus into my heart and be born again—my mother also committed her life to Christ.

Through my affiliation with the Baptist church, I spent two summer stints at evangelist Jack Wyrtzen's Word of Life Ranch on Schroon Lake, New York. This holy-roller boot camp reinforced my experience as a "new creature" and thoroughly indoctrinated me in fundamentalism. I liked the idea of Jesus living in me.

Anyone who wasn't saved before arriving at Word of Life was likely to be converted before leaving. And the believers who attended were pushed to go out and become soul winners for Jesus.

Sunday is the Christian fundamentalist Sabbath. Like the Jewish Orthodox Sabbath, activities are strictly limited on that hallowed day—including hiking, swimming, softball, and ping pong. Two things about this day of rest puzzled me. Why Sunday, and not Saturday, as in the Bible? And what was it about Sunday that made an innocent game like ping pong evil?

At Word of Life, good soldiers of the Lord learned how to fight back. To "turn the other cheek" emerged as something allegorical, not something one really did. The camp offered boys a week-long course in boxing. As a skinny kid, used to being pushed around, I immediately knew this sport was for me. After five days of training, boxing matches were held on Saturday. Boys were matched up with opponents in the same weight classification. My opponent, tall and slender, towered over me. While the training gave me some bit of confidence, I was still pretty scared. Taking advantage of a surge of adrenaline, I charged into the ring like a wild man. Within seconds, I knocked the boy to the mat. That wasn't good enough, though; I wanted to finish him off so he wouldn't get back up and take out his revenge. So, I jumped on him and pounded away. Several counselors rushed into the ring and pulled me off the dazed youngster.

Beating the devil out of that boy at the fundamentalist camp gave me a tremendous boost in confidence. For my efforts, I returned home that summer with a "Word of Life Boxing Champ" patch for my windbreaker.

During my second stint at Word of Life, a new convert and former Golden Gloves boxer attended the camp with his unsaved wife. As far as I know, he was not involved in the camp's boxing program.

Prior to his visit to Word of Life, the man failed the New York State bar exam and turned to Jesus for solace. Then he dragged his wife up to the fundamentalist camp in the mountains.

While still trying to cope with "this 'saved' jag" her husband was on, she said he had "become a fanatic," and all he did was "read the Bible all day and sit around and talk to Jesus." At that point she told her husband, "I'm a nurse. I recognize schizoid tendencies when I see them, and I think you're sick." Well, if he was sick, she caught the disease, too. Before Dede Robertson left Word of Life, she succumbed to the pressure and became a born-againer just like her husband, Pat Robertson.

The Baptist church and Word of Life ranch turned me into a disciple of Jesus, a die-hard Christian fundamentalist. As such, I accepted their teachings on "personal separation." An unwritten list of "do's and don'ts" guided the way towards holiness. The "don'ts" included: don't drink, don't smoke, don't dance, don't gamble—which included any type of card playing—don't go to movies or the theater, and, if you're a woman, don't wear pants or wear makeup. Additionally, don't have sex —or even think about it—until legally married in the eyes of God. The list of permissible activities was shorter. They included: pray without ceasing, read the Bible daily, attend church three times a week (Sunday morning and evening, and Wednesday night prayer meeting), tithe 10 percent of your income, and witness regularly to lost souls.

For the most part, the rules didn't bother me. In fact, I believed that those who followed them showed their unwavering dedication to the Lord.

After my second summer at Word of Life I was a certified fanatic. I wanted to save a lost and dying world for Jesus. Shortly after returning home, I revealed my plans to my mother to preach the Gospel on a street corner in Hillsdale. However, as committed to Christ as I thought she was, she forbade me, wanting to spare our family the embarrassment.

4

A Man or a Mouse?

After my experience at Word of Life I continued to zealously serve the Lord—for a while. On several occasions I tried to convert my friends. Unsuccessful at that, I immersed myself in the Bible, particularly the New Testament and, especially, the Gospel of John—a copy of which I always carried.

Mature and long-standing members of the Baptist church lugged large, well-worn, leather-covered King James Bibles. They marked their favorite passages in various bright colors. As my faith grew, I became determined to someday get a big King James Bible with fine onionskin paper.

Then, something strange happened. About the same time that I outgrew "cops and robbers" and "cowboys and Indians," I tired of Christianity; all of my interest in the Bible disappeared. Soon, I passed my religious experience off as mere childhood foolishness.

The only complete Bible I owned, containing both the Old and New Testaments, was a Revised Standard Version given to me by the Methodist Sunday School. Inside the front cover I had pasted a copy of the painting of the blond-haired Jesus which hung in the Methodist church. One evening, while rearranging my bookshelf, I came across that Bible. When I opened the cover I saw the picture of Jesus. Underneath the picture I had written, "I love Jesus" in red pencil. I might as well have written, "I love Mickey Mouse," because now Jesus was as real to me as the Disney character. Both were childhood fantasies.

Embarrassed by it, I tore the picture off the page and erased the inscription.

Shortly afterward, while sitting on the porch one Sunday night, I observed a carload of Baptists driving by my house on their way to Sunday night services, perhaps to see another Billy Graham movie. My pity for them bordered on ridicule.

While I continued some of my favorite pursuits—painting and drawing, hunting and fishing, and reading—girls, rock and roll, and cars emerged as the hottest of my new interests.

My birthdays were usually marked by a small, traditional party, and perhaps a movie. Though my sexuality developed at eleven, it wasn't until I was thirteen that I invited a girl to a birthday party. In seventh grade, Ann, a cute, blond eighth-grader caught my eye. When my next birthday arrived, I invited two guys, and Ann, to my party.

After cake and ice cream, Mom brought us to the Mahaiwe Theater in Great Barrington, to see *Sayonara,* starring Marlon Brando. I wasn't interested in the movie, but only in how to slip my arm around Ann without her rejection. It didn't take long to come up with a clever, though age-old, tactic. Nonchalantly, I rested my right arm on the back of Ann's seat. Then I could let it slip ever so slowly down to her shoulder; if she didn't jump with alarm, I could proceed further.

My cleverness was greater than my nerve. An hour into the movie my arm was asleep! I mean, it was dead; as much as I tried, I simply couldn't move it.

When the movie ended, and we stood to leave, my arm just fell to my side, useless. It was numb for several days. Discouraged by my performance, I never asked Ann out again.

Elvis reached instant stardom in 1954, when I was ten. Within three or four years, my cousin Jeff and I were among his most loyal fans. While we both collected his records, Jeff's collection was more extensive than mine. Jeff had a real hi-fi on which to spin his records; my record player was an old wind-up Victrola with an acoustic speaker.

Presley's early hits were recorded on 78 RPM platters, but because of the popularity of 45s, we discarded the obsolete 78s. Most of these were shattered against trees and rocks as we tossed them through the air as flying saucers. One of these vintage platters, though, served as a prop in our greatest caper.

A new minister installed a public address system high in the steeple of his church. Every evening, huge speakers blasted the village with sacred music and recorded chimes. The sound carried for miles. One summer evening, well after dark, Jeff and I walked the two blocks from his house to the church. Under his arm, Jeff tucked one of his last 78 RPM records. In my pocket, I held the key to the church—I still worked there as sexton.

Standing outside the church, we looked around for observers, then quickly slipped into the basement unnoticed, and climbed two flights of stairs to the balcony. The sound system's record changer was controlled by a timer on a shelf in the choir robe closet. By the light which filtered in from the street through a window, we removed the recorded sacred music and replaced it with our specially selected record. After some effort, we managed to reset the timer. Jeff and I then left the church as surreptitiously as we had come in.

The good reverend was one of those "early to bed and early to rise" people. He was sound asleep at midnight when, up in the church balcony, a switch clicked on and a tiny motor hummed to life. As the turntable built up speed, the arm came down, the needle touched the record, and—amplified by 100 power-packed watts—Elvis wailed, "You ain't nothing but a hound dog!"

The parsonage was located two houses down the hill from the church. By the time the minister threw on a robe, ran up the hill, let himself into the church, and climbed the stairs, Elvis was all played out.

Although girls thought I was cute, I developed a problem which seriously hindered my social development and adversely affected my studies. At the time my voice should have changed, it stuck in soprano. When I spoke, I sounded like a member of the Vienna Boys Choir. Sometimes, if I could speak at all, I simply squeaked. This plight caused me untold misery in junior high. One day, as I left the boy's room, a senior said, "Skipper, are you a man or a mouse? C'mon, squeak up!"

School became hell. I refused to participate in class discussions. If a teacher directed a question toward me I simply shrugged my shoulders. Oral reports were out of the question; I'd accept a failure rather than have to stand before a class and speak.

And though my interests in girls heightened during this time, overwhelming fear prevented me from striking up a conversation. Before long my parents surmised something was wrong. They took me to a pediatrician who theorized I caught a mild case of polio in my vocal cords. She recommended a speech therapy clinic in Albany.

For several months my mother and I made the weekly 100-mile round trip to the Northeastern New York Speech Center. Through counseling, topical medication, and vocal exercises, a new, deeper voice slowly developed. I could only maintain it for short periods of time, however.

Finally, at what turned out to be my last morning speech session, the therapist said, "When you leave here today, I want you to keep speaking in your new voice. Don't permit it go high again."

Mom took me back to school that afternoon. I tingled with fear and excitement. It was my misfortune to enter a World History class right in the middle of an oral quiz. I was horrified. In an effort to remain unnoticed, I slouched down in my seat as far as I could without falling off. It didn't work. The teacher, with expectant eyes, looked directly at me, "Charles" (that's what some of the teachers called me), "what happened in the year 1588?"

Dead silence permeated the classroom. And there I was, slouched in my chair, with all eyes on me. I knew the correct answer, but could I speak it?

"The English defeated the Spanish Armada," I said slowly and deliberately with my new, deep voice. Everyone was stunned. Then, smiling, the teacher turned and directed questions to other students.

My theory is that my voice problem related directly to adolescent sexuality. For example, the emergence of pubic hair is one sign of puberty; however, that remains quite hidden. A boy's change in voice, though, is evidence for all to see that a boy has reached puberty. The church caused me to view sex as dirty. Subconsciously, I didn't want my family to know I'd matured, that I was a sexual being. The only way I could cover the fact was not to let my voice change.

As I mentioned, some teachers called me by my given name, "Charles." Generally, though, everyone called me "Skipper." With the arrival of manhood, I thought "Skipper" sounded childish. So, I dropped the "er" and became "Skipp."

Now that my voice problem was fixed, I looked forward to school dances. During my tenure at the Baptist church I was taught that dancing was evil, and practically akin to foreplay. Only husbands and wives should be that physically close, I was told. Yet that didn't explain why the married couples in the church didn't attend dances. I had heard that Fundamentalist couples were forbidden to engage in sex while standing up because it might lead to dancing.

While some of my friends took dancing lessons, I stayed home. So, when I first started attending school dances I usually hung out in a dark corner. Eventually I got enough nerve to approach girls for the slow dances, because they were easy to fake.

When Chubby Checker's "Let's Do the Twist" swept the nation, the kids at our school were too shy to "twist." So, one Friday night I grabbed a girl by the hand and dragged her onto the dance floor. As we twisted away, a hand-clapping crowd gathered around us. And not for a moment did I think hell awaited me.

Girls became my passion. I was smart though, because I sure didn't want to get a girl in trouble—for then I would be in trouble, too. So, in preparation for the anticipated big day, I hid a condom and a jar of Vaseline under a rock behind our house. I found the condom— a Trojan—in a drawer in a room vacated by a former boarder at our house. Since it was hermetically sealed, I couldn't open it until just before using it, so I didn't even know what the condom looked like. I stole the Vaseline from the medicine cabinet. I'd heard somewhere that plenty of Vaseline was necessary for intercourse.

What I imagined would be a breeze, proved quite a challenge, with many rebuffs along the way. And, as far as I know, the Trojan and small jar of Vaseline are still where I placed them many years ago.

On wintry nights Jeff and I often hung out in a rear booth of the Roe Jan Diner in Hillsdale. One evening, while we dined on greasy hamburgers and fries, and sipped Cokes, an old man entered and sat in the booth next to ours.

Moments after he ordered a bowl of Campbell's soup, he nodded off. As he slept, he tilted sideways. We thought this was funny and made up silly schemes to taunt him. Just as we were about to sprinkle salt on the man's head, he woke up from his brief nap.

The man sensed our amusement over his snooze. "How're you boys tonight?" he queried.

We quickly altered our behavior and acknowledged the gentleman.

One thing led to another, and when his hot soup arrived he invited us to join him. The stranger's gift of gab held us enthralled for over an hour. When we realized the lateness of the hour we told him we had to go home and said good-bye.

A white 1955 Thunderbird was parked by the doorway of the diner. Because of our conversation, which included car talk, we knew it belonged to the stranger. As remarkable as the auto was, its license plate intrigued us even more so. The New York plate consisted of a single digit. This was before the days of vanity plates.

We went back into the diner. The man was draining a cup of coffee as we approached him.

"Who are you, sir?" I asked.

"I'm sorry, I didn't introduce myself. I'm Thomas E. Dewey. I used to be governor of New York," he replied.

Forgetting the time, we slid into his booth and sat at the feet, so to speak, of the old story teller. The story I remember most concerned a trip the governor once made from Albany to New York City. His chosen course was Route 9 south to 23 east, then south on 22. This was, perhaps, because Dewey had a home off Route 22 in Pawling. Nevertheless, his chauffeur proceeded south on 22, which was undergoing work at the time. Several seemingly endless detours made the going slow. Dewey had just completed a hectic week at the state capital and, because of his weariness, he soon fell asleep.

Suddenly, jarred awake by a large pothole, and unaware of his location, the governor exclaimed, "Are we still on that damned detour?"

"No sir," his chauffeur replied, "we've been back on the state road for some time now."

Dewey told us, at that very moment he conceived the idea for the New York State Thruway.

My encounter with Governor Dewey was significant; it was the first time I had met a person from a history book. In school we talked about Dewey's surprise defeat by Harry S. Truman in the 1948 presidential election. While that was interesting, meeting the man, and talking casually with him at length, brought history to life. From that time onward, I developed a new interest in current world events.

Besides girls, cars became another of my worldly attractions. As a teenager, I found myself moving further and further away from the church. I still prayed regularly, but church, and the kind of people that attended, were offensive to me. So, as an automobile enthusiast, Dewey's snappy car appealed to me all the more.

On certain summer nights, the thrill of fast cars drew me to the stock car races at the Lebanon Valley Speedway. On Wednesday nights the speedway hosted the "bombers," an event for amateur racers who couldn't afford the thousands of dollars required to maintain a typical stock car. I spent most of my sixteenth summer readying a '51 Chevy for an amateur night.

A local gas station owner let me work on the car, parked next to his garage. I painted the car black, and because it was a "bomb," I named it TNT, which I painted on both sides of the vehicle in bright orange paint.

Dad got a welder to cut off part of the car's front and replace it with a solid steel bumper and radiator protector. Inside, after we removed the seats and upholstery, heavy roll bars were welded into place.

A search through a couple of junk yards yielded a bucket seat and a seat belt—both hard to come by in those days. Finally, a friend fine-tuned the engine, and, to keep the car from swaying, we chained the axles to the frame of the vehicle.

My excitement mounted as I gazed upon my racing machine. I was the only kid in town to own a real race car. While that felt good in itself, Dad's help with the car served to heal the ill-feelings and mistrust I'd held against him for so long—ever since learning the story of Abraham and Isaac.

One Wednesday night remained before the end of the racing season, and TNT was ready to show its stuff. Being under eighteen, the minimum age for racing, I asked my friend Jerry to act as my driver.

Dad volunteered to tow TNT to the speedway with his station wagon. Late in the afternoon, we hooked a tow chain between his wagon and the race car. I steered TNT as Dad towed. The 25-mile trip gave me my only chance to "drive" the car.

As we slowly made our way on the winding road between Hillsdale and New Lebanon, I smelled a vaguely familiar odor. Then, a redlight caught us as we approached the town of New Lebanon. Dad braked to a stop. I tried to imitate him, but, instead, smashed right into the back of his car.

Now, I recognized the odor—brake fluid! No harm was done to

either car, but Jerry, who was riding with Dad, crawled under TNT to survey the problem. A chain we used to hold the axle fast to the car's frame cut a brake fluid line; now the race car had no brakes. So, carefully, we continued on to the track, using slow, coasting stops.

Track officials inspected each car before a race. Because of the amount of pressure in brake lines, they can't be repaired, so they must be replaced. Installing new brake lines was out of the question if we were to race TNT that summer.

Jerry hastily came up with a plan. He managed to find some brake fluid, crimped the broken line, and refilled the system. He figured he could stop the car a couple of times before the system was depleted again. Although the car would be racing with no brakes, at least we could get into the race. Jerry was willing to take the chance.

TNT passed a cursory inspection. I watched from the pit area in the center of the track as Jerry pulled into position. An official motioned for him to pull up more closely to the next car. He did, and bumped the car in front of him. I knew the brake fluid had leaked out again.

The bombers, lined up in their designated starting order, circled the track, and returned to the starter's flag. The flag came down. And with a loud, rumbling roar, amidst thick, gray clouds of exhaust fumes, they were off.

Too wide on the first turn, Jerry scraped the wall. Sparks flew into the night, but he kept the racer under control. Coming high out of the corner, Jerry floored the gas pedal. The old Chevy screamed as it met the demand for more speed.

Taking the back turn on the inside, TNT gained much needed distance. Suddenly, a car coming from behind closed the gap between the two racers. It collided with the rear bumper and sent TNT spinning out of control. With the sound of crunching steel, TNT plowed into the wall.

"Jesus," I said aloud, "protect him!"

Jerry was unharmed, and after the other cars raced by, he managed to back the car away from the wall and drive it to the pit. With the front bumper dragging, the hood pushed up, and the radiator spewing steam, TNT was finished.

I thanked Jesus. He seemed to be there when you needed him.

Once again, I sat in TNT as we pulled it back to Hillsdale. The lack of brakes made the trip a long one. During the ride, with a certain satisfaction, I pondered the short history of my career as a racing promoter.

The next morning I left my house earlier than usual. Normally, I waited for the school bus across the street from the house.

"Not today," I said to myself.

Another bus stopped in front of the post office. The night before, we parked TNT at the gas station across the street from the post office. As I headed down the street, I envisioned the scene. Sure enough, as I rounded the corner I saw a group of kids peering into my seasoned racer. I knew they were imagining the spectacular race of the night before. It felt great.

5

Mannequin Boy

Half way through my senior year I still hadn't decided where to go or what to do after graduating. Years earlier, I wanted to be a cop; then, in junior high, I gave the Navy some thought.

College was of no interest, because school was so unpleasant and such a struggle. Furthermore, no one ever encouraged me to go to college. That I was about to finish high school was a big relief to my parents. Once, when I turned sixteen, I asked Dad if I could drop out of school and get a job. When he told me in no uncertain terms that that was out of the question, I never entertained the idea again.

As a senior, only two things interested me, Liz, my girlfriend, and art class. My relationship with Liz was torrid and tense; at once, it both stimulated and drained me. Always fearful of losing her, I often cowered to her jealous rages and demands.

Art was the only class in which I found satisfaction. While I enjoyed using various media, I especially liked painting with water colors and oil. A group of artists, writers, and musicians formed an association called the Community Activities League (CAL) to promote art and other cultural activities. I knew some of these people, and they invited me to join.

CAL arranged for the use of our school gym to put on an art show, and invited artist Norman Rockwell to come over from nearby Stockbridge, Massachusetts to give a talk. Rockwell offered to exhibit one of his well-known works, and when he arrived, he asked me to carry the painting in from his car. As we walked from his car, we talked about art, and he encouraged me to pursue my interest in painting and sculpting. (One summer I worked as an assistant to a New York metal sculptor who had a home in Hillsdale. That experience sparked my interest in the medium.) My one and only sculpture appeared in the show. It was a piece I had made in art class.

Later on I was selected from among the other members of the senior art class to design a Christmas centerpiece for the school library. After the holidays, Mr. Colclough, a history teacher and the librarian's husband, requested a meeting. I couldn't imagine what he wanted. Curiously, he asked me if I'd ever seen the windows in New York's Saks Fifth Avenue, or Lord & Taylor? I told him that after Thanksgiving, several years earlier, our family had visited New York City for a weekend. The brilliant Christmas lights, magnificent department store windows, and other wonderful sights and sounds dazzled me. A walk through Greenwich Village, and conversations with several of the Village's denizens, convinced me that New York was really the place to be if I wanted to pursue an art career. But, like many of my childhood fantasies, the romance of living in New York had long since worn off.

Mr. Colclough said people have lucrative careers in window display, and he thought that my centerpiece in the library indicated I could do well in the field. A spark ignited in my soul. Although I knew nothing certain about window display, design, or decorating, I was sure I could learn. Bob Inglis, the school's able guidance counselor, discovered that the Pan America Art School in New York offered a fifteen-week course in window display. I called the school and made an appointment. Shortly after my eighteenth birthday I took the train from Hillsdale to New York's Grand Central Station. Filled with excitement, I quickly walked the fifteen blocks or so to West 57th Street.

Nestor Castro and his wife, a Cuban couple, ran the school. Castro based the window-display course on an illustrated book he'd written on the subject. The Castros assured me that the school helped its graduates find work in the field. Great, I thought. I imagined myself working for one of the big department stores like Saks Fifth Avenue or Lord & Taylor.

Convinced that this was the right move, I enrolled, and left a downpayment for my tuition. I also learned that the uptown Y.M.C.A.—the "Gentleman's Y"—was close by. So, before I left the city, I checked out the Y and found it to my liking.

I threw a small party upon graduation from high school. An erstwhile French poet—Jacques Pillionel, a man who frequented the Hillsdale library—provided the entertainment. I imagine mine was the only class of 1962 graduation party in the area—perhaps the state—with a poetry reading in French. And I didn't know a word of French.

In the fall I packed all my clothes, my Elvis tapes, and my "I love Jesus" Bible, and with three suitcases and a large reel-to-reel tape recorder, I moved to New York City. My only worry involved Liz. From the beginning our relationship had been rocky, but I lost my virginity to Liz, and found it difficult to let her go. She felt differently, however, and wanted to end our relationship. Although I knew this, I couldn't accept it, and managed to keep it alive. My inflexibility caused me much anxiety. However, with the little money I'd saved, and with some help from Mom and Dad, I began a frugal life in New York. Most of my main meals consisted of pasta; and entertainment was pretty much limited to self-guided walking tours.

Then Curtis, a fellow art student, found a little efficiency unit at a hotel near the school. He asked if I'd like to share it with him. It sounded better than the Y, so I took him up on it.

My roommate, a Southern Baptist, came from Montgomery, Alabama to study window display. Always animated and talkative, yet polite and charming, I admired him. As Curtis had no plans for Thanksgiving, I asked Mom and Dad if he could come up with me.

They found him amusing, and, of course, he was well-versed in the Bible. This impressed Mom, and she was thrilled that my roommate was a born-again Christian.

From time-to-time, back in New York, Curtis blurted out derogatory remarks about blacks. Unused to such prejudice, I first thought he was making thoughtless jokes. Then, one morning we went out for breakfast. After placing food orders, we sipped our coffee. A black man came in and sat on the stool next to Curtis.

Curtis jumped up and yelled, "I ain't sitting next to no nigger!"

As he fled the restaurant, I sat there bewildered. Curtis may have been a Southern Baptist, but if there was such a place as heaven, I kind of doubted he would make it.

Though it was the 1960s, the display techniques taught at the Pan America Art School dated to the 1940s and 1950s. Nevertheless, my attendance there paid off.

In November, Lord & Taylor called the school seeking two students to fill temporary holiday season positions in their display department. The school sent me and another student to the chic downtown department store. While I thought we went for just the experience—as volunteers—to my added delight the store added us to the payroll.

I began each day enthusiastically. The wonderful Christmas windows, planned many months in advance, were the main focus of activity. I worked as a "gofer," and became involved in almost every aspect of the process.

Naive as I was, it came as a surprise to discover that gays dominated the display world. As a youth, at various times I'd been accosted by homosexual men in rest rooms and other public places. I vividly recall my dismay on two occasions after being propositioned by men that I knew; both were married, had children, and belonged to the church.

The gays in the display and decorating world, for the most part, were out of the closet, living in their own habitat. Social pressure caused most of these men and women to flee families, friends, and small towns in search of understanding and camaraderie. In New York they found it.

Working with gays was fun, because, as the term implies, they were gay—or festive and merry, most of the time.

I observed, however, that gays often live under tremendous emotional pressure. Families, religion, and society in general condemn homosexuals. Enormous harm is created by the public's lack of understanding of homosexuality. Depression, caused by unnecessary guilt, too often results in drug and alcohol abuse, even suicide.

Employment at Lord & Taylor allowed me to take a hefty discount on purchases I made there. Much of my earnings went towards Christmas presents for Liz, my parents, and sisters. When I went home for Christmas, I didn't have the five dollars for a train ticket to go from Grand Central to Hillsdale.

So, one morning a couple of days before the holiday, I left the city with a suitcase in one hand, and two Lord & Taylor shopping bags in the other. One bag held gifts, the other, some potted flowers. A fifteen-cent token took me to the end of the subway line at 230th

Street in the Bronx, and from there I hitchhiked northward to Route 22.

A light snow fell as I trudged along the highway. It was wet, cold, and slushy. In between rides, the passing cars walloped me with brown slush.

The going was slow, for, even back then, few people dared to pick up a stranger. The best lift, about ten miles, was from a cop. By late afternoon, I arrived in a small town called Wingdale, about an hour south of Hillsdale.

Darkness fell as I stood outside a long, ominous building. Car after car passed me by, but not one even slowed down. With wet feet, and snow falling on my uncovered head, I stood there shivering. Out of the corner of my eye I saw someone approaching. I turned to face a uniformed security guard. He was an employee of the state mental hospital, the long brick building behind me.

"Where're ya goin' bub?" he asked.

Before he sized me up as an escaped patient and threw on a strait jacket, I quickly explained my situation.

"Nobody'll pick ya up in front of this place," he told me.

I thanked him for the information, and walked down to a brightly lit gas station where I'd spotted a phone booth. Mom accepted my collect call, and an hour later, I was in a warm car with my parents, headed home for Christmas. Regardless of how far I'd backslid, Christmas always made me feel close to the Lord.

Within a few months, the inevitable happened; Liz and I broke up. My initial hurt and anger turned to relief as I contemplated the relationship: our mutual trust, lamentable from the beginning, had vanished; she was still in high school; and we lived so far apart that we only saw each other on weekends—if I had money for the train.

With my new-found freedom, I determined to find new relationships in New York. This led to some wanton adventures.

One Saturday night in Greenwich Village, I walked by a tavern filled with women. Curious, I turned back, entered, and found a vacant stool at the bar. After a second beer, it dawned on me that I was sitting in a lesbian bar. Amused at my naiveté, I ordered a third beer and watched the action.

An attractive brunette approached and began a conversation. She was nineteen, I learned, and came down to the Village from the Bronx with her aunt. Pretty soon the aunt came over and joined us. The nineteen-year-old's forwardness betrayed the fact that we'd just met. While her hands wandered over me, the aunt, too, got into the act.

Things got too hot for the nightclub, and they invited me to their apartment in the Bronx. We caught a cab, and, in the back seat, fondled one another as we rode uptown. What a ride!

In their neighborhood, we picked up a bottle of red wine before going to their apartment. It looked like I was in for the time of my life. Then, for some reason, the women became angry at each other, started cursing, and a fistfight ensued. I tried to break them up, and received some cuts and bruises for the effort. Then, the aunt ran into the kitchen. Frantic, the younger woman grabbed my hand and said we had to flee, because her aunt would kill us.

As we bolted down the stairs, the aunt screamed obscenities. On the street, we spotted a bus, and raced to the corner to catch it. Down the block, the aunt came flying off the stoop of the brownstone apartment house.

Our bus pulled away as the mad woman pounded on its door. The driver didn't stop.

On the way downtown I learned that the two women were lovers, and not relatives at all. I don't know why they chose me for their game—perhaps I was a victim of reverse sexism—but I guess I asked for it.

Downtown, I walked the girl to the YWCA, and went home alone, a little bit wiser for the experience.

I completed the course at the Pan America Art School, and Lord & Taylor kept me on after the holidays. Before long, though, it seemed as if I wasn't going anywhere at Lord & Taylor.

Someone I met at a party called to tell me that a position was open in Saks Fifth Avenue's display department, and provided the information I needed to arrange for an interview. During lunch hour I went for the interview, and the next day the assistant display director at Saks called and offered me a position fondly referred to as "mannequin boy," fulfilling my dream of working both in Lord & Taylor and Saks Fifth Avenue.

Henry Callahan, the late, acclaimed display director at Saks Fifth

Avenue, was intense about the mannequins—or, as he called them, the "girls." The dozens of mannequins came equipped with several sets of arms, hands, and legs. Most of them came apart at the waist. They could be set up in different positions by switching body parts. Generally, mannequins are bald. A numerous selection of styled wigs are kept on pegs in a long closet.

When I assumed the role of mannequin boy, many of the girls were separated from their original arms and hands. Through the use of the manufacturers' photographs, I matched the girls up with the correct hands and arms, which I hung around their necks in cloth sacks.

From time to time, Henry Callahan wanted to purchase new mannequins. However, his budget restricted him to replacing mannequins that, because of damage, were no longer usable.

Sometimes he called me from his upstairs office to say he was coming down. Soon he'd arrive on mannequin row in Saks' basement, where all the bald girls were stored in bins. Now, when mannequins aren't in a window, they're held upright by metal rods inserted in their rears. The rod attaches to a metal base placed on the floor. (Less sophisticated stores display mannequins in their windows using the rod and its base to support them; Saks Fifth Avenue uses thin, almost invisible wires, for support.)

As I followed him down the row, Henry inspected each mannequin. When he pointed to one, I pulled it out and threw it to the cement floor. After he chose several, I went to work on them. With one of the heavy metal rods, I smashed their bald heads and naked bodies. As I chopped, heads rolled off, and breasts and hips caved in, and Henry watched with glee—and an occasional grimace—while I broke up perfectly good mannequins. Then, red-faced, he went back up to his office and ordered new mannequins to replace the "damaged" ones.

Though they were just mannequins, I felt uncomfortable whenever I did this.

Derek Stuart-Bell, an entertaining, witty, and seasoned window decorator, told me of a "must see" New York attraction. He said Harlem's Apollo Theater hosted marvelous live acts on its stage. Derek raved so much about the performances that I thought he went there all the time. Fascinated, I took the "A" train up to 125th Street to see the Wednesday night amateur show, hosted by Ralph Cooper. When I didn't see another white person in the audience, I doubted that Derek went there very often. Nevertheless, the few shows I saw at the Apollo were electrifying. And there was no way of knowing that someday I'd be on that fabulous stage.

Some of the performances I saw live on the Apollo stage included Diana Ross and the Supremes, the Ronettes, and the black comedienne, Mums Mabley. On one unforgettable occasion, the MC led a twelve-year-old blind child across the stage to the microphone. Although the youngster's single instrument was only a small harmonica, Little Stevie Wonder captivated his enthusiastic audience with his soon-to-be first hit, "Fingertips, Part II."

A Belgian friend at Saks told me about a friend of his who was looking for someone to share a third floor walk-up on West 73rd Street, just off of Central Park West. It wasn't far from the little place I shared with Curtis. Because Curtis, with his hypocritical bullshit was getting on my nerves, I agreed to meet the guy. He came from Paris, his name was Jacques, and he taught at a dental school near Columbus Circle. He seemed like a perfect gentleman, and he asked a fair price for the rent.

With great delight, I left Curtis and moved in with the Frenchman. Jacques did a little moonlighting on the side, and because of his clients, he insisted I make my bed and keep my things picked up. I never knew when someone would be stopping by for fittings of Jacques' home-made, low-cost dentures.

My new roommate was the first atheist I'd ever talked to about the Bible, Jesus, and religion, or anything else, for that matter. He never ridiculed me when he saw me reading the Bible. Although I strongly disagreed with his views, our discussions remained civil.

Jacques was OK. One night, however, after I'd been there for about six months, he made a pass at me while we watched a couple engaging in a nude photography session in an apartment across the street. I guess the excitement was too much for Jacques. His forwardness unnerved me, though, and I looked for a new place to live.

About that time, I met two young women who lived in the apartment across the hall. I quickly got to know them, and became quite enamored with one.

Mary Ellen was two or three years older than I, and very attractive. This, however, along with her advanced education, intimidated me. Also, I was afraid a serious affair might develop, and, frankly, I lacked the confidence to maintain such a relationship.

We spent a lot of time together over meals in her apartment, or on leisurely walks. She belonged to a Christian Science church, and we had some long talks about religion as I probed her about her beliefs. Meanwhile, our involvement remained platonic, although she indicated on several occasions that she wanted it otherwise.

Without notice, Mary Ellen's roommate moved out, and Mary Ellen invited me to move in. In some respects, the timing was perfect, but it didn't seem like the right thing to do. I wondered what my parents would think and where it would lead. I was scared; it was too much to handle.

Then, Mary Ellen accepted a job in another city, and I never heard from her again.

One weekend, Dad told me of a New Yorker who also had a home in Hillsdale, who might have a room to rent in the city. Bob's apartment was at the Ansonia, a New York landmark. He only used it part-time when he came in to give piano and singing lessons in the apartment's living room. I looked him up, and ended up renting one of the large apartment's rooms.

Three other guys also rented space, either full-time or part-time— a Jew, a Muslim, and a Catholic. Remarkably, we all got along. Tony, the Catholic, aspired to sing opera at the Metropolitan. His biggest break came when he sang "The Star-Spangled Banner" before a Yankee game.

While I lived at the Ansonia my grandfather was stricken with cancer. Several years earlier he had survived a heart attack, and after that we always tried to protect him from overwork. For example, after it snowed, I tried to get down to his house and shovel him out before he attempted to do it himself.

I loved and admired Grampa Porteous. When I learned he was in the hospital I went up to Hudson to visit him. Mom and Dad said that Grampa wasn't told that he had cancer and would die. While I thought that such discretion was silly, I promised not to say anything.

The visit was very special. At one point during our conversation, Grampa, with a certain twinkle in his eye, said, "You know, I have cancer, and I'm going to die." I nodded my head. He took my hand, squeezed it, and said good-bye. I wondered if I'd ever see him again. At that moment, I really hoped heaven was real.

Having pets as a youngster is what really prepared me for the reality of death. I've always cared for animals. Over the years I collected a menagerie which included: cats, dogs, hamsters, rabbits, woodchucks, raccoons, tropical fish, birds, snakes, salamanders, turtles, chickens, skunks, a chipmunk, and a duck.

Although I went to extremes to see that they were well cared for, some of my pets fared better than others. My parakeet was doing fine until my mother cleaned its cage with the vacuum cleaner. She should have taken the bird out first.

Some of my pets weren't allowed in the house. Snakes and salamanders were in this category. Originally, salamanders were allowed, but, after Mom saw the salamanders on their way down the stairs as she was on her way up, they, too, were banned.

For a while, I was permitted to share my bedroom with a raccoon. He slept on a branch of a tree which I nailed to the floor in a corner of my room.

Mom heard that raccoons liked to raid people's kitchens. She put her foot down, and insisted that I build an outside cage for the coon.

During the first night in his cage, the raccoon escaped. I felt bad because he was a gift from the owner of the Catskill Game Farm. The thought occurred to me, however, that animals didn't belong in cages, anyway.

When I was three—when I moved to The Gateway—my grandmother gave me a kitten. We named the brown and black tiger cat Chi Chi. Of all my pets, Chi Chi was my favorite, and for over a span of eleven years we developed a strong bond.

Sometimes Chi Chi disappeared for several days, but I never worried, because he always came home. Then, the time came when my old cat didn't return after a week; after two weeks I knew Chi Chi was gone.

Occasionally, I played underneath our long front porch. It ran the whole length of the house. Due to the terrain, the west side of the porch was too low to crawl under. One day while under the porch, I crawled toward the west side. At the narow end I saw Chi Chi. I called him, but there was no response. He was curled up the way he usually slept. In the tight space I could only reach his tail. I put my hand around his tail and gave it a slight tug. The cat's tail separated from its body. Sobbing silently, I laid in the cool, damp earth with Chi Chi's detached tail in my hand. After a while I crawled back outside into the sunshine and left my old friend sleeping peacefully in his final resting place.

Chi Chi's demise was my second experience with death. The first was the old lady whose room I was given after she died. I was quite sure that cats didn't go to heaven. Why this was escaped me. I did know that if I had to choose between who I would see in heaven, Chi Chi, or the old lady, my affections were with the cat. Now, my grandfather was dead. If anybody went to heaven, I was sure he'd be there.

Although my experience in Greenwich Village was enough to scare the hell out of anybody, it didn't stop me from seeking new adventure. Summer arrived, and early one Saturday morning I headed off to New York's most famous beach, Coney Island. I arrived early; but in just a few hours the beach was packed. Had I wanted to catch the surf, I would have had to step over innumerable bodies basking in the sweltering heat, so I simply lay in the sun and read a book all day.

Before I knew it, the sun slipped away and darkness invaded the broad, sandy beach. I dresssed, rolled up my beach towel, and took one last glance at the Atlantic.

Suddenly, a small, dark-complexioned boy hobbled toward me, his right leg in a cast.

"Hey, Meester!" he began. "My mother wants to see you."

"I don't even know your mother," I replied as he scurried away.

"She es over here," the boy said over his shoulder.

Instinctively, I followed. Just ahead, the boy approached two women, apparently Hispanic, and a man laying on a blanket. They greeted me with wide smiles. One woman, whom I figured to be the boy's mother, motioned for me to sit down. She was attractive, with long dark brown hair, and a good figure.

"Please," she said, "could you do a beeg favor for me?"

"Well, ah, sure," I replied.

Unmarried, and with a son with a broken leg, she sought an escort for the evening. She invited me to eat at Nathan's Hot Dogs, and then assist her with her son on the Coney Island rides. And, the evening climaxed quite wonderfully in Spanish Harlem.

While I had friends at work, by and large, I was lonely in New York. The loneliness drove me to seek some sort of higher meaning to life. Long walks took me all over Manhattan. In the Times Square area, street evangelists could be found almost any night of the week. Some were obviously lunatics, and the crowds gave them wide berth.

Any time I saw a crowd gathered around a street preacher I stopped to listen. Some of these itinerant evangelists attracted good-sized crowds. Although often taunted, their sincerity showed through, and I found myself drawn by their words.

Back at the Ansonia, I stayed awake late into the evening reading my Bible. My reading was random and haphazard; I scoffed at some of the stories, but derived pleasure and meaning from others.

One Sunday night I visited a young adult group at a midtown Methodist church. I secretly hoped that I'd be accepted, and could, perhaps, find some sort of spiritual home. Treated as an outsider, they cold-shouldered me, and I didn't bother to go back.

Like many occupations, unless you're at, or near the top, or independent, window display doesn't pay well. Several people I knew worked as free-lance decorators. One of them was Chris, a thirty-year-old lesbian. She hired me to assist her with windows she did every week at various East Side boutiques.

Late in the evening, after we finished the windows, Chris and I invariably went out for a drink. She always drank a mint-flavored drink called a Grasshopper. While we sipped our drinks we talked. Chris was attractive, with thick, straight, natural blonde hair. Sometimes she teased me, and hinted that she'd like to bed me, but nothing ever came of it.

I liked working independently, and quit my job as mannequin boy at Saks Fifth Avenue—Henry Callahan would have to get somebody else to assault his mannequins.

While I enjoyed New York in many ways, I sensed that my fortune would be made elsewhere. Even though my free-lance artistic talents earned me a living—however meager—the competition was great in New York. Others around me had such a flair for the work that I wondered if window display or decorating was really for me.

Meanwhile, Tony, one of my roommates, ended his pursuit of an operatic career and accepted a position as general manager of Villagio Italia, a resort in the Catskills. Before leaving New York, Tony asked me out for lunch. At lunch, he offered me a job as his assistant at the resort.

Once again, the timing was fortuitous. Within two weeks, I found myself on the mountaintop.

6

California Dreaming

In 1964, just before I left New York, the Ford Motor Company unveiled its exciting new Mustang. I saw one in a Manhattan showroom, fell in love with it, and convinced Dad to co-sign an auto loan. Because of my new job at the resort, he figured I was good for the money and guaranteed the loan.

So, here I was, single, with a hot new convertible, and living at Villagio Italia, a popular mountain resort. Life was never more promising.

One weekend, while visiting Hillsdale, about 40 miles away, I attended a friend's graduation party. The bash was good, so good that at its conclusion the merrymakers wanted to continue their revelry. I invited the group to my grandfather's cottage on Prospect Lake—which, of course, I had no right to do.

For me, going back to Prospect Lake represented a new start. In reality, though, I went around in a circle, ending up right back where I started.

At that very lake, three years earlier, I had lost my virginity, and began a relationship for which I paid a high emotional toll. When that affair ended, the hurt remained.

At times, I ached for a steady, intimate relationship with a woman. And other times, I wanted a bevy of girlfriends; I wanted to play the field. Two needs motivated my search for romance: a hardy sexual appetite, and the need to love and be loved. My low self-esteem, though, clouded my judgment and made me vulnerable to unhealthy liaisons.

The party included everything that a wild beer party at a lake should include: a radio blaring rock and roll, beer-drinking contests, ribald jokes and conversation, skinny-dipping, and sex. I spent the first half of the night with a fifteen-year-old high school girl. Then, later, I became engaged in conversation with Linda, one of her friends of the same age. Linda and I talked for hours. Our conversation was deep and serious, about God, the meaning of life, and our hopes and dreams. Before we knew it, the sun rose over the lakeside cottage.

One of the girls invited the whole gang to her house for breakfast, assuring us that her mother would be glad to feed all of us. Sure enough, her mother did.

After breakfast I took Linda to her home, and then returned to Villagio Italia. Before I left, we made plans to see each other again. Soon, Linda and I dated regularly. Because of her age, her parents tried—though inconsistently—to restrict her activities, but we always managed to circumvent their interference.

The school year was about to end, and I asked Tony if Linda could work at Villagio for the summer. He gave her a job at the resort's day camp.

That summer I worked hard. At first, as Tony's assistant, I performed a myriad of jobs for seven days a week. Then, Tony made me the sole purchasing agent for the resort. This meant that I had to keep the place supplied with its daily supply of pasta sauce, spumoni ice cream, Chianti wine, toilet tissue, and everything else needed to keep a resort running. It was a daily headache, and often chaotic.

Every week I drove the Villagio panel truck to Manhattan for fresh meat, a 250-mile round trip. On some days I drove a dump truck to Long Island City to pick up Italian wines, then over to the lower West Side of Manhattan to load up with liquor.

When we could get away, Linda and I went out at night. Almost any time I was at the resort I'd be paged to come and help with one crisis or another. If we left the grounds, I caught hell from Tony the next day because I wasn't there when he needed me.

With an average fifteen-hour, fast-paced day, seven days a week, I became run-down and ill. I ran a fever, and had no strength at all. A doctor made a house-call and, after an examination, said I had mono and needed to rest for a few weeks.

My Aunt Barbara, the Franciscan nun, visited me. A nun in full regalia at an Italian resort causes some stir! While I don't remember her saying any prayers at my bedside, I had a suspicion that she talked to somebody up there about my condition. After a few days I was out of bed and back to work again.

Meanwhile, Linda and I became quite an item. The other employees viewed us—the two love birds—in a charming sort of way. The admiration, however shallow, was nice. On the surface, our relationship carried all the allure of a wonderful romance. And in some ways it was a good romance. However, we were blinded by both our youth and the moment. While our time together qualified as the classic June-to-September romance, I wanted more. I didn't want Linda to leave in the fall.

As the summer neared its end, Linda and I fought often. On several occasions, while parked in my Mustang in the woods, just off some back road, she cried and told me that it wasn't working, that it was getting too serious. I cried too, and told her that I loved her and we could make it work. This caused tremendous tension between us.

I lost one girl, and it hurt a lot; I didn't want to lose another. I fought hard to keep her, not for her, or us, but for me. For every argument she threw at me about why our relationship couldn't work, I argued hard and long why it could, and would.

Finally, I convinced Linda to stay on at Villagio Italia. A local family, whose members worked at the resort, offered her a spare bedroom in their home. Because Linda just turned sixteen, and agreed to stay in school, her parents let her leave home for the Catskills.

Our romance continued through the fall and winter. In February, I reached the age of 21. Now, as the war in Vietnam escalated, Uncle Sam wanted me.

Several months earlier, my draft board had ordered me to report to the village of Catskill for a pre-induction physical. Upon learning that I'd had mono within the year, they deferred me for six months.

Then they called me again and this time I passed the physical with flying colors and became a prime draft candidate. Horrified, I sought a way to avoid being shipped off to Vietnam.

As a kid, military service, particularly the Navy, seemed to be a good option. I was very willing to defend our country in the event of an attack, or even a threatened attack. I couldn't, however, understand what threat the North Vietnamese posed to America. The Vietnam war never proffered a "bad guy," like an Adolf Hitler or Saddam

Hussein. My conscience told me that there was no valid reason to go to these people's land and shoot them. It didn't matter whether they happpened to be from North Vietnam or South Vietnam. I wrote to my draft board and requested conscientious objector status; I told them, except in self-defense, I could not kill a person.

Soon, I got my reply. They rejected my request without explanation. Extremely angry, I was determined to avoid the draft. Then, I learned that before his assassination, President Kennedy had issued an order deferring married men from the draft. I had found my answer.

Though Linda Silvernail was only sixteen, I proposed to her. While our problems hadn't gotten any better, she agreed to marry me. Her father, Wally, a kind man, almost collapsed when we asked permission for Linda to wed. He granted it under one condition, that she finish high school—because her older brother and sister hadn't. Others, though, warned us that teen marriages didn't work, because people changed over time. Well, I wasn't a teen, I reasoned, even though she was. But we were in love, and we just *knew* everything would work out.

By now both of us had enough seniority at Villagio Italia to have Sundays off and we began attending the United Methodist Church in Tannersville. Rev. J. Filson Reid, the church's minister, became fond of us, and agreed to perform the wedding in March. Meanwhile, he tried to coax me into studying for the ministry. While he knew nothing about my background, he detected something of my scuttled bornagain experience. Although I almost succumbed to his cajoling, I successfully resisted a call to the ministry.

After a congenial candlelight wedding on a cold and rainy March evening, we went off on our honeymoon—to another Catskill resort. Sadly, the respite away from work was the brightest thing about our honeymoon. Immediately afterward, I informed the draft board of my marital status, and that year, 1965, I received my long-awaited deferment.

Linda and I were romantics at heart, and that was one of the few things we had in common. Because of Hollywood's portrayal, and the tales we'd heard, California beckoned us westward. Perhaps I'd go back into window display, I thought; Palo Alto's Saks Fifth Avenue was near San Francisco. So, with part of an inheritance from Grampa, we made some advance car payments, threw our scant possessions into the back of the Mustang and headed for San Francisco—to live happily ever after.

California Dreaming

The trip to California was grand. With AAA road maps to guide us, we crisscrossed the country following old Route 66 much of the way.

As often as we could, we sacked-out at night in our sleeping bags under the stars. One night in the Ozarks, a sudden thunderstorm drenched us before we took refuge in the car. In the morning, some other happy campers, warm and dry as they emerged from their tent, offered us hot coffee and breakfast.

In Arizona, while searching for buffalo on some dusty road, we got stuck in the sand. After a National Parks ranger's truck pulled us out, we were on our way again.

At the Grand Canyon, while we marveled at the views, two Jehovah's Witnesses passed out copies of *Watchtower* and *Awake!* magazines. While I'd known about Jehovah's Witnesses, this was the first time I'd ever met one. I took their literature and read parts of it, but wasn't impressed; something about it didn't ring true. The sincerity and dedication of the Witnesses, though, impressed me strongly.

A quick self-examination revealed that my life lacked positive direction; I had no firm foundation upon which my values were based, and there were many questions about life to which I had no absolute answers. While I was a free spirit, I wondered if I was, perhaps, too free.

Awestruck by America's scenic beauty, and the wonderful possibilities that lay ahead for us, Linda and I remained harmonious for the duration of the trip—our problems temporarily overshadowed.

We passed through a dozen states on our two-week trek, and arrived in California broke. My inheritance amounted to $2,000, but because of litigation over the will, I only received half of that. With the advance car payments, and the expenses of the trip it had all disappeared.

A friend from high school now lived in Southern California. We looked him up and he offered us the couch as a place to sleep. From there, I hoped to get a temporary job, save some money, and continue on to San Francisco.

My friend told me that American Electric, a war plant that manufactured bombs and land mines for use in Vietnam, was hiring. So, dressed in a gray suit from Saks Fifth Avenue, a white shirt and my best tie, I applied for a job. Duly impressed, they hired me on the spot, and at seven the next morning I began my new position—sweeping floors in a long warehouse at two dollars an hour.

After cashing my first paycheck, Linda and I moved into an efficiency unit at the Arizona Motel, in Harbor City, California. Before long, we had saved enough to rent a one-bedroom apartment in Harbor City.

As required by law, I informed my draft board in New York of my new address. To my dismay, President Lyndon Johnson rescinded Kennedy's order exempting married men from the draft.

By return mail I received an order to appear in Catskill for another pre-induction physical. I couldn't believe they were so stupid to ask me to travel from Los Angeles to Catskill for a physical. So, hoping to avoid this, I wrote and asked them to re-schedule my appointment at the Los Angeles induction center.

They didn't waste any time; within days notification arrived ordering me to report for a physical in Los Angeles. Induction was getting too close for comfort.

At the induction center hundreds of young men were ordered to strip bare and parade from doctor to doctor for various examinations. During the process I unsuccessfully feigned deafness and blindness.

While standing in the long line before the final doctor, I acted out of desperation. My right toe suffered perennially from a slight ingrown nail; with clenched teeth, I stomped on that toe with my left foot. The pain shot through my leg and tears welled up in my eyes; I looked down at my toe. The ghastly thing throbbed, and blood dripped from under the nail onto the floor.

The doctor took one look and said, "Boy, you ought to have that taken care of." He deferred my induction for thirty days, but it would be six months before I heard from them again.

Sweeping floors for a living in a dark and dingy warehouse wasn't my idea of life in sunny California. However, I made the best of it, and when an opening came up for a forklift driver I got the job and soon mastered the utility vehicle. All day long, trucks arrived from American Electric's various plants, while others came by to pick up parts for shipment to aircraft companies and the armed forces—to ultimately end up in Vietnam.

All incoming components needed to be inspected by the company's quality-control people, and then by U.S. Government inspectors, before being shipped out. Large wooden crates and wire baskets went from the trucks to a special area for initial inspection. From there they went into storage, where they were kept until they were needed.

One day Deak, an American Electric inspector, asked me to move a crate of metal nose cones into a better-lighted area so he could inspect them. Deak showed me where to put the very heavy crate, and because he stood so near, I acted with extreme care. Upon his indication to lower the forks, I performed the maneuver very slowly. With a gentle thud, the heavy crate met the floor; I shifted into reverse and backed the forklift away. Suddenly, Deak hollered.

"Owww! Goddammit, you put the son-of-a-bitch on my feet!"

In a panic, with grinding gears I rammed the floor shift lever forward, dropped the fork, and popped the clutch. As Deak continued to holler I lifted the heavy crate from his feet.

Shaken, I jumped from the forklift to examine the extent of Deak's injuries, certain we'd have to call an ambulance. Deak was doubled over —laughing so hard he couldn't speak.

My fear quickly turned to bewilderment, then relief, as I learned the truth behind Deak's prank. With prosthetic feet and lower legs— crafted of solid wood and hardened steel—Deak didn't feel a thing; he wasn't hurt at all. After that, we became fast friends.

From time to time I noticed Dave, the warehouse's shipping clerk, walking through the echo-filled corridors singing gospel songs. Always extremely courteous and helpful, Dave, a black man, seemed at peace with himself and the world. I wondered what kind of church he attended.

I soon tired of the dank warehouse, and when a truck driver quit, the foreman offered me the position. I readily accepted it, and the accompanying raise—my second.

An identical building to American Electric's warehouse sat directly across the shipping yard; it served as some sort of light-assembly factory for another company. When my truck was being loaded or unloaded, I parked it in this yard between the two buildings. The women who worked in that building came out for air during their breaks, and if I was there with my truck, they'd engage me in conversation.

Soon after arriving in California, I wished I wasn't married. The 1960s in California, and, I suppose, in much of the country, were freewheeling and radical. Many of the women I met flirted openly, even some of Linda's friends.

For the first time, I felt like I held some attraction to the opposite sex. While the feeling bolstered my ego, it presented a dilemma; I was a married man. Nevertheless, I didn't let that hinder me for very long. Five months after my wedding, I began an affair with Ann, one of the women from the assembly plant across the shipping yard.

Logistically, affairs are usually difficult, and this one was no exception; there are only a certain number of cover stories one can concoct. Very briefly, I entertained thoughts of sending Linda home, and then getting a divorce, but, despite my actions, I believed marriage was a lifetime proposition. Before long I felt the emotional pressure of living a dual life.

While I drove a truck, I kept up my contacts with Deak and some of the other people in quality control. Deak encouraged me to learn a little technology so I could transfer into quality control. He taught me how to use various precision measuring instruments. I picked up some library books on elementary engineering, which taught me how to read schematic diagrams and blueprints.

One day I learned of an opening in quality control; I made an appointment with that department's director. After convincing him I could do the job, I was hired. The next morning I was back in the warehouse, not sweeping the floor, or moving parts around with a forklift, but as an inspector. The new position paid more, and offered some degree of prestige, as no parts were moved without approval from quality control.

Quite reasonably, guilt overtook me as my affair with Ann continued, and I knew I needed some sort of guidance. During a coffee break one day, I sat on some boxes next to Dave, and I queried him about his church. He told me that he attended The People's Tabernacle of Faith in Los Angeles. Dave acted somewhat uncomfortable when I asked him if I could attend a service, but he indicated that anyone could attend. I had a feeling—and private hope—that Dave's church might offer something extraordinary; I got the Temple Street address.

The next Sunday I asked Linda if she'd like to go to church with me, that a friend at work went there, and it sounded interesting. She agreed to go, so, dressed in our Sunday best, we drove from Harbor City to Los Angeles, a distance of about twenty miles. My expectations, and more, were realized at The People's Tabernacle of Faith.

7

The Rapture

The People's Tabernacle of Faith, a large wooden structure with peeling gray paint, reverberated with lively gospel singing, a hard-driven organ, and enthusiastic hand-clapping. As we left our convertible in the small parking lot next to the church, I cringed as I imagined the scene inside. I think Linda felt the same way, but even more so.

We slipped inside inconspicuously and found seats in the back. Even from that distant vantage point the pervasive music jolted our senses. Many of the people stood, clapping and waving their hands in the air, while others remained seated and just rocked back and forth. A heavy black woman in a white nurse's uniform danced, with closed eyes as if in a trance, in the front of the church.

Feeling uneasy, I decided we should leave, but a glance toward the exit revealed two large men—one black, one white—with folded arms standing on either side of the door. Guards, I thought. Realizing we'd have to stay until the conclusion of the service, I hoped we weren't in any great danger from this strange cult.

Every time the singing subsided, the radiant red-robed choir inspired the church members to go on a little bit longer. Spontaneously, spirited soloists stepped out, and worked the congregation into a frenzy. The black organist, animated and full of energy, was obviously enjoying his gig. With its several rows of keys and numerous foot pedals, the organ resonated with seemingly impossible sounds; it was so unlike the church music I was used to back home. The music in the Methodist church, with its doleful organ, dragged; and the Baptists, although they couldn't afford an organ, performed the same dreadful music on their upright piano.

With such flair, I thought, this choir must be professional. Memories of the Apollo Theater flashed through my mind. Beginning to enjoy the show, I relaxed a bit, and before long, the merriment came to an end.

As the choir members took their seats, the minister stepped up to the microphone and announced the offering.

"Bring your tithes and offerings to the Lord!" he shouted.

With that, the organ burst forth with cheery music that brought the audience to its feet again. From all over the church people stood, with cash in hand, and walked to the front of the church, where they dropped their offering in a basket.

Then, after some announcements, the minister read some scripture passages and launched into his sermon. And what a sermon! In black churches, the minister and congregation have a sort of dialogue during the sermon. Whenever the preacher uttered something the congregation liked, they said so.

"Alright now."

"Preach it!"

"Amen, brother."

This was unheard of in my tradition. If someone tried that back home, they'd surely be asked to leave, but here it was encouraged. Sometimes the minister actually said, "Can I hear an 'Amen'?"

After a brief warm-up, the minister got into a rhythm, pulling the audience along with him; it seemed as if a spell came upon the minister and the congregation. While the minister preached, many members of the congregation cooled themselves with funeral-parlor fans. I observed this with rapt attention.

At times the preacher broke away from the prevailing mood and thundered his utterances. Excitedly, he removed his eyeglasses, and now, like a 250-pound ballerina, jumped around the raised platform while continuing to shout. The audience, out of its trance, stomped its feet and clapped its hands. Suddenly, with a whoop, he threw his glasses into the air; they bounced off the ceiling and came crashing down on the floor. The congregation went berserk.

Now, with tears streaming down his cheeks, the minister wrapped up his sermon and made a plea to those who sought to know God to come down to the altar.

As the organ came alive again, people came down to the front of the church. Two ladies tearfully knelt at the altar. The lady in the white nurse's uniform came bouncing down the center aisle, half dancing, half running; she picked up speed as she approached the altar, and, to my amazement, fell to her knees and slid about two yards, right up behind the two kneeling ladies, and with the palms of her hands, slapped them both on the back of their heads. Now, with her hands raised in the air, she blurted something in a strange language. Dazed, the two women lay across the altar.

Apparently none of this came as a surprise to anyone else; most of the audience began to break up and turn toward the door. Anxious to leave, I grabbed Linda's hand and made a beeline for the exit. A large white woman with an exuberant smile stepped into our path. I smiled at her and was about to say "Excuse me," as we attempted to go around her. No such luck; she threw her heavy arms around me and applied a bear hug.

"Where are you dears from?" she asked after letting me go. Almost before we could answer, other people either hugged us or pumped our hands. Linda and I became separated as enthusiastic parishioners greeted us. Everyone invited us back, and reminded us that their next service was that evening. It was difficult to imagine that after two hours of what we'd just witnessed they'd go back that night for more.

When the dust settled, Linda and I regrouped and headed for our car, and as we left the parking lot people were still waving at us. We drove back to Harbor City in stunned silence.

During the week that followed I thought often about the previous Sunday's experience. While totally strange, perhaps fanatical, the event imparted a warm inner feeling. I arose early on the next Sunday and asked Linda if she was coming to church with me. Surprised that I was eager to go back, she declined.

About the only difference I noticed from the previous Sunday was in my own response. Although not quite at home, I didn't feel like a stranger; the people accepted me like I was a member of the family. My friend Dave from work was absent both of these Sundays.

After the service a number of the mostly black church members approached me; they called me by name, and several asked where Linda was. This impressed me, and brought to mind my visit to the Methodist church in Manhattan a few years earlier; those people totally ignored me. I didn't know it at the time, but I was already hooked by this new-found church home.

I learned that the minister's name was Rev. Harley Akers. He recently left the African Methodist Episcopal (AME) Church to start the independent People's Tabernacle of Faith. His sister, Doris Akers, a gospel recording artist, joined his venture to lead the choir; her previous choir, the Sky Pilot Choir, reached considerable fame among California churchgoers. Isaiah "Ike" Jones was the organist.

Bolstered by my new church affiliation, I told Ann I couldn't see her any more, that our affair was over. Hurt, she asked why? I told her I'd found the Lord again. At first she didn't believe me; then she said I was crazy. Crazy or not, it came as a relief.

Determined to begin life anew, I immersed myself in Christianity. Southern California has several Christian radio stations, with KGER being the most prominent at the time; I listened to this station whenever I was in the car. (Incidentally, because of transmission problems with the Mustang, we traded it in for a Volkswagen bug. I think the sale of the Mustang was significant, marking the end of an era for me.) With the VW radio always tuned to KGER, I became a regular listener to Kathryn Kuhlman, the healing evangelist; Garner Ted Armstrong, the voice of the Worldwide Church of God; J. Vernon McGee, the Bible-teacher from Los Angeles's Church of the Open Door—the first Fundamentalist church in America; Demos Shakarian, founder of the Full Gospel Businessmen's Fellowship International; and a number of others.

The Sunday I attended People's Tabernacle of Faith alone was the only one Linda missed; she came with me the following week and we thoroughly enjoyed the services. A new soloist performed a riveting gospel number called "There's Power in the Blood." After the service we met him. Richard Durfield, a wiry young black, was a bit shy, but had a certain magnetism which made him extremely likable. Ric held a position as a court clerk at the California Superior Court in Santa Monica.

Ric was impressed that we had left New York, not really knowing where we were going or what we would do, to come to California. He indicated that he'd never do anything like that, but his inner strength was evident, and I figured he was just being modest.

In the weeks which followed we never missed a Sunday morning service, and even began attending the Sunday night services and Wednesday night prayer meetings. I felt good in my new environment and absorbed everything I could.

After one Sunday morning service, Rev. Akers and some other men prayed for a lady to be healed of some ailment. I wasn't invited to join in, but, out of curiosity, I hovered nearby because I'd noticed that they always put their hands on people when they prayed for them, and sometimes they spoke in a strange language, which I guessed was probably an African dialect, perhaps Swahili.

I asked Ric about this and he said the Bible says "The prayer of faith will heal the sick," and also, "You shall lay hands on the sick and they shall recover." Well, I knew that those things happened in the New Testament, but I didn't know the practice still existed today. Ric also said that the Holy Spirit gives some Christians a special language to pray in called "speaking in tongues." It comes, he said, with the "baptism in the Holy Spirit." Although I was pretty open to all these new spiritual things, this was a little too bizarre for me to swallow.

Just about the time all the new excitement began to wear off—not to say we didn't still enjoy going to church, because we did, with Rev. Akers' lively sermons, and the rousing choir, but it peaked and became a routine—a dramatic conversion took place at People's Tabernacle. Rev. Akers preached in his typical manner, the choir carried on as usual, and Ric sang "There's Power in the Blood." Then Pastor Akers gave the altar call, and nobody responded. He instructed Ike to keep playing while he pleaded for someone to respond to the Lord's call. As he pleaded, a young woman stood up in the back and practically ran to the front of the church. Sobbing, she fell to her knees at the altar. Several members of the church joined Rev. Akers at the altar to pray with the young woman.

Everyone breathed a sigh of relief because of the response to the altar call, for if there was no response, it could have meant that someone was disobeying God. And she seemed genuinely sincere, which made it even better.

Afterwards, Linda and I met the new convert. Her name was Renee King, and she, like us, came to California searching, except she was from Pittsburgh, Kathryn Kuhlman's hometown. Renee was an attractive, very light-skinned black, so light that she often passed for white. Linda and I liked Renee immediately because she was so outgoing and friendly.

A week later Renee arrived well before the service was to begin. We were glad to see her, and the three of us sat together. Afterwards, Ric approached us, and to our delight, we learned that he'd seen Renee during the week. Someone suggested we have lunch, and so the four of us went out and had a nice time. It was obvious that Ric and Renee had hit it off, and even at this early point, it looked serious. Linda and I were thrilled to have another couple close to our age as friends.

Ric grew up in the Church of God in Christ, in Pacoima, a black church out in the San Fernando Valley. From his youth he had been exposed to a variety of Pentecostal doctrines and practices. And like me, he experienced periods of wavering, commonly known as backsliding. His mother, a very spiritual woman, exerted a strong influence on Ric, which always drew him back to the church whenever he wavered.

Renee, in Pittsburgh, had some experience with spiritual things, but she too had fallen prey to the things of the world. She recounted the time when she stopped believing in God; she said it happened when she realized her parents lied to her as a child about Santa Claus; if they lied about that, then, she reasoned, the story of Jesus dying for her sins must be a lie too. Renee's new-found salvation marked the end of the road for her waywardness.

More and more, the four of us did things together. Soon, Ric and Renee announced their plans to marry. This solidified the bonding among the four of us.

Renee joined Ric in the choir, and our relationship as a foursome continued to grow. Ric, full of stories about evangelists and faith healers, stimulated our interest in learning all we could about this new born-again life. He told tales of Oral Roberts raising people from the dead; of the Christian mystic, Brother William Branham, who, after finding a dying turkey in the woods, laid his hands on the stinking bird, and the bird jumped up and ran off, completely healed; of A. Earl Lee and his supernatural visitations; of A. A. Allen's Arizona community called Miracle Valley, where it was common to see angels on the street;

and many more amazing events which demonstrated the power of God. In addition, he seemed to know something about every evangelical Christian group or activity in Southern California. Night after night, he took us to various evangelistic services and healing meetings.

At the old Embassy Hotel in downtown Los Angeles, we went to see the healing evangelist Leroy Jenkins. Jenkins used prayer cloths and anointed oil to inspire the faithful to believe. I was amazed how God used this man to help others to make shortened legs normal, to give sight to the blind, hearing to the deaf, and the power to walk again to the crippled—right before our eyes. At one point during the service, Leroy, as he was always referred to by Ric, picked out three people from different sections of the audience. He said the three would each be healed, one in the name of the Father, one in the name of the Son, and one in the name of the Holy Ghost. As Jenkins prayed the prayer of faith, one lady fell to the floor. He went over to one of the others and laid hands on the man, and he too, fell. The third person, even with Jenkins' hands on him, didn't fall down, so Jenkins ordered the man to go home to claim his healing, without stopping to talk to anyone. Immediately, the man left the auditorium.

I asked Ric why the people fell down, and he said they were being "slain in the Spirit," or "going down under the power," as some people put it.

On the way back from the meeting, as the four of us cruised happily down the Hollywood Freeway in Ric's long and loaded Pontiac, he told Linda and me about the Rapture.

The Rapture, we learned, was a world-wide miraculous event about to take place—at any moment—in which every born-again Christian would suddenly be swept into the sky to meet Jesus in the air. For some reason, in all my years in and out of church, I didn't remember ever hearing about this. We were astounded at such a possibility, but Ric, always certain about spiritual things, spoke with such authority that we believed every word of this incredible thing. (Ric's air of certainty was such that even Superior Court judges sought his counsel on court decisions.) When Ric said we were in the last days, the end times, and that it was all in the Bible, Renee dutifully turned on the car's inside lights, opened up Ric's red, leather-covered Scofield Reference Bible, and turned to the appropriate scriptures. I noticed that Ric had been telling Renee everthing he knew about the Bible, and of his extensive religious experiences.

Learning about the Rapture was a milestone for me; it was awesome to think that millions of people were totally unprepared for such an event. I felt privileged to have knowledge of this, and realized that, for some reason, the Lord had held this knowledge back until now; perhaps, because at any other time in my life I would have laughed at it. Now, though, I could handle it responsibly and use it to win souls for Jesus. At that moment, I made a secret decision to become a minister and serve the Lord full time.

8

Cults and Isms

Everything in our lives seemed to be going well: Jesus saved our marriage, we had close friends, my job was challenging, and my salary was decent. Linda completed high school, as she promised her father she would, during our first year in California and, after graduation, she got a job with Pacific Telephone. I also confessed to Linda about my affair with Ann and received her forgiveness.

Los Angeles Harbor College was located in Harbor City, near our apartment. Both of us enrolled in the junior college's night courses to study business administration. The prospect of a college education was now exciting, and the state of California's educational system made it affordable.

Our relationship with Ric and Renee continued to grow. Ric told us of a missionary organization which presented live broadcasts on KGER. Once a week, participants gathered at a church in Long Beach, and after a pep talk and prayer, teams witnessed door-to-door about Jesus. At a designated time, the teams returned to the church, where they had a live hook-up to the radio station. Team members testified of the night's events on the radio.

The four of us listened to the broadcast one time and became convinced that we should all go to Long Beach to participate. The first night, Abe Schneider led our team. He referred to himself as a "completed Jew," that is, a Jew who has accepted Jesus. Abe was dedicated to the Apostle Paul's admonition to bring the gospel "to the Jew first."

A fast talker with a lisp, Abe invariably used one line when introducing the subject of salvation to strangers who opened their doors to him.

"Hello, my name ith Abe Thighter; ith an athomic bomb were dropth on Loth Angelith tonith, where would you spenth eternithy?"

Usually, Abe engendered a fast response to his hypothetical question; annoyed home owners slammed the door in his face.

The missionary organization employed a training technique called "faith treks," to create a practical, individual faith in God as a provider. All their missionary candidates had to go on a faith trek before engaging in overseas missionary work. Candidates, without a dime in their pockets, or any possessions other than the clothes on their backs, were driven out to the desert, about one-hundred-fifty miles away from Long Beach. After being dropped off on some isolated highway, they had to make their way back, relying on God to provide rides, food, and drink, or whatever needs they might have. Everyone always made it back safely in a day or so, and hearing their testimonies was exciting.

Linda and I realized a certain sense of security in our relationship with Ric and Renee, and I'm sure they felt the same way. Soon after we began attending the missionary group's meetings, the idea came up, "Wouldn't it be wonderful if the four of us became missionaries together?"

"Yes!" we replied spontaneously.

Barely into college, Linda and I quit our classes, and prepared to enroll in missionary school. Perhaps, in a year or so, Ric and Renee and Linda and I would be sitting in the African bush together, watching the sun set, and reminiscing about how many natives we saved that day. The thought was romantic.

Enthusiastically, we told Brother Akers (by now we'd begun to address mature Christians as "brother" or "sister") of our decision. He didn't like the idea because the missionary group required us to attend its church while undergoing training. For one thing, both of our families had become tithers, giving fully ten percent of our income, before taxes, directly to the church; while the loss of this income wouldn't break the church, it was significant. Akers posed several tough questions which made us re-evaluate our rationale about becoming missionaries. Ultimately, he won, and we dropped the idea.

When Christmas Eve arrived, Linda and I vented some of our missionary zeal at LAX—Los Angeles International Airport. In just a few hours, we handed out 500 religious tracts to travelers headed home for the holidays, telling them of the true meaning of Christmas.

Harbor City was a good distance from my job, the church, and most of our activities, so we found a one-bedroom apartment in Inglewood, much closer to LA. Then, American Electric relocated to La Mirada, in Orange County, again making my daily drive longer. About the same time, a couple of executives left American Electric to join the Whittaker Corporation's Advanced Metals Division, in Gardena, near Inglewood. One of these men called me at home one night and offered me a position in quality control at the Whittaker Corporation. I thanked the Lord, and accepted the position.

A man named Lloyd worked in quality control at the Whittaker company; with his outgoing personality and cowboy boots, I liked him immediately. Then I learned that Lloyd was a former Assemblies of God minister who now lived with a woman much younger than himself. It hurt me to think that a man could stop serving the Lord, especially in such a wonderful Pentecostal denomination as the Assemblies of God. Convinced that God sent me there to win him back, I tried to befriend him, but Lloyd saw through my ruse and avoided me.

That year, 1967, our first child, Angela, was born; Linda, 18, quit the phone company shortly before the birth of our daughter.

More and more, Ric talked about the baptism of the Holy Spirit— or "the Baptism," as he usually put it. He said that after one is regenerated by the Holy Spirit and born again, there remains a second act of grace by God for the believer, and speaking in other tongues always accompanies the experience. Upset because Ric claimed to have something from God that I didn't have, I rejected this notion; I loved God as much as he did, so why should he have something from God that I didn't have?

Pastor J. Vernon McGee, of the fundamentalist Church of the Open Door, reinforced my viewpoint. Fundamentalists believe you get it all when you accept Jesus, and that seemed perfectly logical to me. I listened to McGee's noon Bible study on the radio every day and Linda and I attended his downtown church on one occasion.

Ric, always persistent, suggested that the four of us attend a Full Gospel breakfast on a Saturday morning in the upper room at Clifton's Cafeteria in downtown Los Angeles. These prayer breakfasts were organized by Demos Shakarian, a Christian dairyman. Shakarian, an unassuming kind of guy, used the breakfasts to launch the powerful Full Gospel Businessmen's Fellowship International, an international lay ministry.

I'd heard some of their broadcasts on KGER; it sounded kind of interesting, except I didn't want to get involved in this tongues business.

The Pentecostal movement began in earnest on January 1, 1901, at a little Bible school in Topeka, Kansas, run by Charles F. Parham. While Christians had spoken in tongues before on other occasions, Parham encouraged his students to consciously make an effort to speak in tongues. After many hours of working themselves up, the students finally began blurting out in this strange "language."

In 1905, after his school in Topeka failed, Parham moved to Houston, Texas and opened another Bible school. In Houston, he taught his students about Pentecostalism, and they, too, spoke in tongues.

A year later, a former student of Parham's, a black preacher named William J. Seymour, opened a mission on Azusa Street in Los Angeles. Under Seymour's direction a group of believers sought to have an experience from God, and some people received the "baptism in the Holy Spirit" with the evidence of speaking in tongues. When word of this got out, ministers from across North America flocked to LA to check it out. They picked up the hysteria and brought it back to their churches, and the Pentecostal movement, along with all the supposed supernatural manifestations, was launched.

About the time the commotion waned, it broke out again in the 1940s in Canada. This time it was named "Latter Rain." When that died out, it came alive again in the 1960s and 1970s as "Neo-Pentecostalism," or the "Charismatic" movement.

Several Saturdays—and numerous testimonies about healings and miracles from God—later, I became convinced that there really was something to this baptism in the Holy Spirit. I read the classic Pentecostal book on the subject, *They Speak With Other Tongues*, by John Sherrill. At my next breakfast at Clifton's I was ready; an evangelist named Joe Jordan prayed for people to receive the baptism. He moved down a long line of people, placing his hands on their heads, one by one; he shook them and shouted in tongues into their ears; some people dropped to the floor—slain in the spirit—and babbled in a strange language, while others made sounds as if they were stuttering. Jordan grabbed my head with both his hands and shook me violently, all the while speaking in tongues. "Just say what I'm saying, listen to me," he said. After several attempts, I imitated him. Praise God, I had the baptism!

Linda and Renee, too, sought the baptism that day, but were disappointed that either God chose not to give it to them, or that they failed God because they didn't have the faith. Their disappointment robbed me of the joy I had hoped we could all share together.

By now, my secret ambition to preach was out in the open. I was not only sure of my own calling, I was just as sure of Ric's call to the ministry; after all, he already knew much more about the Bible than I did, and he was sort of my mentor. While not fully convinced that it was the right thing for him, Ric agreed to go to Bible college. To help convince him, I paid for his first year—the rest of my grandfather's inheritance had finally come through, and I used it to pay for our first year at LIFE Bible College. LIFE is an acronym for Lighthouse of International Foursquare Evangelism, the school founded by the late Aimee Semple McPherson, who died in 1944, the year I was born. When we chose LIFE, I didn't know about the scandals that plagued her ministry. McPherson once ran off with one of her church employees, and to cover the episode, faked a kidnapping; later, she died of a drug overdose. Ric assured me that God's anointing was on LIFE, and its mother church, Angelus Temple, both located in the Echo Park section of Los Angeles.

The People's Tabernacle of Faith, though vibrant, found it difficult to pay the rent in downtown LA, and pay Rev. Aker's salary and benefits as well, so the board voted to relocate. A little storefront, which we shared with a barber shop in south-central Los Angeles, became our new church building. In that area, storefront churches exist on almost every block. In America, anyone can start up a new church on a whim; if one wants to serve the Lord, a church is a great tax-free business.

Rev. Akers wasn't hot on the idea of Ric and me attending Bible college, because the school wanted us to serve as volunteers in one of their Foursquare churches. Once again, Akers argued to keep us in his little flock, but this time we prevailed. Nevertheless, before we left our beloved church home, Rev. Akers asked me if I'd like to preach on a Sunday night.

Old high school friends, including my cousin Jeff, arrived in LA. When they called to see if we could get together, I invited them to hear my first sermon; I was certain they would turn down the invitation, but they didn't. With the prospect of having at least four unsaved people in the little church that night, I prepared diligently. After preaching my heart out—along with the presentation of some clever show-and-tell object lessons—I gave an altar call, and depended on the Holy Spirit to move hearts. While Ike played the organ, I pleaded, but no one responded, I didn't yet have the know-how to make a successful altar call.

Wisely preferring the security of his job over full-time Bible school, Ric opted to attend Bible college at night; the Whittaker corporation allowed me a certain amount of flexibility so I could attend school during the day. With our two-month-old daughter, Linda and I moved from Inglewood to Echo Park, just a block from the school.

Right after I enrolled in LIFE, Mom, Dad, and my two sisters came to Los Angeles to visit us. Their visit meant a lot to me, because I felt their support in my choice to become a minister. As a token of that support, Mom and Dad presented me with a new briefcase to carry my school papers.

Working and going to school full-time was difficult. The little time I spent with Linda and Angie was usually in church, or perhaps we'd take a walk along Echo Park's little lake. After that first year I left the Whittaker Corporation and took a night job with the Transamerica Corporation selling home owner's insurance over the phone. My small salary was enhanced by sales commissions. Selling on commission is sometimes unreliable, because every week isn't a good one. When Christmas came that year, we were broke. We didn't even have money to buy a Christmas tree. For the first time in either of our lives, we faced the prospect of celebrating Christmas without a tree. Our way of thinking had changed, though, and we saw the hand of God in our poverty; He wanted us to see the miracle of his Son, and not the glitter of a worldly Christmas tree.

About nine o'clock at night, just a couple of days before Christmas, I was on the Hollywood Freeway, coming home from downtown Los

Angeles. As usual, traffic was heavy. Just before my exit, cars in front of me braked, and then swerved to the right or left in order to avoid an object in the road. To my astonishment, a Christmas tree stood right in the middle of the center lane of the Hollywood Freeway. Right away, I knew it was God, that he'd been testing our faith, and now he'd placed the reward right where I couldn't miss it. I turned the Volkswagen onto the shoulder, and dodging the cars, sprinted out to the center lane and retrieved the tree. Although it was difficult to drive with the full-sized Christmas tree stuffed in the small car, I was home in five minutes. Linda and I cried together as we praised God for his blessings.

By now I was so completely dedicated to serving the Lord that I forgot what was happening in the world around me. The Vietnam War raged on, but no mention of the conflict was ever made in Bible college. If it hadn't been for the draft board, I would have forgotten all about Vietnam. One day, another notice arrived. (Earlier, I had written and told them I was a full-time ministerial student.) To my delight, a new draft card came in the mail marked 4-D—Divinity student—a classification which put me beyond the draft.

Before Bible classes one morning, I listened as some students discussed an up-and-coming Virginia minister named Jerry Falwell. There seemed to be some sort of controversy about him; I don't know what it was, but part of the discussion concerned his rigid fundamentalist beliefs. The LIFE students wondered how God could bless Falwell if he didn't believe in the baptism of the Holy Spirit.

"He'll never amount to anything," one of the students assured the group.

Although committed to Christ and filled with the Holy Spirit, many unanswered questions remained, and I still retained some openness to other ideas and beliefs. One evening, Mormon missionaries showed up at our front door. I was anxious to hear what they had to say.

There were two of them, as there always are, with dark suits, white shirts, and black ties. They were Elder Smith and Elder Benson.

"Oh, you both have the same first name," I said jokingly. Mormon missionaries—always men—are addressed as Elder. They give two years of their lives to serve as missionaries while their families foot all their expenses. During this two-year period they systematically go door-to-door trying to make converts for the Church of Jesus Christ of Latter-day Saints.

Linda offered Elders Smith and Benson some coffee or tea, but she was politely informed that Mormons didn't drink beverages containing caffeine. And we assumed that alcohol was also forbidden, which was fine, because we had recently stopped all use of alcohol ourselves.

After being invited in, the Mormon visitors got right down to business. As good salesmen, they launched their pitch from a point where we all agreed, and from there they worked their way into new territory.

To my wonder, according to Mormon theology, the Bible is the Word of God, and Jesus died for our sins and rose from the dead. That was good, for so far there was nothing unusual about their beliefs.

The Elders set up a flannel graph—a tripod that held a flannel-covered story board—and placed a map of the Old World to the right on the flannel graph. Above the map, Elder Smith positioned a picture of the Bible. As they continued to talk, one of them fastened a cardboard cutout of Jesus with outstretched arms, right in the middle of the flannel board.

Jesus appeared to the inhabitants of the Old World to offer them salvation from their sins, they said. Some accepted him, others rejected him, but everyone had a chance. Linda and I agreed with that.

"But, what about the inhabitants of the undiscovered New World, the Indians?" Elder Smith asked. Good question, I thought, for that had never occurred to me before.

Of course, such a leading question demands a good answer, which the Mormons readily provided. They said that after Jesus died and rose from the dead, he took a lightning-fast trip over to the New World to preach to the Indians. Noticing the puzzled look on my face, the Elders moved quickly to resolve any doubts I had.

"Between the time Jesus died and rose from the dead," Elder Benson asked, "and the time he ascended into heaven, where did he go and what did he do?" Again, a good question. I had no idea; the Bible was silent on this.

The next item added to the flannel graph—a map of the New World, the American continents—provided the obvious answer. This is where Jesus spent that unaccounted-for time, according to the Mormons, preaching the Gospel to the Native Americans. All this, they claimed, is detailed in the Book of Mormon. As a sort of grand finale, Elder Benson applied a picture of the Book of Mormon above the map of the New World. So, we have the Holy Bible for the Old World, and the Book of Mormon for the New World. That concluded the first lesson. Before leaving, the Elders made an appointment to come back in a week. Linda and I looked forward to the next session.

A week later, promptly at seven o'clock, the Mormons arrived, lugging their story board and books. This time they told the story of Joseph Smith, the angel Moroni, the Golden Tablets, and the magic eyeglasses used to translate the "Reformed Hieroglyphics" inscribed on the Golden Tablets. The resulting translation supposedly became the Book of Mormon. Their preposterous tale was more than I could swallow. While the explanation of how Jesus brought the Gospel to the Old and New Worlds seemed to make a certain amount of sense, I resisted the rest of the message. The far-fetched tale of Joseph Smith and the Golden Tablets he found in the woods of upstate New York almost completely turned me off. Yet, there remained a little bit of curiosity and wonder about all these things.

"But," I said, grasping at straws, "there are many contradictions between the Bible and the Book of Mormon." The Bible, being my standard, would be the last word in this matter. At the moment, I couldn't think of any, but I imagined there were some contradictions between the two books. So, before departing, the Mormon Elders made an unusual agreement; if I could find one contradiction between the Book of Mormon and the Bible, they said they would eat the Book of Mormon.

Later that evening I went out to our small back porch and sat on the railing. A full moon stood out brightly in an unusually clear sky. "God," I prayed, "I'm willing to accept your truth. If the Mormons have the truth, please let me know." With that said, peace settled over me.

As the next few days passed, I didn't bother looking for contradictions between the two books; I trusted the Lord to take care of it. Then, when the punctual Mormons failed to show on the designated night, I came to two conclusions: God answered my prayer, and Mormons don't like to eat paper.

With the proliferation of so many religions in California, I was delighted to take the mandatory course during the second semester called "Cults and Isms." Walter Martin's thick book, *Kingdom of the Cults*, guided us through the fascinating study. The lessons taught me why we were right and everyone else was wrong. Now I could spot a false cult almost immediately.

This knowledge came in handy not long after the Mormon episode. One afternoon while I was studying, two ladies who were Jehovah's Witnesses knocked on the door. Boy, was I ready for them! I countered their every argument, point by point. I was flipping through my Bible and reading verses to them until they reached a point of exasperation.

Finally, the lady who seemed to be the leader of the two, grabbed the other by the arm. As they started down the sidewalk, she turned her head back toward me and shouted over her shoulder, "You son-of-a-bitch!"

It felt good to know the truth and to belong to the correct religion.

9

Seeing Isn't Believing

After rededicating my life to the Lord, my greatest passion was to win souls. Being the quiet, undemonstrative type, public preaching didn't appeal to me as much as dealing with people one-on-one. Pulpit preaching also frightened me because I had a soft voice, and found I had to strain to be heard; audiences made me nervous, too. The Personal Evangelism course taught by Jack Hayford at LIFE Bible College really fit the bill. With the Word of God, the Holy Spirit, and a little psychology, I quickly learned that soul-winning was fairly simple, and I became proficient at it.

C. S. Lovett, a Southern California evangelical minister, authored the textbook used in the class. A true soul-winner, he perfected the art of soul-winning for Jesus. Lovett's soul-winning scheme is based on four main scriptures, with clever lead-ins from one verse to the next.

Brother Hayford taught Lovett's system with great enthusiasm, enthralling me as I watched it for the first time. He used a student—who pretended to be unsaved—for the demonstration.

An important feature of the strategy included the use of an open New Testament, even though the soul-winner previously memorized the four Scripture selections. While talking to the unsaved prospect, the soul-winner should point out the verses as he spoke, thus enforcing from the beginning the fact that the discussion was based on God's Word.

As the student stood before him, Brother Hayford read the first

Scripture: "All have sinned and fall short of the glory of God." A brief discussion easily convinced the student that he had sinned at least once in his life.

"Can you picture Jesus standing here in the flesh—right here next to us in all his glory?" Hayford said with the greatest sincerity. The awesomeness of that vivid picture caused a hush to fall upon the class—yes, we do fall short of God's glory.

"The wages of sin is death," read the next Scripture. Hayford explained this "death" as eternal separation from God.

"Would you like to be eternally separated from God?" our teacher asked. The answer was so obvious, the question required no reply. So much for the negative, the guilt-building. The picture changed with the next Bible verse.

"The *gift* of God is eternal life through Jesus Christ our Lord."

"How do you feel," Hayford asked, "when you receive a gift?" The student's countenance brightened.

"God wants to give you a *free* gift." Hayford emphasized the word "free," because salvation can't be earned by doing good works.

"The gift," he added, "is eternal life—and it's through a person, Jesus Christ; the gift comes wrapped in a person—Jesus."

"I want to give you this New Testament as a gift," Hayford told the student. The student looked down at the small book in the teacher's hand.

"Well, do you want it?" the teacher asked.

"Well, uh, sure," the student responded.

"Then *take* it," Hayford commanded. The student took the small Bible from the teacher's hand.

Hayford explained that it was the same way with the gift of eternal life; it is a free gift, but it must be taken through an act of the will. The point was demonstrated well. (Hayford later sold the whole class cheap little New Testaments, for us to give away during the "gift" portion of the spiel.) The next dramatic step contained an element of surprise.

" 'Behold, I stand at the door and knock, if any man hears my voice and opens the door, I will come into him.' Now this is Jesus speaking," Hayford intoned.

"This very moment, He is knocking at your heart's door. He wants to come in," Hayford implored. And, as he said those words, he reached out and tapped the young man's breast. Unnerved, the poor student almost fainted.

"What do you do when you hear a knock on your door?" Hayford continued.

"Why, I say, 'Come in,' " the student sputtered.

"That's exactly what Jesus wants you to do right now. Just say, 'Come in, Jesus,' " the teacher directed.

"Do you hear his voice?" the teacher queried. Now, completely wound up, tears streamed down Hayford's face.

"Yes, yes, I hear his voice," the student stammered.

Although the student had been converted for years, the demonstration moved him tremendously. While it was obvious that some of the Scriptures were taken completely out of context, it didn't matter; the end justified the means, and the Holy Spirit uses them anyway.

I memorized the plan, including the Scriptures, and placed plastic tabs in my New Testament as an aid to help me find the verses quickly, and to stay on track during face-to-face confrontations out on the streets.

While at LIFE, Jack Hayford began to write and publish hymns and gospel songs, and he insisted that the entire school learn his works. Now, many of these young men and women went out to pastor Foursquare churches, or to work in other ministries. Over time, their influence would further Hayford's success as a songwriter. While that was very clever of him, his high-pressure tactics really bothered me.

At LIFE, a Pentecostal school, we properly expected the Holy Spirit to fall on us when we worshiped. With great enthusiasm, Brother Hayford worked the students into a great emotional state in his efforts to get us to worship the Lord. In my way of thinking, worship involved deep, inner reflection and thought, not an outward show of exuberance, but, against my inclinations, I went along with the Pentecostal practice. Because of my inner conflict, though, Hayford's dominance and overbearing personality as a group leader often repulsed me. And, because as a Christian I was supposed to love my brother and sister, guilt and self-hatred filled my soul.

According to Pentecostal practice, the Spirit's presence appeared in various ways. Sometimes the Spirit was manifested in ecstatic displays where worshipers brought forth messages in tongues and others presented their interpretations, and sometimes worshipers prophesied.

When the music became especially lively, some—with closed eyes—

danced in the Spirit. I watched these people closely, because I wondered why they didn't bump into things. At first I supposed that the Holy Spirit guided them. Although it wasn't polite to stare, when I did I invariably caught them peeking as they danced about as if they were in a trance.

While Jack Hayford knew how to work an audience, he discouraged too much Holy Roller exuberance such as dancing in the Spirit. Hayford championed repentance. The Bible says the Holy Spirit convicts (convinces) of sin, and Hayford played it to the limit; he gloated while everyone cried on their knees before God. He constantly pushed the students to worship God, then harped on sin until everyone fell to their knees. Thinking that Jesus had forgiven all my sins, Hayford's machinations were discomforting.

Hayford, as dean of students, knew what we did behind closed doors, and as our spiritual leader he thought nothing of bringing our secret activities out into the open. Once, an under-the-mattress inspection in the boys' dorm yielded a small pile of *Playboy* magazines. Living off campus, I wasn't directly affected by this titillating discovery. Hayford really came down hard on sin in the next chapel service. I was embarrassed for the other students as they tearfully slobbered in repentance over their worldly ways.

The most unrestrained chapel service occurred when Kathryn Kuhlman, the healing evangelist from Pittsburgh, spoke. Kuhlman's evangelistic endeavors started when she was sixteen. She operated a church in Denver for a few years. Then she married another evangelist, who had left his wife for Kuhlman. The move all but destroyed her ministry. So, after about six years she left him and ended up in Pennsylvania, where she revived her flagging ministry.

During one of Kuhlman's services a woman claimed to be healed of a tumor. Pretty soon all sorts of healings were claimed. In 1965, Ralph Wilkerson, of Melodyland in Anaheim, California, convinced Kuhlman to come to California. Her monthly trips became a sensation.

Before I enrolled in Bible college, I'd seen a number of her performances at the 7,000-seat Shrine Auditorium in Los Angeles, where she packed the house for ten years.

A front man—sometimes Ralph Wilkerson—always worked up the audience before Kuhlman appeared on stage. Accompanied by a vibrant pipe organ, he led the audience in rousing hymns, then, at the correct moment, Kathryn literally rushed onto the stage. Always adorned in flowing white gowns, her countenance shined.

"Ohhh, the Holy Spirit is here today!" she exclaimed.

Her voice went from wails to whispers, with her words accented in unexpected places. She held the audience spellbound.

Kuhlman preached simplistic sermons, which I suspected were not always theologically correct. Seldom preaching more than an hour, she would suddenly stop.

"The Hooooly Spirit is moving over this entire audience," she moaned as her hand slashed through the air, slowly and deliberately. Then, Kathryn Kuhlman called out sicknesses which she claimed were cured that very moment.

"A lump on a breast! There, over there!" she cried out while pointing to a section of the vast auditorium.

"A spinal injury over there!" Then, "God's healing a thyroid condition in a, a woman . . . oh, thank you, Jee-saws!"

She encouraged the healed ones to come up on the stage. Elated, a steady stream of tearful worshipers walked across the broad stage toward Kuhlman. With her arm stretched forward, she placed her hands on their heads. One by one, the people fell over backwards into the arms of a stocky little man who lowered them gently to the floor. This continued for four or five hours without pause.

Once, while observing this spectacle, I was amazed to see a cigar-shaped light directly behind Kuhlman. The apparition stayed with her for several minutes, following her as she moved about with microphone in hand. Apparently the only one to see this phenomenon, I almost left my seat for the stage. I wanted to tell the vast audience that I'd seen the visible manifestation of the Holy Spirit on His anointed servant.

Some time later, I realized that the reflection of the bright theater lights on Kuhlman's shining white robe played tricks on my eyes. It took a long time, though, to admit it, because I desperately wanted to believe I'd seen a miracle.

Word got out that Kuhlman was to speak at LIFE Bible College. To contain the crowd, the service was held at Aimee Semple McPherson's Angelus Temple, adjacent to the school. Ironically, both of these female evangelists were redheads, and controversial. The overflow crowd had to be seated in the student auditorium, where she was heard via loudspeakers.

What an event! Everyone at LIFE knew Kuhlman couldn't preach worth beans, but the floor show was worth seeing. We weren't disappointed.

After her little sermon about the Second Coming, the tall evangelist approached the choir with her hand outstretched, touching the person seated at the end of the row. Like dominoes, everyone in the row fell over. Then, row by row, she literally knocked them off their seats. The audience gasped. She left the platform and came toward them, touching many as she moved among the crowd.

Kuhlman continued to climb through the audience, and people keeled over by the row-full. By now, scores lay all over the place. It was mayhem. And Jack Hayford was ecstatic.

Feelings of guilt over my extreme dislike of Hayford left me unsettled. While I thought his soul-winning techniques were brilliant, something about the scheme made me uneasy. However, I let that pass, because so many other things about him bothered me.

I made an appointment to see Brother Hayford. In humility and shame I confessed my bitterness toward him, and asked him to pray for me. He listened but failed to understand why I felt the way I did. I couldn't find the words to tell him that his actions usurped the Holy Spirit, and that God didn't require man's shenanigans in order to move in people's hearts. This manipulation included the way he taught soul-winning, but I didn't see it at the time. I left his office feeling foolish.

During my second year at LIFE Jack Hayford accepted a position as the minister of the First Foursquare Church of Van Nuys. Located on a street called Sherman Way, it had only eighteen members. Cleverly, he renamed it The Church on the Way; under Hayford's leadership the church attracted some former Hollywood celebrities, such as the singer Pat Boone and Disney actor Dean Jones. As his church grew, I saw less and less of him at school.

10

Hollywood Harvest

In the mid-1960s, Hollywood's famous Sunset Strip became a hippie mecca. The *Los Angeles Times* called it a "snake-like, fun alley." The Strip is a several-block-long section of Sunset Boulevard, crowded with cafes, head shops (stores selling drug paraphernalia), bars, nightclubs, record stores, and apparel shops. Rock and roll, and Eastern music emanated from the record stores, and incense floated through the air amidst flashing, psychedelic strobe lights. Roving crowds of sightseers and locals packed the narrow sidewalks, under the watchful eyes of helmeted Los Angeles County Sheriff's deputies who patrolled the street on foot. Nevertheless, drug deals and prostitution took place openly.

The nightly denizens came in an array of sizes, shapes, and colors. Young runaway girls from other parts of the country wore skimpy cotton blouses and micro-mini skirts. Most of the young men sported long hair, beards, and sometimes, colorful costumes. Surrealism pervaded the scene, as many were off in another world, tripped out on drugs.

Ric and I viewed the Strip's lost souls as fertile missionary ground ready for the harvest. With our ultra-conservative, Bible-college look, we stuck out like sore thumbs, and, at first, few people listened as we attempted to witness to them. After several missionary attempts, some of the Strip's regulars began to trust us, concluding that we weren't undercover narcs.

In the beginning, I found it unnerving to approach strangers and tell them about Jesus. The hardest part was getting started. My own version of Abe Schneider's opening line about a bomb dropping on Los Angeles turned out to be the best method. "Excuse me," I'd say as I approached a person. "If you died tonight, where would you spend eternity?" That usually stopped them dead in their tracks.

While I was on my way to Hollywood one night, a pizza delivery van side-swiped my VW. The driver pulled over to the curb and I pulled up behind him. A quick inspection revealed that neither vehicle sustained any damage. Always trying to be alert to cues from the Holy Spirit, I saw the Lord in this incident, and jumped at the opportunity.

"If you die in an auto accident tonight," I started, "where will you spend eternity?"

"I don't know," the pizza man exclaimed, "but if I don't get these pizzas delivered soon I'm going to catch hell!"

Unswayed, I whipped out my little New Testament and opened it to the first Scripture in the soul-winning plan. As I went through the spiel, the pizza deliverer kept glancing at his watch. At the conclusion of the presentation, I asked him if he wanted to receive his free gift, salvation through Jesus?

"Sure," he responded.

I asked him to bow his head and repeat a prayer to ask Jesus into his heart. He followed my leading, word for word. Then, I ran to my car and pulled out some Christian literature for my new convert. When I got back, he was already in his van, anxious to deliver the now-tepid pizzas. He took the material I shoved through the window, and left in a hurry.

As I praised God for sending a hungry soul my way, I pulled a small date book out of my pocket and made a special mark. Like a gunslinger who carves a notch on the barrel of his six-shooter for every victim, I carefully recorded every soul I won for Jesus.

Witnessing to sinners in Hollywood always provided us with the ultimate challenge. Few of these people wanted to hear about Jesus. While Christianity is actually an Eastern religion, the other Eastern religions attracted more attention at the time. My Cults and Isms class at Bible school helped me a lot as I argued and reasoned with numerous prospects about sin and salvation.

The subject of reincarnation came up often, and, as usual, I had a pat answer ready for every situation. "The Bible says," I always began with those who believed in reincarnation, "there is one life to live, and after that, the judgment." The pat, Bible-based answers were usually taken out of context, and thus, the truth of the matter was that the Bible didn't have all the answers, but I couldn't see that.

One warm spring night, an odd, bearded character stood on a Hollywood street corner lecturing anyone who stopped to listen to him. His shoulder length hair hung from beneath his wide-brimmed leather hat. I worked my way through the small gathering and listened for a minute. He obviously didn't know what he was talking about, so I interrupted him.

"If you died tonight, where would you spend eternity?" I asked.

"Heaven and hell are right here on earth!" he shot back.

"Jesus said hell is a place," I returned, "a place where there is weeping and wailing and gnashing of teeth."

"I am Jesus, I am the son of God!" he cried out.

With that, I knew I faced a formidable challenge. We continued to argue, and, as our theologies clashed, I sensed some support from the small crowd.

The sinister character's intense eyes burned into mine, then darted from passerby to bystander as he continued his tirade. His ramblings included fragments from the book of Revelation and other parts of the Bible; and he prophesied of dire times to come, but none of it made any sense. In a short time, I realized the guy was hopeless, probably crazy. Not wanting to waste any more time with such an unreceptive person, I said, "Look, I've got to move on, maybe we can talk again."

"Any time, man," he said with a grin, adding something about being on the Strip every night.

"What's your name?" I asked.

"Charlie," he said.

I put my hand out, and he returned a weak handshake.

"See you around, Charlie," I said, departing.

Charlie's fervor and egotism left a lasting impression on my mind. About a year and a half later, I saw Charlie again, but not in person. His photo, looking like the madman he was, appeared on the front page of the *Los Angeles Times*. Charlie's last name was Manson.

Charles Manson, mass-murderer, was in a class by himself. While Manson, by his own hand, may have murdered as many as thirty-five people, his uncanny power controlled others to the point where they killed for him.

Through mind control, Manson led a cult called the "Family," consisting of a band of young girls and a few young men, who carried out killings ordered by Manson.

Manson carried a certain presence, a charisma, which I observed first hand, and he used classic mind-control techniques to influence others. Scouring Southern California highways, and Hollywood's Sunset Strip, Manson recruited Family members. Then, taking advantage of their needs, he used sex, drugs, guilt, fear, love, repetition, isolation, an amoral philosophy, and even the Bible, to dominate their minds so that they did whatever he ordered. His power over them was so complete that he sent them out on nightly murder sprees, which they performed gladly, and without any apparent feelings of guilt. In one month, in the summer of 1969, Manson and his Family brutally murdered nine people. Even after Manson and six Family members were arrested and indicted for seven of the murders, the killing continued, carried out by other Family members.

A Hollywood actress, Sharon Tate, the pregnant wife of film director Roman Polanski, was one of the first victims. Sandra Good, a Manson family member, said the group killed thirty-five to forty people. Many bodies have never been found, and technically, those murders remain unsolved.

Manson was convicted and sentenced to death, but the death penalty was abolished in California, and his sentence was commuted to life in prison. Today, Manson remains in maximum security at Folsom Prison in Northern California.

Apparently, at the time I encountered Manson, he was in Hollywood recruiting members for his self-styled cult.

While Ric and I zealously served the Lord, our wives were left out of most of our activities, and had to fend for themselves, seeking their own niches while living in predetermined molds. I'd been assigned to assist the pastor of a little Foursquare church in Los Angeles, and Linda volunteered as a teacher in its Sunday school. Linda and Renee attended few events at the Bible college, and came once or twice with us to Hollywood. Renee, too, had a child, so, as good Christian women, they stayed in their proper place at home.

While I served God, our home was often rife with discord. I blamed the difficulties on Satan, who, I was certain, was trying to hinder my ministry.

One night, not long after Ric and I began to frequent Sunset Strip, two attractive blonds approached us and tried to lead us to Christ. When it became apparent that we were all there for the same purpose, like true Pentecostals, we threw our hands into the air and praised the Lord.

Cousins, in their late teens, Liz and Ann came from Sweden with their families. After living in California for a short time, they discovered Sunset Strip and became regulars. Their lives, filled with drugs, sex, and rock and roll turned into a blur—until Jesus turned them around. It happened, they claimed, one night when they were parked in a car in the Hollywood hills with some guys. All of a sudden, the car shook wildly and a huge, shining angel from God appeared before them. (Today, I suspect that drugs had something to do with this.)

Having been reared in the Pentecostal church in Sweden, they reckoned that God was trying to send them a message. In response, they were now out on the streets trying to save souls. They even went so far as renting a large office on Sunset Strip as a place for prayer and spiritual counseling. Across the street from the Playboy Club, they called it the Chapel on the Strip.

The four of us agreed to join forces for God in Hollywood. Soon, we met others who saw the district's plight and sinfulness, and came to save souls as well.

The Chapel on the Strip was located in a portion of a U-shaped building, with a courtyard in the middle, and open at the street end. Across the courtyard, Arthur Blessitt, a handsome young Baptist evangelist, rented an office shortly after the Chapel opened. While Ric criticized Blessitt because, as a fundamental Baptist, he didn't believe in the baptism of the Holy Spirit, Arthur brought new drama into Christian ministry. By sneaking into nightclubs, he witnessed and preached until he was thrown out. Out on the streets, whenever he convinced someone to accept Jesus, he made them kneel down on the sidewalk with him to pray. Later, dragging a large wooden cross, he trekked across the United States.

A haughty young Pentecostal couple by the name of Tony and Susan Alamo also ventured into Hollywood. They checked out the Chapel on the Strip, but rather than work with us, they pursued their own ministry.

Before the end of my second year at LIFE, I felt the call to serve

God so strongly, that when final exams came, I didn't even bother to show up for them. And, while my program involved a full three years of study, I never returned, and no one at LIFE even noticed.

If the Chapel were to succeed, I saw that it needed to become more visible, and I offered to make that happen. Because of my zeal, the others elected me as the Chapel's director, a volunteer position. First, I approached a Christian sign painter I knew and convinced him to donate a large and colorful sandwich-board sign, which we placed on the street whenever the Chapel was open. Inspired by the sign, the same man also designed flyers, which we passed out by the hundreds.

A Hollywood original—movies—became our biggest attraction. One of the girls suggested we show Christian films. Very few people, though, were willing to come into the Chapel to see Billy Graham films. Taking note of the Chapel's natural setting, I had a brainstorm. Directly behind the Chapel loomed a smooth-faced, forty-foot rock, which at some point someone had taken the trouble to white-wash. Seeing this as a natural movie screen, I moved the projector out to the sidewalk, right on Sunset Strip, and beamed Billy Graham up to the rock. An immediate hit, our outdoor movie theater became quite a crowd stopper.

Next, I thought, we needed some publicity, and I called John Dart, the religion writer for *The Los Angeles Times.* He interviewed us over coffee in a Hollywood diner. When the story about our ministry to hippies came out, our phone started ringing off the hook, and mail poured into The Chapel. Complete strangers sent donations, and national magazines called for interviews. One well-known author wanted to write a book about our work. I was excited because our ministry was taking off like a rocket, and, if we pursued the publicity, much-needed funding was sure to follow.

Ric, though, to my dismay, cautioned us to avoid the ways of the world. He thought continued media coverage of our activities would do more harm than good. I strongly resented his attempts to scuttle my efforts. Ultimately, we brought the question up for a vote, and Ric's effective arguments against the worldly media caused the others to vote against further publicity.

This was the first clash I had with Ric. Without a doubt, jealousy sometimes came between us as we both pursued our individual goals. Ric's strong and serious authoritative manner appealed to those who needed assurance and firm direction. I tended to be more jocular and easy-going.

Nevertheless, we continued to work and fellowship together. When not involved with the Chapel, Ric and Renee and Linda and I took day trips with our children, or shared meals together.

For a while, Ric and Renee lived in a small one-bedroom apartment over a garage in Los Angeles. About that time, the ministry of Kenneth Hagin began to influence us. Hagin was a "name it and claim it," or "prosperity," evangelist. He taught that a Christian could ask God for anything, and by standing fast and believing, would receive the request.

One afternoon I went over to Ric's to return some Hagin books. Ric introduced me to Fred Price, a former Jehovah's Witness who converted and now pastored a little Christian and Missionary Alliance church. Fred, a tall, handsome black, had also discovered Hagin's teachings and was very excited about them. I found this interesting, because, by-and-large, black Christian theology bordered on the primitive and folksy. Now, here was this guy Price, ready to take the teachings of a particularly extreme white evangelist into the black community. Crossovers like this were rare.

As our work in Hollywood continued, I despaired at the need I observed. Hundreds of young people roamed the streets night after night. Many of them were runaways; their parents didn't know their whereabouts; they had only the clothes on their back, and didn't know the source of their next meal.

At our next board meeting I presented a plan to help these young people with their temporal needs. First, we'd call a young person's parents to assure them that their child was alive and well. We'd feed them, clothe them, and then help them find a job and a place to stay. This, I thought, was what God wanted us to do for his lost children.

This is when I received my second great disappointment as I endeavored to minister the way I thought was proper. Led again by Ric, the others thought my plan wasn't what God wanted us to do in Hollywood. "Jesus said, the poor you always have with you," they said. And with that, they thought it was all right to ignore the temporal needs of the poor. Our mission was, they said, to save lost souls so they don't go to hell.

With that, I told them that someone else should take over the Chapel on the Strip and left.

Linda and I moved to the Highland Park section of LA, where some friends told us about an exciting new church they'd found. The pastor,

Dale Young, with his own hands, restored an old movie theater, turned it into a church, and called it Glad Tidings Tabernacle. It was affiliated with a small denomination called Harvest Fields Missionary and Evangelistic Association, which grew out of the Latter Rain movement.

After one visit, we joined, and offered our services, which Pastor Young gladly accepted. Linda and I became Sunday-school teachers, and I headed the youth and outreach ministry.

On Saturday mornings I met with several ladies of the church, and after I taught a short Bible lesson and instructed the ladies on how to witness, we methodically combed the neighborhood to seek new souls and church members.

To teach the ladies at Glad Tidings Tabernacle, I employed the soul-winning strategy taught by Jack Hayford. None of them were very bright, however, and they just couldn't seem to understand the technique. Nevertheless, they didn't have much else to do; they liked the church, and were determined to bring in some new folks—though we never did.

I used to chide my friend Laverne Campbell. Laverne pastored a successful Foursquare church just down the street from Glad Tidings.

"Why aren't your members out winning souls?" I said.

"I'm trying to reform them first," he replied.

I knew what he meant, because while success has its rewards, it can also bring its share of idiosyncrasies. Laverne told me of a woman in his church who always left the service during his sermon. She returned after a few minutes, her face flushed. Concerned that she might have some sort of physical problem which might benefit from prayer, one day he tactfully confronted her about her brief absences during his sermons. As it turned out, when he preached, with microphone firmly gripped in his hand, she became highly aroused and went to the ladies room to masturbate.

Soon, Ric and Renee followed us and became members of Glad Tidings. I was a bit miffed because Pastor Young had taken me under his wing and given me a lot of responsibility and authority in the church, and, I knew, when he got to know Ric—who had also dropped out of LIFE Bible College—he'd recognize the possibilities of using Ric's natural charisma to help build the congregation.

I was correct. Dale wanted Ric to preach, but he couldn't have him preach without asking me also. Dale always preached on Sunday morning, so he asked Ric and me to alternate on Sunday nights.

From time to time, Glad Tidings received a visitor or two, and due to the small congregation, their presence was obvious. One Sunday night, when it was my turn to preach, I noticed a middle-aged Chicano woman in the church. I was delighted that someone new would hear me preach. Some of the people had already tired of me, I knew. One man actually told me that my preaching was boring.

As I preached energetically, I looked toward the visitor—she was sound asleep. I blamed myself for preaching another dull sermon and quickly wrapped it up.

At the conclusion of the service the woman awakened. I walked over to her and introduced myself. She expressed a desire to talk privately. We moved to the church office and sat down. Then, she told me her horror story. She had an alcoholic husband and two juvenile delinquents for children. That very night, while on her way to kill herself, she saw the words Glad Tidings Tabernacle displayed on our lit, yellow plastic sign.

She apologized for falling asleep while I preached, but added that it was the first time she'd been able to sleep in several days. That made me feel good. (Eventually, she became a productive member of the church. I met her husband, and helped him work through some of his problems.)

The effectiveness of our ministries grew, and in recognition of God's calling, on May 9, 1968, Ric and I were ordained at Glad Tidings Tabernacle by a group of ministers representing the Harvest Fields Missionary and Evangelistic Association.

11

Heaven's Number One Salesman

"Billy Graham will hold a crusade in Southern California next year," Ric told me one day. I was delighted. Although Billy Graham movies were the vehicle which brought me to Christ more than a dozen years earlier, I had never seen the evangelist in person. What a great joy it was to learn that Billy, as he was affectionately referred to, was coming to Southern California. He was my champion.

Someone once said, "Billy was the most dedicated salesman the Fuller Brush Company ever had." That was in 1936, when, fresh out of high school, Billy Graham sold brushes in the hills of North Carolina. The tall, handsome young man moved on to become heaven's number one salesman.

As the story goes, in 1949, Billy Graham held his first big evangelistic meeting in a tent set up in a vacant lot in downtown Los Angeles. Although the meetings went well, they weren't phenomenal. Then, a lady who had been praying for the success of the meetings felt the Lord telling her to phone the newspaper mogul William Randolph Hearst. She phoned San Simeon, Hearst's fabled California estate, and somehow got the legendary newspaperman himself on the phone.

The woman, a Mrs. Edwards, excitedly told Hearst about Graham and the tent crusade. He thanked her and hung up. Then he did something very unusual. He wired the words "Puff Graham" to his entire newspaper syndicate. The two words were, of course, newspaper jargon for "build up Billy Graham."

That evening, reporters from the *Los Angeles Examiner* and the *Herald Express* covered Graham's meeting. Headlines in both papers the next day featured the event. Overnight, literally, Billy Graham became a nationally famous evangelist.

Through the Billy Graham Evangelistic Association, and later World Wide Pictures, Graham became the biggest and most successful evangelist on the planet. He has preached about sin and salvation through Jesus to more people than any other human being.

I always remembered a story Ric told me about Billy. Graham often traveled the country by rail. His public relations people made sure the local press knew when he was going to arrive in a particular city. As is their function, the reporters fired questions at Graham as he stepped off the train.

On one occasion, a reporter called out to Graham, "What do you think about sex before marriage?" Graham, as Christ's model ambassador, replied firmly, "It doesn't matter what I think; the Bible calls it sin!"

"Wow! What a man of God," I marveled. He put his own thoughts aside and simply accepted what the word of God said. I resolved to do the same in my life and ministry. It sure made things a lot easier. Although there was more about the Bible that I didn't understand than what I did understand, I was taught to believe that the Bible held the answers to all of life's problems. As a result, I made a conscious decision to wait on God in order to grasp the concepts revealed in His Word.

This blind acceptance gave me a matter-of-fact outlook on life, and even more so, enabled me to speak with power and authority. The Bible says of itself, "The Word of God is quick [meaning alive] and powerful and sharper than any two-edged sword." I could use it to cut down and out-argue almost anyone in any circumstance. "God stands behind his Word," I assured myself, as I memorized hundreds of verses by their correct numerical reference. "The Bible says . . ." became my favorite phrase.

Now, I had the opportunity to see and hear Billy Graham preach. I looked forward to the ten-day Crusade slated for Anaheim Stadium in nearby Orange County.

The next day I stopped at the church to check the mail. I'd ordered some of Jack Chick's new comic book tracts, and waited anxiously for them to arrive. There was nothing from Chick Publications, but there was a letter from the Billy Graham Evangelistic Association. I opened it and was thrilled with the letter inside. "Dear Pastor, you are invited to participate in next year's Billy Graham Crusade at Anaheim Stadium."

As our church's evangelistic leader, I filled out an information card, shoved it into the enclosed business reply envelope, sealed it, and walked to the mailbox on the corner.

Soon, another letter arrived accepting me as a counselor for the upcoming crusade. "What a privilege!" I thought.

For many years, Billy Graham has held the largest and most successful evangelistic crusades. These crusades are carefully orchestrated for emotional impact. Nothing is left to chance.

The city slated for a crusade is often chosen several years in advance. The Graham organization's machinery is put into gear a good two years before the event.

After a city has been selected, the ministers of that city and the surrounding areas are contacted and asked to participate, along with their congregations. That was how I got invited; our church was on some mailing list.

An advance team from the Billy Graham Evangelistic Association moved into Southern California and established a local office. In addition to meeting with the ministers and congregations, the local crusade office provided reams of material to aid the local church's participation. This material included Bible studies on salvation and witnessing. These studies, coupled with prayer meetings, served as pep rallies for the coming crusade. I attended all of these meetings, along with several people from my church.

A typical eight-day Billy Graham Crusade costs a couple of million dollars. Long before the big week, we, the local participants, were encouraged to contribute money towards the crusade. Most of the funds needed to cover expenses were raised before the event. Then, during each nightly service, a bucket brigade passed cardboard pails throughout the audience. (It is common to raise $50,000 or more a night—about $2.00 per person.)

Money raised above and beyond the cost of the crusade went back to the Graham organization. Later, some of this money was used to broadcast the crusade on regional or national television. It wasn't a wash though. Long after Billy Graham leaves town, regular appeals for money go out to those on the newly enhanced mailing list garnered from the names and addresses of the participants.

By working with the local churches, the Graham organization was able to inform every Bible-believing Christian in several counties of the impending crusade, well before any paid advertising was placed.

Church members were encouraged to invite their unsaved friends, relatives, and neighbors to the crusade. Transportation was arranged through car pools and busing. Buses came from as far away as 150 miles. Batches of tickets, though not actually required for admission, were given to each participating church.

Just prior to the crusade, a final push was made. The event was announced in church bulletins, posters were plastered around the city, and some newspaper, radio, and television advertising was purchased.

Because of the meticulous planning, Anaheim Stadium was packed to capacity every night. The stage was carefully arranged with lush, green plants. The area's most well-known ministers sat on the platform, to one side of the podium, in full view of the throng. High in the stadium, an American flag was prominently displayed.

As the service progressed, soloists presented rousing renditions of gospel songs. Personal testimonies from well-known entertainers and sports figures were presented. They recounted their salvation through Jesus. All of this carefully calculated hype had one purpose—persuasion.

The purpose of every crusade is to persuade people to accept Jesus Christ—and to support the Billy Graham Evangelistic Association. Success is measured by participation and response to the altar call.

Every evangelist, early in his or her career, at one time or another, has made an altar call which fell flat. Trial and error has virtually eliminated that embarrassment. What has developed is the foolproof altar call.

Billy Graham is a master at this. His technique is based upon the same methods and principles of group psychology and crowd motivation that all successful evangelists employ.

Graham preached a rousing sermon each night. Through his Bible-based sermon, he convinced many people that their lives were out of control in some way. He came down hard on sin; he convinced people that they had missed the mark. He named some sins. By calling enough sins by name, especially the more popular ones, he hit the nail on the head every night.

Billy won his audience through agreement. He told them the country has gone downhill since prayer was taken out of the schools; he reminded them that pornography is vile; he also said that someday we would all die and meet our maker. Everyone agreed; Graham had them in his pocket.

Billy Graham also had sex appeal. He stood tall in his expensive silk suit. His eyes flashed, his mannerisms were precise.

Graham's sermon contained just the right amount of humor. And, at the right times he became very serious.

Soon the sermon ended. "I want you to bow your heads and close your eyes—with no one looking around," the evangelist ordered. I knew that this routine helped to avoid distraction and embarrassment. The audience believed that no one was looking. (They couldn't see the powerful telephoto lenses of the TV cameras. The close-ups would look impressive later when the crusade was broadcast.)

While every head was bowed, Graham said he was going to pray. Then he prayed audibly. The sermon he had just preached was condensed in his prayer. He hit all the highlights, especialy the sin and forgiveness parts. Billy asked God to speak to the people's hearts. The invocation of God's name caused the people to attribute their nervousness to the presence of God.

The evangelist asked all those who needed prayer to raise their hand. Since just about everyone could use a little prayer, many hands went up. The ice had been broken; they began to participate. As he saw the hands go up, he said somberly, "I see that hand over there, and there, and there. Thank you, thank you."

Now, Graham asked those who once walked with Jesus, but had fallen away, to raise their hands. The poignant sermon, the testimonies, the gospel songs, the size of the crowd, and the mood of the moment inspired many to raise their hands. Again he softly spoke, "Thank you, thank you."

Next, he implored those who had never accepted Jesus as their Lord and personal Savior to just hold up their hands. He didn't even ask them to accept Jesus, only to indicate that they had never accepted Jesus. Because everyone snuck peeks, those who had never been saved witnessed many around them raise their hands. So, it was very easy for the few in this last group to hold up their hands. They thought that no harm could come from an upraised hand. They were snared.

Now, Billy Graham had everyone in the stadium stand, and they did so obediently. With a great sense of melodrama he said, "Jesus is here, right now." This really spooked them.

While the people remained on their feet, Graham said, very sincerely, "I want to pray with those who've raised their hands. God wants to touch you tonight, he knows your needs." Then he asked all those who had raised their hands to come forward, walk down, and stand before him.

It is most difficult to get those in the back moving, so he started with them and said, "Starting in the back, and way up in the top balconies, come down, right now, hurry!" If he had started with the front the whole altar call could have fizzled out. The folks near the front responded as they saw the people coming down past them. By now everyone had opened their eyes.

Each night, at the very moment Billy asked the people to come forward, he nodded to the choir director and soloist to begin the hymn "Just As I Am," a tried and tested hymn for altar calls. At the same moment, all of the volunteer counselors, myself included, who were planted throughout the audience, began to move forward. The momentum grew.

Like sheep, those who raised their hands followed us volunteer workers. Some wept, like an adulterer caught with his pants down. Others felt foolish and quite unsure about what they were to do. This is where we volunteer counselors proved our worth. As we spotted the uncertain ones, we threw an arm over their shoulders, or took them by the hand, and led them down to the altar.

Graham praised the Lord. Slowly and deliberately, he said, "Thank you Jesus, thank you Jesus."

As the people gathered before him, he offered the television audience (it was being videotaped for future broadcast) his free booklet by calling the toll free number displayed on the TV screen. The TV audience would be very impressed by the number of people who had come forward.

Now, Graham spoke to those who had come forward. He asked them to bow their heads, and led them in a rote prayer to accept Jesus into their lives. It was a sort of swearing-in, a vow.

We volunteers were now busy collecting the names and addresses of those who had come forward. These were given to Graham's organization and would be added to his mailing list.

Volunteer counselors included, an average of 2 to 4 percent came forward each evening. This figure sounds small, but out of a crowd of 30,000, a group of 600 to 1,200 looks large on television, especially since the altar area was fairly small.

The actual number of new converts at the altar was as little as one-half of one percent. This is because most of the people who came down were volunteer ushers and altar counselors, backslidden Christians who felt inspired to give it another try, admirers who wanted to see Billy Graham up close, and Christians who dragged unsaved friends and relatives to the altar.

Follow-up activities help keep the Billy Graham Evangelistic Association alive. People are kept active through their enrollment in Billy Graham's Bible correspondence courses, and by subscriptions to his *Decision* magazine.

Unfortunately, the crusade didn't add a single soul to our church. Although I was uplifted by the experience, the realization that very few were actually converted was a big disappointment to me. I still admired Billy Graham for his showmanship. He is a true star.

12

No Hope Street

As hard as we worked to build the attendance at Glad Tidings Tabernacle it remained small. Visitors attended on a regular basis, but seldom returned. I searched for a reason to explain the lack of numerical growth.

Perhaps our homosexual pianist brought God's displeasure. My experience, however, told me otherwise. While Pentecostal preachers often lash out against homosexuals, the prevalence of gays in Pentecostal church music departments is commonplace. Not only was our current pianist gay, several lesbians sang in the choir at my other church, People's Tabernacle of Faith, and a number of gays have made the successful transition from church choirs to secular pop music. No, homosexuality didn't seem to bother God.

The Durfields and Linda and I often discussed the impasse at Glad Tidings. We all recognized the problem, but, at first, were reluctant to say what we knew in our hearts. While Pastor Dale Young preached with great zeal and earnestness, his sermons were generally shallow, or they simply made no sense. A product of the Latter Rain movement, Young came to Los Angeles desperately yearning for another great revival. He named his church after Glad Tidings in Vancouver, British Columbia, pastored by Rev. Reg Layzell, an early leader in Latter Rain. And, fondly, Young often referred to his former mentor, Thomas Wyatt, and his Wings of Healing Temple in Portland, Oregon. Wyatt also participated in the fabled Latter Rain movement, and upon Wyatt's demise, Dale Young hoped to take over the Wings of Healing ministry.

That didn't happen, however, and Young came to Los Angeles, where he was determined to launch another revival.

Well, God wasn't cooperating. Pastor Young lived in the past, an imaginary time when the Holy Ghost fell on churches and miracles happened by the bushel full. Through his boring sermons he continually recounted the glorious days of old, but offered very little that one could grasp and apply to daily life.

When we couldn't take it any more, we met with Dale and told him our feelings. Rather than take it graciously, he lashed out at us and said we were hindering the Holy Spirit.

After that, though, his sermons did change. Now he went on prophetic binges, warning of God's impending judgment on those who resist the Spirit. He told of people falling out of trees, off ladders, or down the stairs, and of others run over by automobiles, all because they rebelled against the will of God.

When the threats didn't frighten us into repentance, Dale took Ric and Renee aside and, to them alone, accused me of causing division in the church. Upon finding this out, Linda and I quit Glad Tidings Tabernacle, while Ric and Renee stayed on for a while longer.

Before leaving Glad Tidings, I found employment in the customer service division of the Los Angeles Department of Water and Power on North Hope Street. The city job paid well, and left me time to pursue my ministry. While at work, I made it a habit to discreetly witness to anyone I thought was receptive.

The Department of Water and Power described my position as a Customer Service Representative. In actuality, I collected delinquent water and electric bills. While I found the work to be demanding, it had its good moments.

Most of my collection duties were performed by telephone and mail, without direct contact with customers. Recipients of my letters often called to offer explanations for their tardiness in paying bills, and to work out payment schedules. Sometimes they were simply billed in error. Our receptionist, Raynie, screened the incoming calls and forwarded them to the proper representative.

I soon became immune to abusive callers, hard-luck stories, and outright lies, and took every call in stride. So, the afternoon Marie Bailey's desperate call came through, I treated it routinely. In soft, but urgent tones, she told me that she was blind, broke, and without food.

"What is your name?" I asked.
"Bailey, Miss Marie Bailey."
"Please spell that."
"B-a-i-l-e-y."

"Will you hold, please," I said. As the little white light on the phone's row of buttons flashed, I looked for the "Bailey" file. I looked in every possible location, but to no avail. Giving up, I picked up the phone and pushed the button with the flashing light.

"I have no file on you, why are you calling?" I asked.

"Because I am blind and have no money or food," she responded.

Puzzled, I asked her what she expected me to do. Miss Bailey indicated that she thought I was in a position to help her. Still confused, I asked for her address and told her I'd see what I could do.

"Thank you, but don't come at night. Watts is very dangerous," she added.

Watts. How could I forget Watts? In the summer of 1965, shortly after we arrived in California, a riot erupted in Watts. Ominously, the smoke, clearly visible from the Harbor Freeway, rose above the area. The riot raged on for seven days; thirty-four people were shot and killed; a thousand were injured; and 800 buildings were destroyed or damaged. After the police lost control of the rampage, 13,000 armed National Guardsmen, along with tanks and helicopters, finally brought order. Linda and I watched the live coverage on the TV in our motel. (I didn't know it at the time, but it would be ten years before we watched TV again.)

Later, after church one Sunday, Dave, from the People's Tabernacle of Faith, took Linda and me on a tour of Watts. The devastation from the riot was still evident. So, when Miss Bailey mentioned Watts, I knew where she meant.

After Miss Bailey's strange call, I walked across the room to Raynie the receptionist and asked why she assigned the call to me, as I had no file on the woman.

"Oh," she replied, "she asked for the pastor, and knowing that you're a minister, I figured she was calling you."

Well, that made sense, sort of, but still left a lot of questions unanswered, especially since I didn't know the woman. When I got home that evening I told Linda of the curious incident. We both sensed that God was somehow involved in this, and we agreed that we should act on our intuition. After buying two large shopping bags full of groceries, we headed for Watts.

Now dark, it took some time to find the unlit street. About ten o'clock we finally located a small, shabby cottage with the correct street number. I climbed the sagging porch and knocked on the door. Curiously, the door bore several splintered, dime-sized holes.

After knocking several times, and getting no response, I went to the house next door to inquire if Marie Bailey was their neighbor. Yes, I was at the right place, but Miss Bailey never opens the door after dark, I learned.

So, going back to Miss Bailey's cottage, I knocked again, and then announced, "Miss Bailey, your pastor's here." In a moment I heard movement from inside, then the door slowly opened, revealing a small and frail black woman, illuminated only by a bare bulb which hung from the ceiling.

"We brought your groceries," I said.

"Praise the Lord! Praise the Lord! Oh, thank you Jesus, thank you Jesus!" she shouted while dancing around with her arms raised in the air.

"Come, come in," she said, tugging my sleeve.

As we introduced ourselves, she showed me where to put the groceries. Explaining that she hadn't eaten in two days, she asked if we could prepare something.

While Linda heated some soup, I sat down and talked with Marie Bailey. I asked her if she knew I worked for the Department of Water and Power.

"You do? I thought you were a minister."

"Well, I am, but you called me at the Department of Water and Power."

"I did?" she replied quizzically.

As Miss Bailey talked, the puzzle unraveled. She explained that she was legally blind, and although she could see forms as shadows, she couldn't seen the numbers on a telephone. When making calls, she dialed the operator, gave the name of the party to be called, and the operator made the connection.

Linda brought a bowl of soup and placed it on a chair in front of Miss Bailey. Between slurps, she continued her story. For two weeks, she said, she existed on oatmeal. Then, the day before she called me, she ran out of the cereal. All her life she trusted the Lord to meet her needs, and believing she'd starve to death without a miracle, she fell on her knees and asked the Lord to help her. Years earlier, Marie Bailey attended Angelus Temple. So, in desperation, she tried to call the sizable Los Angeles church. Not knowing the phone number, she asked the operator to connect her with Angelus Temple.

"When you came on the phone," she said, "I thought you were one of the pastors at Angelus Temple."

Somehow, the operator dialed the wrong number and got the Los Angeles Department of Water and Power on North Hope Street. I had to laugh, because the street sign read "No. Hope St.," which gave the street the nickname of "No Hope Street." Now, I knew there was hope on "No Hope Street." (Sometime later, George Burns played the role of God in the movie *Oh, God!* In the film, Burns kept an appointment with John Denver in the same North Hope Street building.)

In talking further with Miss Bailey, we learned that she lived in fear and solitude. Youngsters often threw rocks at her house in order to frighten her, and at night people attempted to open the locked door. Somehow, she obtained a handgun, and the next time someone tried to break in through her front door, she emptied the gun through it. That explained the door's splintered holes. Later, after shooting herself in the leg, the police took the gun away.

Actually, Marie Bailey had money. In her mail, we found several uncashed welfare checks. The next day, we took her to the local market to cash the checks and buy more food. We talked to the store's manager and he agreed to look out for her on a regular basis.

One Saturday afternoon, while taking Marie out for ice cream, she said she had something for me, and stuck a tightly rolled bill into my hand. I glanced down at the rolled greenback and saw the number "10." Embarrassed at the thought of taking money from her, I gave it back, telling her I couldn't accept it.

She insisted, saying, "The Lord told me that he would tell me who to give this to, and last night he told me to give it to you."

Realizing that Miss Bailey would be offended if I said no, I took the money.

Later, when we got home, I unrolled the bill. It wasn't a ten dollar bill at all, it was a hundred-dollar bill. Because I didn't need the money, and because it came as a result of my ministry, I decided to hold it in my wallet until I found direction from God about what to do with it.

As my zeal for the Lord increased, I endeavored to make up for lost time. There had been so many missed opportunities to tell people about the Lord. The Bible told me that the blood of those whom I failed to witness to would be on my hands. With this in mind, I remembered my friend Thomas E. Dewey. He was kind enough to send me a congratulatory card when I graduated from high school. Because of my backsliding at the time, I never bothered to tell him about Jesus. I sensed that God was telling me to write him and share my testimony about how I had come back to the Lord. I meant to do it, but I never got around to it.

At lunch time I usually left the Department of Water and Power's downtown office for a walk and a bite to eat. One day I passed a newsstand and a newspaper headline turned my head. "Dewey Dead!" it read. I just stood there and sobbed. Before he died, had someone else reached him for the Lord? I didn't know, but I took this as a harsh lesson in obedience. I determined to never disobey the Holy Spirit again.

After Charles Manson was arrested, his Family, the so-called "Manson girls," held a vigil outside the Hall of Justice, where he was being held for trial. Several of them camped in a van parked in front of the building. During the trial, they carried out various stunts to capture media attention. When Manson appeared in court one day with an X carved on his forehead, the girls on the street imitated him. After his murder conviction, they shaved their heads bald.

I took it upon myself to tell them about the love of Jesus. Each day during lunch I sat with Crystal, Mary, Kitty, Ouisch, Sandy, and Squeaky on the sidewalk and talked to them. While a couple of the girls refused to talk to me, others listened intently, and then countered with their Manson-taught philosophy. They warned me of the judgment which was about to come, which I sensed as a veiled threat or warning.

One day they handed me a manuscript which they said Charlie wrote while in jail. I don't know how they got it, but they said it was smuggled out. It was signed by Manson. I asked if I could borrow it, thinking I might learn something to help me achieve a breakthrough in my talks with them. With the stipulation that I return it the next day, they loaned me Manson's article. At work, I photocopied the twenty-odd pages, and returned the original. I was tempted to keep the original and return the copy, but I was truly frightened by these girls. Even during Manson's trial, the murders continued. Besides the killings, there were attempted assassinations, including that of witnesses and one attorney. Squeaky (Lynette Fromme) and Ouisch (Ruth Ann Moorehouse) were subsequently arrested in connection with the attempted murder of a prosecution witness. Squeaky received a ninety-day jail sentence and Ouisch was released on her own recognizance, only to disappear. And after that, in 1975, Squeaky was arrested once again after attempting to shoot President Gerald Ford when he visited Sacramento. So, I believe my fears of these girls was reasonable.

Unfortunately, today I cannot locate the copy of the Manson document. From what I remember, it contained Charlie's fantasy of a coming race riot, which his trial, and something he called "Helter Skelter," would ignite.

Besides our attempts to convert total strangers, Linda and I were both zealous in our efforts to bring old friends and acquaintances to Jesus. Together, we composed a letter explaining our feelings about sin, salvation, and Jesus. Linda wrote it in her hand, and we had it printed, and sent it back East to every single person we could think of. For the most part, no one responded. A couple of people perceived our letter as a nice gesture, but one indignant person in Hillsdale wrote back and warned us to never send such a letter again.

After leaving Glad Tidings, I began a Wednesday-night Bible study in our home. Several city employees from the Department of Water and Power attended.

Sundays were still free, and we used the time to visit other churches. Soon after meeting Miss Bailey, Linda and I were at the Faith Center church in Glendale. After the service, I met a man by the name of Don Widmark, whose display in the back of the church intrigued me. Don operated an electronics business and recording studio across the street from Billy Graham's Worldwide Pictures in North Hollywood.

He showed me a new portable radio-sized machine called a cassette tape player. It played hour-long sermons and Bible teaching on small plastic cassettes which were simply inserted into the machine. With closed eyes, I picked up a player, stuck in a cassette, flipped a switch, and, presto, I heard Bible teacher Bob Mumford. How simple, the blind could use this with ease, I thought.

I told Don that I'd like to buy one of these things to lend to a blind lady, and asked what I could buy for a hundred dollars. For a hundred bucks, he sold me three players, and ten prerecorded audio cassettes.

Miss Bailey was thrilled with the tapes. She told me of another blind lady, whom I met, and I also lent her a player and tapes. I kept the other player for my Wednesday-night Bible-study group. The tapes caught on quickly, and I received contributions to purchase more tapes. Before long, we had a dozen cassette players circulating, and the tape library grew to more than a hundred selections.

Operating my little ministry from home had its ups and downs. One week an unprecedented number of people told me of their plans to attend the Bible study. Excited by the prospect of having so many people coming, right after dinner on Wednesday, Linda and I set up every available chair in the house. The couch easily sat three; the overstuffed chair, one; the dining room chairs, six; my desk chair, one; a kitchen stool sat another; plus ten folding chairs, totalling twenty-two seats.

With nervous excitement, we waited for all the people to show up for the seven-thirty P.M. Bible study. About quarter to eight, one young couple pulled up in front of the house. Realizing by now that they were the only ones coming, in vain, we tried to cover our embarrassment and put all the chairs away before they knocked on the door.

However, that wasn't my most embarrassing moment. As the Bible studies continued, several couples attended regularly. And others came. Soon, the group doubled in size, and, eventually, doubled again. Now, with so many people coming, we used all the chairs, plus some new ones we bought. One Wednesday night Linda prepared a quick dinner of baked beans and hot dogs. Afterwards, while doing some last minute vacuuming to pick up some dirt on the floor, I got a terrible gas attack. At that dreadful moment, a half-dozen people from the group approached the house.

To conceal the potent gas about to be unleashed, I quickly disconnected the floor attachment from the vacuum-cleaner hose and placed the hose's nozzle to my backside. Had God's grace been with me at that moment, I might have at least measured up to St. Augustine's clever verse in *The City of God*, "There are those that can break wind backwards so artfully you would think they sang." However, that wasn't the case. Instead of containing the smelly methane gas, as I mistakenly thought it would, the vacuum cleaner dispersed it throughout the house—just as the people came through the door.

13

Exorcists and Flying Prophets

As the Wednesday-night Bible studies grew they took on aspects of Pentecostal church services. Participants brought their own instruments, including guitars, tambourines, a flute, and an autoharp. Surprisingly, the neighbors never complained about the noise. In fact, one elderly neighbor enjoyed sitting by her open window listening to the music and Bible teaching.

Most of the people who attended the Bible study were unchurched, that is, they didn't attend a church. They got a lot out of the meetings, though, and wanted to meet more often, so I began Sunday afternoon services.

Now, our house church offered as many services as some regular churches. Offering four hours of Bible study a week meant even more time spent in study and preparation. Then there was follow-up. Christians often need constant help and encouragement to stay on the straight and narrow path. They want visits at home, and while in the hospital, and prayer and counseling at all hours of the night and day. And soon, I was performing weddings and funerals. Before I knew it, I was putting nearly as many hours into my ministry as I put in at the Department of Water and Power.

Linda and I discussed the situation, prayed about it, and then decided we should take a leap of faith. (Truthfully, decisions reached as a result of prayer are no different than decisions made without prayer. We do what we want to do, regardless. Prayer is often used to justify the rightness of our decision. In other words, if we prayed, then the decision we made must have been the God-approved one.) I quit my job and looked entirely to the Lord to support my work as a minister. Because I considered it my life-line to God, prayer became a focal point in my life.

Each of my days began with prayer. At first, I tried to stay in bed while I prayed, but then I always fell back asleep. As a solution, I placed the alarm clock under the bed. When it went off, I had to get out of bed to retrieve it, and then, of course, I was already on my knees.

To help defray the expenses of the cassette-tape ministry, I put an offering basket by the door. Now, that basket would have to provide enough for our family of three to live on. The Lord came through, and the people rallied behind me as their full-time pastor. We received little money, but it was always just enough.

Although we had some couples, my house church attracted mostly women. Some of them were successful in dragging their husbands or children along. For the most part, husbands resisted any involvement whatsoever. Yet, on the other hand, a few husbands became involved without their wives.

The introduction of religion into a home usually divided it right down the middle. The only times religion nurtured a family was when a husband and wife worshipped together. When only one participated —which was most of the time—it created much disharmony.

At this same time Ric and Renee were off chasing new rainbows. We saw them from time to time, and on each occasion we heard about something new they were pursuing. Their pursuits sometimes involved new ways of acquiring material possessions. When they got involved with people who sold Amway and Shaklee home products, we heard that the head of Proctor & Gamble was a practicing satanist. As proof, a couple who were Ric and Renee's new friends offered a document which showed that the Proctor & Gamble logo represented a satanic symbol. At first, the strange story sounded credible, but then I realized the probable motive behind it. If Christians could discredit Proctor & Gamble, then it would be easier to sell Amway, Shaklee, or whatever other like products they peddled. Of course, this was an individual thing. Amway or Shaklee had nothing to do with the scheme.

Many Christian groups have published statements from Proctor

& Gamble that disclaim any tie to satanism. Yet, the rumors persist as unscrupulous people take advantage of some Christian's religious paranoia.

Proctor & Gamble has lost tens of thousands of dollars because of the deceptive practices of some fundamentalist Christians. In an effort to fight back, the company has sued couples for spreading the malicious, false rumors.

From the time I first met Ric, he seemed attracted to various conspiracies and intrigue. And it wasn't difficult for him to convince Renee of the special secrets he claimed to know. Through the Durfields, I learned of the Protocols of the Learned Elders of Zion, an anti-Semitic tract which purported to prove that Jewish bankers conspired to take over the world and create a one-world anti-Christian government. The group they were involved with at the time passed the booklet among its members.

Ric and Renee's search for new things didn't end with the material. In pursuit of new truth they also followed certain charismatic Christian gurus. For a while, they became very involved with a man who called himself "Dr." Grimes. Grimes, employing a series of manuals he wrote, taught about supernatural spiritual gifts and ministries. We attended some of his meetings with Ric and Renee. Grimes once prayed over me, and God supposedly spoke through him and said, "I have given thee the heart of a pastor. Feed my sheep."

After Grimes, they went after a Jamaican named Cecil Ducille. Ducille proclaimed the end-time message. Claiming special revelation from God, Ducille said God was calling a special people from within the body of Christ, the church, to bring forth his message for the last days. This teaching had an appeal to Christians who wanted to go all the way with God—versus lukewarm Christians who were satisfied in their churches. It made them feel very chosen, very special. Because of their advanced spiritual maturity, God, through his prophets—such as Ducille—was giving them revelation that other Christians weren't yet ready to receive.

Sam Fife, another end-time preacher, came to California from Florida. He, too, claimed to have a special revelation concerning the body of Christ. With great enthusiasm, Ric and Renee became involved with Fife, also. We attended one meeting with them, but something suspicious about Sam Fife made us wary, and we tried to stay detached.

God seemingly blessed my ministry, and it branched out into several directions at once.

Some new members of my house church, Jon and his family, had a burden for the lost souls in Mexico. As Jon spoke fluent Spanish, we went to Mexico to preach the gospel to the poor. Our mission was successful, and we started a new church in Camalu, on the Baja peninsula. Members of the congregation and I made numerous trips bringing food, clothing, and medical supplies for the people of Camalu.

One family left the area and moved out to Indio, just beyond Palm Springs. Once a week, I made the trip out to the desert to teach a Bible study in their home.

Renee became pregnant again, and the group she and Ric were involved in at the time believed in having babies at home. After they shared their ideas with us about home birthing, we wanted to have our next child at home. As it happened, Linda was also pregnant. Soon, our son Mark was born at our home and house church on North Avenue 53 in Highland Park.

Our landlord came by one day to tell us that he wanted to sell the house. He offered us the first option, but it was already too small for the services, so we turned it down, and began looking for another rental.

Bill and Lorraine, a couple who worked at the Department of Water and Power, lived a few miles away in Eagle Rock. Their good-sized garage came with a small addition on the back. They offered us the use of the small building for our church. The men of the church tore down an interior wall and paneled the complete inside of the building. I named the little church Eagle Rock Assembly (which, in retrospect sounds like a small factory)—but most people called it "Skipp's church." I appointed elders to help me run it.

We found a house to rent on Echo Street, and the church's ministry in the garage continued to grow and reach out. An Indian family joined, and soon we helped support a mission in India and made plans for me to visit there.

Linda, Angela, Mark, and I spent a few weeks away to visit our folks back home. During that time I spoke at a Full Gospel Businessmen's breakfast, several churches, and some home Bible studies. By the time we started thinking about returning to California, I'd cultivated a substantial following in New York and Massachusetts. In order to continue my ministry to these people, I went to WHUC, a Hudson, New York radio station, and bought time on Sunday mornings. Although it was a contemporary music station, they sold time to anyone. I did the first two broadcasts live from the Hudson studio. After returning to California, Don Widmark let me use his studio to make tapes which I mailed each week to Hudson.

People from Ric and Renee's group started attending our services, which really pushed the walls out. Before long, we found ourselves getting involved again with Sam Fife's ministry. Although I seriously questioned some of his teachings, a lot of what he had to say seemed to make sense. Of course, it appealed strongly to everyone's ego, including mine. I already believed we were in the last days, and if God was ready to wrap things up, it was logical that he'd send messengers to his people. I came to believe that Sam Fife, Cecil Ducille, and others were his messengers. By now, thoroughly addicted to religion, I lost all the joy I once had, including my invaluable sense of humor.

Fife's network spread across the United States, and the more important ministers in his group owned their own small planes. Most of "the body" regarded these men as prophets. The prophets claimed to receive dreams, visions, and words from God for specific individuals. People even called them long-distance on the phone to get a word of personal guidance from the Lord.

During Christmas week in 1971, Fife's end-time group held a convention at the Fairpark Coliseum in Lubbock, Texas. The date was fine. By then we had given up celebrating Christmas because of its pagan origins. The delegation from my church included thirteen people, counting the children.

We traveled in two vehicles, an old Dodge van, and a new Chevrolet sedan. Way out in the middle of nowhere, between El Paso and Odessa, the van broke down—about 360 miles from Lubbock. A man in a tow truck came from a ramshackle garage just a stone's throw from where the van died—I sensed that many vehicles broke down along that stretch of desolate highway. The mechanic said it would take a week to get parts, and the price he quoted to repair it was more than the cost of buying another van. So, we just left the thing there in Texas and all thirteen of us somehow crammed into the car. After that, whenever we stopped for gas, food, or bathroom calls, people stared in disbelief as we all spilled out.

The convention was disastrous. First of all, it became evident that Fife and his end-time prophets were either self-deluded, or on some kind of power trip. Their teaching violated everything I knew about the Scriptures. People became more and more dependent on the ministers for a word from the Lord, and as they did, they found every aspect of their lives controlled by these end-time prophets. The prophets and elders in the body decided who one should marry or divorce, where they should live and work, and made other choices of a personal nature for them.

To make matters worse, like a Biblical plague, a flu virus spread through the gathering and hundred of people became violently ill. Mark and I got so ill that our family had to stay in Lubbock an extra five days, finally returning to Los Angeles by Greyhound.

After Lubbock we separated our church from the end-time movement. Others who stayed with it left the United States, moving either to the jungles of South America or the harshness of northern Canada. The Canadian faction, even though they didn't believe in observing Christmas, made their living by raising and selling Christmas trees.

Later on we heard that some of the end-time prophets were flying to a meeting in New England when their plane disappeared. People we knew actually believed that those in the plane had attained such an exalted place in their spirituality that God simply took them home, plane and all. While I didn't believe that for a minute, I felt better when, many months later, their bodies were found in the plane's wreckage on a mountaintop.

In the summer of 1972, Marylisa, our third and last child, was born at our Echo Street home. This was about the time we got involved in exorcism. Besides the tales I'd read in the New Testament about casting out demons, I had no knowledge about the subject. I didn't even know such things happened today.

The Durfields, through two books, introduced us to the phenomenon of demon possession and exorcism. One was *Between Christ and Satan*, written by a Lutheran pastor named Kurt Koch, and another, *Angels of Light*, by Hobart Freeman. Freeman's teachings especially whetted our appetites for a deeper walk with God as we delved into these spiritual truths. The books seemed to present valid answers to questions concerning the actions of many Christians who were never helped by traditional pastoral counseling. These people were demon possessed, or at least, controlled in some way by demon spirits.

As we studied demonology, our church came to believe that demons —which we understood to be spiritual beings—operated through a hierarchical system, and that different geographical areas were controlled by certain types of demons. For instance, a demon of lust controlled Los Angeles through pornography; a demon of chance controlled Las Vegas through gambling; a demon of violence controlled Chicago through organized crime; and a demon of greed controlled New York City (where most of the Jews in America live).

Popular Charismatic Bible teachers such as Don Basham and Derek Prince reinforced our quest to hunt down and drive out demons. Just reading about or listening to tapes on exorcism didn't satisfy our need for this spiritual power. It's easy to find supposed demonized people in Charismatic or Pentecostal congregations, as the very nature of these groups tend to attract eccentric people.

Exorcisms are long, arduous, and often violent. The church elders and I usually went to private homes to perform exorcisms. On some occasions our wives went with us, to add extra spiritual power. In one home, an average, middle class housewife knelt on the wall-to-wall carpet. As a dozen hands were laid on her head, we at first prayed in tongues.

"Shun-da da-da-ma hun-da. On-di, ma-kai-on-do," someone babbled.

"Come out! Come out in the name of Jesus! I command you to come out of her!" one elder shouted into her ear.

"You evil spirit of lust," he continued with great power and authority, "And you spirit of witchcraft, leave, in the name of Jesus!"

By now the atmosphere was charged and everyone continued to speak in tongues. The pitch grew louder as we feverishly prayed for the woman's deliverance from evil spirits.

Someone started to sing, "In the name of Jesus, in the name of Jesus." Everyone joined in and lifted their hands toward heaven. The woman slumped to the carpeted floor and sobbed.

Seizing the moment, an elder clutched the woman with his burly hands. He blurted loudly in tongues and vigorously shook the woman. The rest of the group stopped singing and shouted incomprehensible utterances. The woman sat up, her knees digging into the carpet as the elder continued to shake the demons out of her.

"Come out! In the name of Jesus, I command you!" he yelled into her ear.

Overwhelmed, she screamed and fought back. Now, everyone held her by the arms and shoulders as they yelled for the demons to come out.

"Fuck you, fuck you all!" the woman screamed. "You're all going to hell!"

While some of the women were shocked by the vulgarity, this outbreak only encouraged us—because a Christian wouldn't talk like that, we were now certain it was the demon speaking through her. Discovered, he was obviously ready to come out, but not before a last ditch effort.

Then, she screamed again, and started to cough and gag. Having been through this many times, we had the barf bag ready, but she missed it and vomited on the carpet.

Ecstatic, we shouted in unison, "Thank you Jesus! Thank you Jesus!"

The woman we delivered from evil spirits had normal problems—she fornicated and smoked cigarettes—which to us indicated a rebellious nature and was one major door demons used to get into a person. Also, she admitted to reading her horoscope in the newspaper, and as a child, she played with a Ouija board. We believed these activities resulted in demon influence.

The antic of cursing is very common during an exorcism. Sometimes the subject spit, bit, punched, and even attempted to choke would-be exorcists. The wilder the exorcism, the more convinced we were that it was really a demon we were dealing with.

One man, whose family tricked him into coming to the exorcism, leapt over a coffee table and grabbed me by the throat. It took four men and their wives to wrestle him to the floor, where he finally obliged to throw up, thus expelling the supposed demons.

Once, while waiting for the elders to arrive, Linda and I had to hog-tie a woman to a chair. Suicidal, she kept running to the kitchen to grab a knife. We performed several exorcisms on her, all to no avail. Ultimately, she was committed to a mental institution where she received shock treatments.

One attractive twenty-one-year-old was thought to be possessed by demons. Her unnatural craving for food caused her to gorge herself at meals, and during the night she raided the refrigerator and ate everything in sight. Strangely, she never gained any weight. In fact, she was malnourished. Why? Because after eating she forced herself to vomit. Twice, we attempted to cast demons out of her, but her symptoms remained unchanged. Then, a doctor diagnosed her as having bulimia, but treatment came too late. Before her twenty-second birthday she committed suicide.

I've known of occasions where minsters have called dozens of people forward at the conclusion of a service. Those who had been involved in the occult, false religions, had uncontrolled lusts or habits, and even women who had had an abortion participated in a mass exorcism which concluded with everyone engaging in the obligatory vomting. Yards of church carpet have been ruined in this manner.

Over a period of almost three years, we performed dozens of exorcisms. Our victims included men, women, and children—as young as seven and eight.

After a while, it became clear that everyone we thought we delivered of demons reverted back to their old ways and still had the same problems. In fact, several ended up in mental institutions or died through suicide. Rather than admit to the severity of our destruction, we just let it go and went on to emphasize something else.

14

California Adieu

After word of the Lubbock fiasco got around, the Durfields joined our congregation and became fully involved. Renee introduced a new book to the congregation called *Dare to Discipline*, by Dr. James Dobson, a born-again Christian psychologist. Dobson's book emphasizes strict, authoritarian discipline. In it he describes how his own mother abused him, and he stresses the necessity of pain when administering corporal punishment.

With so many children in our church, some of the young parents saw Dobson's book as a godsend. All of my church elders and their wives, and several other parents, met every week to study *Dare to Discipline*. I never liked hitting my children, but Dr. Dobson used Scripture to back up the practice, so I accepted it.

One afternoon one of my church elders called on the phone.

"Skipp, you've got to help me, I'm in jail." I registered surprise and started to ask questions, but he said he'd explain everything when I got down to the police station.

At the jail he told me that while in school that morning, his eight-year-old daughter felt ill and went to the school nurse. The nurse noticed marks on the girl's legs. Suspecting child abuse, the nurse called the police, who, in turn, went to the hardware store where my friend worked and arrested him.

The elder told me that after church the previous Sunday, his wife observed their daughter playing with a twenty-dollar bill. Upon questioning the little girl, they learned that she had stolen it from the offering basket. So, they applied the appropriate punishment according to their understanding of Dr. Dobson's *Dare to Discipline*.

I assured him everything would be all right, that there was no way the court could punish him for exercising his religious freedom by rearing his children according to the Scriptures. I promised to testify before the judge to my friend's fine character and that he was a faithful worker with me in the church.

On the day of the trial, I sat directly behind the two detectives who investigated the case. As we waited for the judge to call this case, the detectives shuffled through eight-by-ten police photos of the little girl's backside. In living color, the photos revealed appalling abuse. Shocked and sickened, I left the courtroom, and did not testify on behalf of my friend. I just couldn't condone what I had seen in those pictures. The church elder, by the way, received probation.

Of course this experience made a great impact on my own feelings about parenting. Dobson's book went on a shelf as I sought better ways to raise my children.

The church in the garage could no longer accommodate all the people we had drawn so we looked for a new facility. Several of our young members needed more than just a church; they needed a family, so we settled on a large, twenty-four room house in Pasadena. The big house suited our needs so well that we affectionately called it "the big house."

Linda and I enjoyed a warm friendship with Ric and Renee during this time, so we all agreed that our two families (by this time the Durfields had four children, and we had three), along with some of the single young people who attended services, would share the big house. The house's layout consisted of four distinct living areas, a kitchen/dining area, plus a large open living room with another, adjoining dining area. This latter area became the chapel where we held church services. One room became a home school. Our daughter, Angela, and Kimberli Durfield were now of school age. Not wanting to send them to a public school controlled by a satanic secular humanistic system, we started our own school. Angie and Kim were the only two students when the fully certified school began. A public school teacher, and member of our church, oversaw the school. Renee taught the children.

Several other rooms became offices and guest rooms. One guest spent a few nights in one of these guests rooms, and she reported that demons lived in her room and the adjacent room. I believed her because, unknown to anyone else, I'd been on a fast for several days, taking only water during the entire fast. One day as I came to the top of the staircase I saw a demon. It ran away from me and disappeared through the wall, right into one of the rooms the guest claimed had demons. Until she mentioned the demons, I was afraid to tell anyone about them.

Because of the woman's report, the elders met in the demonized rooms and effectively cast them out. At least no one ever saw any again.

Ric's mom attended the Church of God in Christ, in Pacoima where Ric grew up. An invitation came to me to preach at her church on a Sunday night. Although my methods were very much unlike those of black preachers, I went and was well-received by the congregation.

It used to always disturb me how easily congregations accepted whatever they heard from the pulpit, as if they weren't even listening. I developed a ploy to prove my point, and used it in Pacoima.

"How many of you believe the Bible is the Word of God?" I asked. "Well, raise your hands!" I shouted. Every hand went up.

"Do you believe every word in the book?" I implored.

"Amen."

"That's right."

"Praise the Lord."

As they got really worked up, I continued my strategy.

"Well now, do you believe that story in the Bible about Jonah swallowing the whale?"

"Amen!"

"Yes, we do, brother!"

Whenever I've done that, without exception, every congregation has swallowed it. They always fall into the trap and say they believe Jonah swallowed the whale, and not the other way around. It's because they don't really listen.

Our ministry in Indio continued, and sometimes Bill, one of the elders, went out to conduct the Bible study, thus relieving me of some of the work-load. I met Bill and Lorraine at the Department of Water and Power, and they were the first to come to my Bible study in Highland Park. Eventually, Bill became an elder in the church, and quite an enthusiastic Bible teacher.

One week, Bill and Lorraine, their little baby, and one of the young men who lived at the big house made the two-hour trip out to Indio. It was after midnight when they left Indio to head back to Pasadena in their Toyota station wagon. As they sped along the San Bernardino Freeway, a drunk driver came barreling up behind them, catching the corner of their small car and spinning it around. The car spun out of control and rolled several times. Lorraine and the baby, who were both sitting in the back seat, flew out of the car through the rear tailgate and onto the highway.

Bill called me around three a.m., and I left immediately for the hospital. It didn't look good. The men were unharmed, but Lorraine almost lost her arm; the bones from her broken shoulder blade cut the muscles and nerves to her arm, rendering it useless. Her baby suffered severe head injuries, and was in danger of not pulling through.

Back in Pasadena, we called all the members of the church. Many gathered at the big house for a hastily called prayer meeting. We prayed through the day, claiming healing for Lorraine and the baby. As night approached we continued our prayers. The latest report said the baby's condition remained unchanged. We prayed harder, fully expecting the baby to be healed miraculously.

About midnight, almost twenty-four hours after the terrible accident, the phone rang. It was Bill calling to tell us that their baby died. I was stunned. How could God allow this to happen, I wondered. Then, taking strength from the Scriptures, I went into the chapel to make the announcement.

"God hath given, and God hath taken away," I said somberly. At once, I realized that those words were the stupidest I'd ever uttered.

The Volkswagen finally broke down and had to be towed to the shop. The repairs came to $300, which we didn't have. So, I just left it, waiting on God to provide the money. I didn't tell anyone how much it cost, because I didn't want it to sound like I was begging. After a couple of weeks, the car remained at the shop.

After the service one Sunday, a man who came some twenty miles on the bus each week, asked me if I would pray that he could get a car. I asked him how much he could afford for a car should God make one available. He said $300.

"Well, brother, God just provided a car," I told him.

I took his money, picked up my car, and signed it over to him. I figured it wasn't doing anybody any good sitting in the garage, and perhaps God wanted him to have it. So, I gave it to him. For several months afterward, my three-speed bicycle served me well in local ministry. Different people lent me cars whenever I had to travel to Indio or other distant places.

While I received a small salary, the church could barely afford even that. Ric, who had since left his court job, got nothing, so he sought outside employment. Now, Jon, who headed the Mexican ministry, worked as a salesman for a large pharmaceutical company, and thought he could get Ric into the company as a salesman. Ric was delighted at the prospect because it paid well, offered full benefits, and a new car. He told me that if he got the job, he'd give me his fairly late model Volkswagen as a gift.

"Really!" I exclaimed. It would be nice to have a car again. Yes, he said that he and Renee discussed it, and she concurred that if he got the job with a car, they should give their Volkswagen to me.

Several weeks passed, and I forgot about Ric's car. I was in the parking lot in back of the big house one afternoon when Ric came down the driveway in a new silver-colored Chevrolet.

"Hey, nice car," I said. "Where'd you get it?"

"Oh, I got the job, didn't I tell you?" he replied.

"No," I said. "Where's your Volkswagen?"

"Uh, we sold it," he answered.

I didn't say anything to Ric, but that incident served as an eye-opener.

Sometimes when I fellowshipped with my friend Don Widmark we'd visit different churches together. One, Melodyland Christian Center in Anaheim, was a spiritual hot spot where Charismatic Christians from all over Southern California flocked. Another, Orange County Church, rose out of a former drive-in movie. Don introduced me to Rev. Robert Schuller, a Christian positive thinker who used to preach from the top of the outdoor movie's concession stand. Now, his Garden Grove Community Church had a massive church-building program under way.

Through Don, I was introduced to a pastor's fellowship which met in Glendale. For a while, I was a regular participant. We openly shared our victories, heartaches, and then prayed for one another. I got to know several pastors closely. Some things, I learned, weren't shared with the group, but were discussed one-on-one. Now, most of the ministers I knew seemed very honest and sincere. However, I've known several who were less so. For example, most churches have one or two well-to-do old people included in their membership. Some pastors skillfully court these people until the old folks pledge to leave everything to the church after they're gone. And sometimes the pastor himself is named as a recipient in the will. These ministers just can't wait for these old folks to drop dead. What surprised me is how shamelessly some of them will talk about this.

Don called one day to invite me to a special pastor's retreat in the mountains near Arrowhead Springs. An Argentine minister by the name of Juan Carlos Ortiz wanted to meet with local pastors and share with them what God was doing in Argentina.

The informal gathering began early in the morning and went throughout the day and into the early evening. At first, Ortiz seemed kind of odd. He began the session with prayer, which wasn't strange in itself, but his manner of public prayer was . . . different. Ortiz, looking out toward the pastors, prayed to God with his eyes open. He explained that when two people converse, one of the party doesn't close his eyes while the other speaks. Well, he said, it's the same way when we talk to God. God doesn't close his eyes, so why should we?

After that, all the pastors prayed with their eyes wide open, which created an eerie feeling. Here's this guy praying to God, and when you look up at him, he's looking at you, or at other people in the audience. Also, it's not an easy feat, because one becomes easily distracted praying that way. I never went for the idea.

Ortiz went on to tell us of his revolutionary method for making Christian disciples in his home church. In Argentina, Ortiz took several men under his wing and taught them everything he knew about spiritual things and God's order for the church. The men entered a covenant relationship with Ortiz, and because of the love and trust they all shared, they trusted Ortiz to guide them in the knowledge of God's will in every aspect of their lives. In addition to being at Ortiz's beck and call, as his representatives, they carried all of his authority in the church. In turn, each of these men gathered newer converts under them and made them their disciples. These newer converts answered only to their shepherd who answered only to Ortiz. The pyramid continued downward until it had so many levels that the whole church was involved in discipleship. Discipleship included only the men, because married women came under the covering, or authority, of their husbands, and the younger, single women in the church came under the authority and teaching of the older women. On top, Ortiz always remained in control. The pyramid scheme of "discipleship" was also called "shepherding."

Like most of the other pastors at this private gathering in the mountains, I was quite taken by the idea of discipleship. At one time or another, all of us struggled with order and command in church government. Ortiz's method seemed to offer positive solutions to some real problems. Jesus made disciples, so why couldn't we?

Four elders, including Ric Durfield, helped me to run my church. And while I was recognized by everyone as the pastor, schisms and power struggles sometimes developed. If my church put discipleship in effect, I could remain at the top, and each of my elders could develop their own disciples. Their need to teach and oversee would be satisfied, and I could oversee the entire church as it developed and remained intact. The whole idea was so beautiful that I absorbed everything Ortiz said during the next few hours.

When I got back to Pasadena, I called an elders' meeting to discuss discipleship. The idea received a mixed reception. The elders liked the thought of being in charge of individual cells within the church—their own disciples. And, later, some of the young men—newer converts—in the church were enthusiastic about some of the aspects of discipleship. However, some were obviously afraid that I'd have too much power, and didn't like the idea of only answering to me, for which I could hardly blame them.

About the same time another Argentine pastor, Juan Carlos Ortiz's brother-in-law, came to live in the Pasadena area as the result of an affair he had with a church secretary back home. While working on spiritual rehabilitation, he'd occasionally fellowship with us. He tried to help me promote discipleship and convince the elders of its validity.

As it turned out, discipleship soon swept through the Charismatic community across the nation, but it never took root in my Pasadena church. With its obvious drawbacks, discipleship, or shepherding, caused havoc as it disrupted churches, groups, and individual lives. Many churches and families split as a result of this divisive teaching.

Living with so many people caused tremendous pressure on my family. Linda felt the daily stress of having to deal with so many personalities. While attempting to display unselfish love, the members of our extended family often excelled in selfishness. Goaded by Linda—because it's my nature to avoid confrontations—I sometimes flew off the handle in my efforts to achieve discipline, deal with the numerous personality problems, and, generally, work out the logistics of so many people living under one roof.

Behind closed doors, Linda and I fought bitterly over these things. On the surface, it was simply a matter of whose way the problems should be handled—her way or my way. Unknown to either of us at the time, we had becomed mired in the false kingdom of aberrant Christianity.

Our deliverance came unexpectedly. Rev. Fred Musson, a highly regarded pastor from back East, came to California because, through several channels, including my continuing radio show in Hudson, he learned of my ministry in Pasadena. With the knowledge that I was from Hillsdale, he hoped to lure me back to New York to help him with his ministry at the West Copake (Dutch) Reformed Church.

Fred offered me a position as the church's youth minister. The invitation included a small salary and free housing. At first I was reluctant to consider the offer, because my ministry in California thrived—we just began renting a Lutheran church building across the street because the big house could no longer hold the Sunday crowd. With the increased volume of activity, I cancelled my planned trip to India, and sent one of the young men of the church instead.

Recently, though, Dr. Irma Waldo, once my pediatrician, now a family friend, had told me that my Mom was seriously ill. At this point Linda and I had lived in California for nine years—never having made it to San Francisco, our original destination. Never sound, our marriage was now practically in a shambles; I was troubled by the Pentecostal lunacy I had witnessed during the past few years; I yearned for a normal, balanced Christian ministry—which I had started to realize I would not have with my present associates; Mom's condition worried me; and, finally, I thought I needed a chance to escape. After adding all this up, I accepted Fred's offer to return to New York.

Bill and Lorraine said the Lord told them to give me a car, which turned out to be a used, late-model Volvo. After announcing to the church that Ric was going to replace me as pastor, we bid farewell to all our friends. With as much as we could pack in a U-Haul trailer, Linda and I and our three children permanently left California for greener pastures.

As we traveled eastward, Linda and I engaged in constant, bitter arguments over insignificant things. This was symptomatic of a far greater problem. Over the years we tried to serve the Lord together, but as we served Him we grew so far apart that only a thin thread held us together.

Each night we purposefully stopped at a motel with a pool. Even though we were miserable—and knew it—we wanted the children to have a good time. Angie and Mark had just had birthdays, making them seven and four, respectively. Marylisa, the baby, was just two. During that seven-day trip Mark became a proficient swimmer.

Mile after mile passed as we sped along the interstate, trailed by the U-Haul. When we weren't fighting, silence filled the car. During those times I reflected on our nine years in California. In the beginning, everything seemed so innocent and simple. Then, because of my own actions, fear and guilt drove me into an abyss, a bottomless pit from which I almost didn't escape. Before I knew it, I had taken my family with me.

I reflected on the folks at the People's Tabernacle of Faith. Sure, because they enjoyed their religion, they whooped up a storm when they worshipped, but for the most part, they kept it simple. And they lived good lives. How did things get so complicated for us, I wondered? I really looked forward to a normal, sane ministry in New York.

15

Walking Away

From the start, ministry in upstate New York was everything I had hoped for. The church provided us with an adequate little house in Copake, Angie and Mark attended a good public school, and the youth meetings took off right from the beginning.

As an outreach to local youth, our church opened a coffee house ministry called the Agape Inn, *agape* being the Greek word for love. Staffed every night by volunteers, the Agape Inn became a popular hangout for a number of teenagers. Having learned from the best, I showed Billy Graham movies, followed up by Bible studies for all the new converts.

At local holiday parades, the kids who attended the Agape Inn marched proudly with banners which proclaimed the love of God and salvation through Jesus. *The Independent,* the local weekly paper, actively covered all our events. With this, and the radio ministry, I became widely known throughout the area.

Every Thursday morning I taught a Bible-study class in the back of a Christian bookstore in Hudson. Attended mostly by women, up to thirty regulars came out for the lessons and prayer session which followed.

Spiritual trends constantly sweep through Pentecostal and Charismatic groups. These fads include the supposed sighting of angels or demons, physical healings, prophecy, or various forms of church leadership, such as discipleship, or the revival of a five-fold ministry—

apostles, prophets, evangelists, pastors, and teachers.

At the time of my Hudson Bible classes, people were into the craze of being slain in the Spirit during prayer—just like when Kathryn Kuhlman visited LIFE Bible College. This bothered me because I believed the women were faking it. Every time I laid hands on them, they'd fall to the floor and, conveniently, someone caught them and gently lowered them to the linoleum. I didn't believe God ever used me to knock people down to the floor.

One morning after my Biblical teaching, I served notice that catching people who were slain in the Spirit was to cease immediately. If God causes someone to swoon, I said, He will see to it that they don't hit their head on a chair or something. So, from now on, just let them drop. From that time—not so strangely—when I laid hands on people they remained solidly on their feet.

The best thing about serving in a mainline denominational church was that my former colleagues in California shied away from us. That was fine with me. Also, since the Reformed Church was more liberal, it espoused no strongly held doctrinal positions or other radical viewpoints to polarize and split families, as in typical Fundamentalist and Pentecostal churches.

When winter arrived, we closed the Agape Inn, and as an alternative activity for the young people we purchased a bus and started a traveling Gospel singing group called The Agape Force. "Force" came from the hit movie that summer, *Star Wars,* and the popular saying from the movie, "May the Force be with you." *Star Wars* was the first secular movie I had seen in ten years. For that whole time in California, television, movies, popular music, and secular literature had no place in our lives.

Over a year passed, and Fred accepted a call to another church which paid more. He recommended me as his replacement. The board, called the Consistory in the Reformed Church, voted to accept his recommendation. Immediately, I worked to bring Pentecostal tradition into the West Copake Reformed Church. Carol Lee, the leader of The Agape Force, also conducted the church choir. She went along with my plan, and soon after the staid old church was replete with tambourines and hand-clapping. Although some people left the church, many more came in as word got out about what was happening there.

Then I received a call from my friend Laverne Campbell, in California. As Laverne represented what I perceived as a balanced ministry, I was glad to hear from him. He had joined Jack Hayford's ministry at the Church on the Way. Laverne told me that Jimmy and Carol Owens, a song-writing couple from the Church on the Way, wrote a Gospel musical production called *If My People,* based on II Chronicles 7:14. The verse reads, "If my people, which are called by my name, shall humble themselves, and pray, and seek my face, and turn from their wicked ways; then will I hear from heaven, and will forgive their sin, and will heal their land."

Laverne explained that America, as a nation, sinned and left its Christian heritage, and now God was calling for national repentance. The *If My People* production was slated for presentation in more than thirty state capitals as a kind of "God and Country" rally. Hopefully, it might bring God to the attention of state legislatures, and perhaps Christians might even get involved in the political process by voting and running for public office.

Pat Boone, the singer, and Dean Jones, the Disney actor, were selected to lead two touring companies of *If My People.* I'd met Pat once after one of his performances in Anaheim, California, and had a lot of respect for his Christian testimony. Albany, New York, was one of the cities picked for the presentation. Laverne asked me to be their New York coordinator. At first I balked at the idea, but I told Laverne that I'd pray about it.

Although I believed that America was founded as a Christian nation, I also thought it had backslidden so far that God wanted Christians to stay completely out of secular matters. The Bible said that we weren't "of this world." Our kingdom on earth was a spiritual one, which would be manifested later in heaven as a material one. No, I didn't think Christians should get into politics.

Nevertheless, I did pray about becoming involved, as I told Laverne I would. I gave II Chronicles 7:14 a lot of thought. Although the verse really had nothing to do with America, its premise made sense. Also, a fellow from Georgia named Jimmy Carter was running for President of the United States. No one I knew had ever heard of him, but word got around that this Carter was an outspoken born-again Christian. Perhaps God wanted him to run this country according to the Word of God, I thought. God's law, the Bible, certainly was higher than man's law, the Constitution. I knew many other Christians who felt the same way.

When Laverne called back, I told him the Lord spoke to my heart about *If My People,* and I agreed to prepare their way in New York's capital. Carol Lee helped by training a local choir in the Owens' music. Meanwhile, I rented the basketball stadium at Sienna College in Albany. It held 5,000 people.

Although I got the word out to a number of churches in the capital district, my expertise at publicity left something to be desired. When the big night finally arrived, about 2,800 people attended the rally. Dean Jones, the band, and the choir performed well. The audience's enthusiasm was great, but not great enough to fill the 2,200 gaps in the seating.

The California group expected that night's audience to meet most of the expenses of the Albany presentation. Before the offering, someone told me to pitch hard for money, because it was urgent. I've always had a problem asking for money, but I gave it my best shot. After the offering, the choir sang while the cardboard buckets were gathered in a secure room. I stood watching as they counted the money.

"Damn," the California representative said, "we've got to get more."

"Skipp, go out there and take a second offering," he yelled. Nervously, I approached the mike, stopped the music, and announced to the 2,800 people that we hadn't met our expenses. The second offering helped, and later, the Church on the Way made up the difference.

For the most part, things were going fine at the West Copake church, but while some of our former pressures had eased, Linda and I still remained estranged. Then some Reformed Church ministers complained that I wasn't ordained in their denomination. (After leaving California, I transferred my ministerial credentials to the Elim Fellowship, in Lima, New York. The Fellowship is associated with the Elim Bible Institute, an early participant in the Latter Rain movement, and currently a leader in the Charismatic renewal movement.) The real basis of their complaint was that their seminaries were graduating more ministers than there were churches to pastor. As West Copake was a desirable church, they wanted me out.

I saw three possible options. I could attend a seminary in New Jersey; the West Copake church could split away from the denomination; or I could leave. Knowing the Lord and His Word, and having the indwelling Holy Spirit, I couldn't imagine what their seminary could teach me about God, so I quickly ruled that out. Many members, and some of the Consistory, wanted to try to take the church from the denomination. Linda and I put a lot into that little church, and with a good salary, a nice home, and some good people, they gave a lot in return. Any ensuing battle to take the church from the denomination would surely be divisive as people took sides. This was the last thing I wanted to see. I decided to leave.

Since coming back to New York, Dr. Irma Waldo supported all my ministerial efforts—as the youth minister, as founder of the Agape Inn and Agape Force, and as pastor of the West Copake Reformed Church. Also, her husband served on the Consistory. The Waldo's offered me encouragement many times. As a physician, Irma heightened the zeal of many Pentecostal types, because Pentecostals always gloated when an educated person became involved in their fanaticism.

After I resigned my pastorate, Irma approached me with an attractive alternative. An available piece of property in Hillsdale incorporated a twenty-something-room house, two small apartment buildings, and a cottage. If I would consider taking over the estate as a place for a non-denominational Charismatic ministry, she agreed to approach the owner, a local businessman, to arrange terms.

I formed a new ministry, registered in the State of New York as VITAL Ministries, Inc. Irma and several others sat on the new board. VITAL was an acronym for Victory In The Arena of Life, which I invented because I viewed life as an arena in which we must strive for victory.

Like my other endeavors, the Agape House did well from the beginning. The facilities were perfect, and we offered Bible studies, prayer meetings, Gospel concerts, and, eventually, regular church services. Agape House residents—up to forty of them at a time—included battered wives, foster children, homeless people, wards of the courts, and those who simply desired to live in a Christian environment.

Although I'd mellowed somewhat from the California madness, I still witnessed at every opportunity, especially when it involved a celebrity. Norman Rockwell was one of my father's favorite artists and, as a Christmas present, my sisters gave him a book of Rockwell prints. To enhance the gift, on New Year's Day, 1977, I took the book over to Stockbridge to have the artist autograph the large volume.

Norman Rockwell and I sat in his parlor and talked. Our conversation included the time we first met at the CAL art show at my high school, about sixteen years earlier. To be honest, he remembered the exhibit, but he didn't remember me specifically. When he asked what I was doing now, I saw it as my opportunity. I told Rockwell about the West Copake church, and how God was now blessing us at the Agape House. Then, I threw the question at him.

"Mr. Rockwell, if you died tonight, where would you spend eternity?"

With a gleam in his eye, Rockwell responded without hesitation. He said that, although a church member, he doubted that there really was a heaven or a hell, and furthermore, if there was, he wasn't in the least worried about it.

Nonplussed, as politely as I could, I tried to convince him that he was a sinner, and sin meant eternal separation from God. He would hear none of that, and employing his gentle wit, Norman Rockwell rebuffed my every effort to convert him.

Before I left, Rockwell signed the book for my father, and thanked me for coming over. He died about a year later.

While I operated the Agape House, the opportunity arose to run for a seat on the local school board. This was a chance to create a greater Christian influence in the school district. Already we had taught the youth group how to witness in school and encouraged them to pass out Jack Chick comic-book tracts. Now, if I could get on the school board, we might be able to influence textbooks and library books.

As it always did, *The Independent* reported my latest venture on its front pages. Support for my candidacy was strong. There were, however, some people who vehemently opposed my venture into politics. At a question-and-answer session after one public debate with other candidates, someone asked me what I thought about the separation of church and state.

"The separation of what?" I replied. I had never heard the term before.

The man angrily explained that the Constitution declared that organized religion was supposed to stay out of government. He said my candidacy violated that provision. Although I understood little of what he was talking about, I disagreed with him, because I knew the words he used didn't appear in the Constitution. And so what if he was right? God's law is above man's, I thought.

In the following days, the battle heated up, and accusations and denials flew. Sorry that I ever got involved in politics, to the consternation of my advisors, I refused to campaign. Even so, I still almost won.

Ric Durfield and his family, and then one of my former elders, came to New York from California to minister. Although I invited them to the Agape House, I feared what new thing they might bring with them. Even though I still held some extreme beliefs, I couldn't handle any more new ones from LA.

Carlton Spencer and other ministers from the Elim Fellowship also ministered at the Agape House, which helped us to keep a semblance of balance, at least in the Pentecostal perspective.

One day, a bearded Jewish man with his wife and infant son came by the Agape House. They reminded me of Joseph and Mary, with their young Jesus. For one reason or another, the family had become homeless, and he asked if we had any place for them to live. As it happened, the cottage had just become available, and I told him he could move his family in immediately. Later, we could discuss his contribution toward the rent, but for now the main thing was to get a roof over their heads.

That night, one of the board members said some of the others wanted to meet with me in the chapel. At the meeting, attended by three board members (Dr. Waldo wasn't included), they castigated me for allowing that family to move onto the premises.

"Don't you know they're Jews?" one said.

Another one piped in, "We can't just let an unsaved family move in without a meeting about it."

Furious, I flatly stated that the family was staying, and that I'd leave before I put that family out.

Sometimes I couldn't believe the callousness of Christians who, to the detriment of humanity, got so wrapped up in their foolish doctrines. I saw it in California when my colleagues refused to provide help to kids who had run away from home, and I saw it when children were abused under the pretense of Biblical discipline.

The incident over the Jewish family finally blew over, and the family proved to be invaluable to the Agape House. That, though, wasn't the end of our problems. Other day-to-day events sometimes made the Agape House a madhouse. At times, chaos prevailed. Linda and I reached the point where we hardly talked to one another. Almost every day we fought, from early in the morning until late at night. Our children felt the tension and became anxious.

After almost twelve years of marriage, I wanted to throw in the towel. I didn't believe in divorce, especially among Christians, but what was I, a martyr? Why could others get divorced, but not me? I searched and prayed for answers. Then, one morning I woke up feeling particularly good about life, and while shaving I made the decision. Divorce.

I knew the going would be rough, that I could even lose my ministry, but wanting to be free of the oppression I felt, I was willing to take a chance. When I told Linda, she was devastated. She asked me to reconsider, adding that she would try harder to make things work. She tried, we both tried, only to revert to constant fighting.

One day I was out and got back a little before Linda expected me to. Her bags were packed, and she was trying to get a ride for herself and Angie to the Greyhound Bus station in Albany. After we discussed it, I offered to take them to the bus and sent them off to California with our MasterCharge card.

Linda expected to stay in California with Angie for a few months. That was good, because I hoped she'd come back a changed person. After a certain age, however, people don't change. I knew I wouldn't and couldn't change, and I should not have expected that of her. We had already changed over the years, and grown further apart. I remembered that when we announced our marriage plans twelve years earlier, some people warned us that teen marriages didn't work. I'm sure some of them do, but the odds are against it.

While Linda was in California, I shared our apartment in the Agape House with Mark and Marylisa. We enjoyed breakfasts together before I sent them off to school, and I told them stories at night. Figuratively, the sun seemed to shine every day. I loved every minute of it. For the first time in years, I felt real peace.

To my surprise, Linda came back in about a month. We endured the rest of the summer together, and in the early fall we even attended one session with a marriage counselor. Meanwhile, we bought a second car and Linda got a job as the county coordinator for the teen mother program. By late fall our situation hadn't improved, and Linda packed her personal belongings and moved out.

Word of our separation spread quickly. Listeners to my radio program, "Pastor Porteous Shares," learned about it. Almost immediately, contributions to support the radio ministry dwindled so that, after five years I had to take it off the air. My outside speaking engagements were cancelled because the various groups and churches said that without my family intact, I was unfit to minister. While Fundamentalism itself tends to split families, its adherents have no mercy on pastors whose families break up. People outside of Fundamentalism may find it hard to understand this, but it is a closely followed tradition.

Still, the authorities at Elim, where I held my ordination papers, assured me that I had Biblical grounds for a divorce—presumably, because my wife left me—yet, in their viewpoint, the possibility for remarriage was out of the question. That was fine, because I didn't want to get married again.

Curiously, even as I write this book, I continue to receive materials from Elim Fellowship advertising conferences for singles. The latest one I received carried the catchy title, "Singles—Searching for a REAL Relationship?"

While I struggled to rear my children, and to keep the ministry of the Agape House alive, the Agape House board called a meeting. A majority agreed that, until my family was restored, I should step down as their pastor. I could still live at the Agape House, but I could not minister there. Their confidence in me vanished.

With that, I packed my belongings and my three children's things and moved out. Fortunately, my parents' house had an empty downstairs apartment. After we moved in, the editor of *The Independent* called and offered me a job at the newspaper.

Rather than pursue my calling, I decided to take a year's leave of absence from all ministry and just work at the newspaper. After that length of time, I reasoned, I should know what the Lord wanted me to do. There was still no doubt in my mind that I was called by God as a pastor. At this point, I didn't know how to pursue this, but I entertained several options. I even—very briefly—thought about how easy it would be to start some sort of aberrant group, a cult, if you will. Nevertheless, I couldn't betray my true, orthodox, Bible-based belief system. There certainly was no place in my life for that sort of thing. Well, that "year" turned out to be my longest year.

The newspaper job was my first secular employment in years. At *The Independent* I quickly learned black-and-white photography, advertising sales, layout and design, reporting, and a little about writing. Being on call to cover late-breaking stories seven days a week kept me away from any formal activities—like church.

No longer a pastor, I didn't have to work at keeping my flock inspired. The absence of sermon and Bible study preparation allowed me to open my mind. This process turned out to be my first step in walking away. Having to feed the sheep had been my own source of spiritual food. Born-again Christians have to work hard at keeping their religious experience fresh. They attend Bible studies and prayer meetings. They devour inspirational books from Christian bookstores, drive around with their ears glued to "anointed" tapes, and gawk at television evangelists. The pump must be kept primed.

Some Christians work full time just to keep the devil at bay. I've known many who had more faith in the power of Satan than in the power of God.

For the first time in many years I allowed myself to take an honest look at the faith I blindly embraced for so long. For instance, my Bible of choice at the time was The Open Bible. This is a slightly modernized edition of the Authorized King James Version. It is published by Thomas Nelson Publishers. At various times, while studying this Bible, I noticed the absence of words from certain sentences.

For example, a sentence in Mark 3:4 should read, "But they held their peace." In my copy of The Open Bible, two words, "their peace," were omitted. Further on, in verse 34, two words are absent. In Matthew 26:64, referring to the appearance of Jesus during the Second Coming, "clouds of heaven" was missing.

On the surface, these seemingly typographical errors may appear innocent and minor. However, when you think of a modern publishing house, with all of its advanced techniques for copyediting and proofreading, this shouldn't happen. Furthermore, as I thought about all the copies of copies of ancient manuscripts (you know, not a single original Biblical manuscript of any book of the Bible exists!) that have been handed down through the years, I realized that we cannot possibly know what the originals said.

For liberal Christians, these thoughts pose no problem. However, for us Fundamentalist/Pentecostal Christians, the accuracy of each word was vital, because we relied so heavily on each word, to "correctly divide the word of truth."

So, now I had nothing to lose by being honest with my intellect. That process led me eventually to examine all the other doubts I'd had over the years. I didn't do this all at once, but little by little. If I went through this process while still in the ministry, as some have done, I may have reasoned myself right out of a career.

The struggle to be a "victorious" Christian ceased. With more time on my hands I read previously forbidden secular novels and nonfiction books. One book, *Courage to Divorce,* helped me a lot. Newspapers took on new relevance as I read them without looking for the supposed fulfillment of Bible prophecy, such as wars and earthquakes. I found reading the Sunday paper more enjoyable than attending church.

Because most of my Christian friends now shunned me, I found new friends. Open discussions with them broadened my outlook.

I eventually filed for a divorce. Linda didn't contest it, and it was promptly granted.

After being at the newspaper for about six months, one assignment led to another near-disaster. I photographed a folk dance held in Harlemville, New York, a Ruldolf Steiner community. (Steiner was a nineteenth-century philosopher, theologian, and educator.) Later, Maile, one of the participants, a professional hula dancer, called me under the pretense of adding information to the folk-dance story. Our long conversation led to a date, then another, and finally we became very serious.

Maile, too, was recently divorced, and like me, had three children. Well, we thought, why not live together with our six children and share resources? While I was hesitant to live unmarried with a woman in front of my children, I agreed to it. We found a house large enough to comfortably accommodate us all, and set a date to move in. That's when the landlord, a Mormon, told us he wouldn't permit unmarried couples to live together in his house. That settled it; we'd just get married then.

Well, we did. And then I learned that my new wife insisted that the children attend the Steiner people's Waldorf School in Harlemville. At first I agreed, and made arrangements for them to enroll in the fall. In the meantime, I devoured several of Maile's books on Rudolf Steiner's teaching. That's when I learned that Steiner, even though some of his educational philosophy appeared sound and reasonable, was a kook. For instance, I read that Steiner believed honey bees originally came from Mars.

As a foreshadowing of what I was getting into, my wife began to manifest some strange behavior. Fearful of entering a life worse than the one I had just left, I took my children and fled, thus breaking up our seven-week marriage.

Maile agreed not to contest the divorce, but left for parts unknown. So, without serving legal papers, a divorce was not possible for some time.

After that, I dated extensively, and made very effort to avoid a serious relationship. Another marriage was the last thing I wanted.

One day my editor assigned a piece on "National Police Week." To do the story I arranged to do an all-night shift in a sheriff's cruiser.

Although I learned how to operate radar—and we chased a few speeders—our eight hours together were more enlightening to the sheriff's deputy than to me. As a pastor, I had known of many families that suffered from the ravages of illegal drugs. Without names or specifics, I related story after story to the Officer.

He was astounded that there were so many hard drugs in the county. I couldn't believe that he didn't know. Twenty years earlier I wrote an editorial in our high-school paper in which I predicted illegal drugs would become a major problem in the area. Time had now proven me correct. Back then, even the teachers thought I was insane.

"Have you told the sheriff about this?" the deputy asked. I hadn't, and he urged me to make an appointment with the sheriff. Several weeks later I did.

Sheriff Paul Proper listened intently and asked a lot of questions. I answered him the best I could without betraying the confidences gained during my ministry. When I left his office I was satisfied that something would be done. In my opinion, illegal drugs could be wiped out by sheer force—just go in there, bust the dealers, and throw them all in jail. They were all hardened criminals, anyway.

The sheriff called me one day and asked if I could come to his Hudson office. I went and I learned that he had checked out some of the things I had told him earlier—and that he was up for reelection. Would I work for him?

We agreed that my employment with the sheriff's office would be a closely kept secret. I knew some of my activities might jeopardize my reputation, but I was now beyond caring what other people thought about me.

Soon, I was enrolled in a basic course for part-time police officers that was given by the Sheriff's Department. In addition, I took two courses at Columbia-Greene Community College, near Hudson. The courses were Criminal Investigation, and Self-defense, which I called, "How to fight dirty."

During this time it wasn't obvious to me that I was in an important transition. In the daytime I worked as a reporter; almost every night I could be found in one bar or another. My undercover territory soon spanned the county. While I investigated stolen guns and arsons, my main task was to find the drug dealers. I was a narc. This entailed my making a lot of drug purchases. My assignment was to buy up the ladder as far as I could, and to learn who the big dealers were. At first, marijuana was the catch of the day.

16

Undercover Capers

Perspiration greased the steering wheel's smooth surface. With a deep sigh of relief, I wiped my hands on my faded jeans and turned the car south on Farm Road, leaving behind the village of Copake. I had just passed the first crucial test. Moments before, in the dusty, unpaved parking lot behind the Copake Pharmacy, I stood face to face with a drug dealer. Our encounter was brief but significant.

The instant he pulled up in his polished black Chevy pickup, I abruptly left my car and approached him—a move calculated to keep him in his truck, and a safe distance from my car.

"Just follow me," he said through the rolled down window.

"Where're we going?" I asked, and then thought, Don't ask too many questions or you'll blow it!

"You'll find out when we get there," he replied tersely.

Any passersby who noticed me saw me alone in the long Ford Granada. Sequestered in the trunk, Undersheriff Jim Bertram and Investigator Bobby DeRuzzio, from the Columbia County Sheriff's Office, lay in wait. A pouch under my seat contained $4,000 in unmarked bills—the going rate in 1977 for twenty-five pounds of marijuana—wholesale, of course.

To protect my cover, I stowed my Smith & Wesson .38 Special in the trunk with my partners. Their arsenal included two 12-gauge pump shotguns, two 9mm semi-automatics, and two .38 Chief Specials. Our "man-in-the-trunk" scheme worked because both men, while muscular, were below average in height. The specially rigged trunk could be opened from the inside.

"Farm Road!" I yelled as I tailed the Chevy pickup.

Faintly, I heard Jim repeat, "Farm Road," into his portable radio. Our backup teams tracked our location.

The backup units consisted of six deputies; two in a green unmarked sheriff's car, two in a black van, and two in an orange Chevy Corvette—a dynamite vehicle for high-speed chases.

What the hell am I doing, I wondered as I followed the dope dealer. Akin to the thrill of one's first roller-coaster ride, fear and excitement consumed me. Only two years before, I ended my career as a well-known, crusading, Bible-thumping, tongues-speaking radio preacher and pastor. The community respected me as a religious leader. Now, at thirty-seven, twice-divorced, with shoulder-length hair, I reflected an unacceptable life-style. And, although I held a respectable job at the newspaper, everyone knew I frequented bars at night. That was not all: rumors abounded that I used drugs; some people even thought that I dealt drugs. Some Christians, in their self-righteous judgment, gossiped about my supposed backslidden condition.

The Chevy pickup turned left into a narrow dirt road that led up a hill. It stopped. The clean-cut, tall, blond driver got out and walked back to my car.

"From here you'll ride with me," he said.

"No way!" I shot back. "Look, I've got $4,000 under my seat and I'm just not going to go on without my car," I protested. "How do I know what you're up to?"

He looked perturbed, but shrugged his shoulders and, to my relief, murmured, "Well, OK."

As we made our way up a long, steep hill, I yelled toward the trunk. "He wanted me to ride with him."

"We heard!" Jim responded. I heard Jim mumble something into the radio.

At the top of the hill we came to a house that was under construction. A hefty German shepherd emerged from a darkened doorway, followed by a seedy, short, stout man. I knew the two men were brothers, and I suspected the location to be their family farm. Both vehicles stopped. Again, I got out quickly and headed toward the blond man as he slid out of the pickup. The shepherd raced toward me. I froze.

The big dog sniffed me and then nosed around the car.

Shit, I thought. The damn dog's gonna find them.

The seedy-looking brother asked if I had the money.

"I've got it. Let's see what you've got," I replied.

"C'mon," he grunted.

They led me into the basement of the unfinished house, about twenty yards farther up the hill. Someone turned on a single bare bulb which hung from the ceiling. Cardboard boxes, two 30-gallon plastic garbage cans, and two saw horses, bridged by an eight-foot plank, were, more or less, the only items in the room. An expensive scale was set on the plank.

What a scam, I thought, low overhead, big profit.

My nightly rounds of local barrooms paid off numerous times. I originally learned about the two pot-dealing brothers in a bar. My first contact with these two characters was by phone—I didn't know how else to get in touch with them. I made a deal to buy a pound of homegrown pot for a hundred bucks. My instructions were to go to a local bar which was popular for its pool table. Anyone who wished to play listed his name on a chalk board. One of the brothers told me to go there and jot my name on the board.

A moment after I scribbled "Skipp," a man came up to me and said, "Buy you a beer?" I accepted.

We stood there and guzzled our beer while we observed the local pool sharks. Then he told me to follow him into a back room.

"Do you have the money?" he asked. I nodded and handed him five twenties. In turn, I expected to be handed a pound of grass, but instead he gave me explicit directions to its hiding place. He knew a narc could bust him on the spot, so his ruse served to protect him, or so he thought.

I left the bar by the side door, and within a few minutes I found the large oak tree my contact had described. A small bush grew at its base. Behind the bush I located a brown paper shopping bag; it contained a pound of Columbia County pot—not the best but illegal. It also laid the groundwork for a bigger buy.

Soon after I made the deal for twenty-five pounds of weed. It should have been all packaged and ready to go. Instead, as I stood nervously and watched, the tall brother pulled marijuana out of the plastic garbage cans by the handful, and carefully weighed each pound on the scale, one at a time. Then he pressed it into small plastic bags and sealed them with wire ties. He repeated this action twenty-five times.

Meanwhile, his stout brother made regular trips outdoors with the dog. Earlier, as we walked up to the house, I noticed the panoramic view. I hoped the backup units didn't attempt to come up unobserved, for it couldn't be done. Also, my concern mounted over Bertram and DeRuzzio in the trunk. A glance at my watch indicated they'd been in there for over an hour. Not only would they be cramped, but they might worry that something had happened to me and come looking. Any number of factors could jeopardize the operation.

Finally, twenty-five hefty plastic bags of marijuana lay at my feet. Hastily, the two brothers crammed them into an oversized suitcase—thrown in at no extra cost.

The three of us walked outside into the pleasantly warm summer night. The stars sparkled in the sky; the view was incredible. For a moment my mind wandered, and loneliness descended on me. With a shudder, I focused on the present reality. I was anxious to get this over with.

I carried the suitcase, twenty-five pounds of marijuana, and more inside the house. What a great bust this is going to be! I thought.

"Let me throw this on the back seat and I'll get your money," I said. I wondered if they thought it was strange that I didn't put it in the trunk. I pulled the money pouch out from under the front seat. The zippered, plastic bank pouch bulged. Will they want to count it? I wondered. I knew there was $4,000, because I had counted it earlier.

We were just moments from the real action, I couldn't botch it now. Two words—my prearranged signal to Jim and Bobby—danced in my mind. I handed the fat one the pouch. The brothers looked at each other; their faces glowed. Without a doubt, they already had the money spent. After all, it wasn't all that much.

I shook their hands and said, "It's been nice doing business with you. By the way," I added, "do you have any turkeys on this farm?"

The deputies in the trunk caught the two code words, "any turkeys." I took several steps backwards, and like jack-in-the-boxes, Jimmy and Bobby thrust their shotguns upward and popped out of the trunk.

"Put your hands in the air!" they screamed as they took aim. "You're both under arrest!"

The brothers threw their hands high, just like in the movies. Shock registered on their faces. I quickly retrieved my .38 from the trunk, pointed the revolver at the fat one, and recovered the money pouch. Jim and Bobby handcuffed them while I kept them covered.

By now reality had set in. "You fucked up!" the fat one yelled at his brother. "You were supposed to search him and have him ride up with you," he screamed.

"I thought it was all right!" the blond blurted.

Jim called the backup units. Way down in the valley I saw their headlights turn onto the narrow dirt road.

It was late at night by the time we booked the brothers at the county jail. Jim correctly sensed the paranoia of Charlie Inman, the District Attorney, because the D.A.'s office provided the drug money for the bust. So, with a mischievous grin on his face, Jim called the D.A. at his home.

"Charlie, this is Bertram."

"Yes?, Yes?" the D.A. anxiously replied.

"Well," Jim said, "everything didn't go as we'd planned, but it's under control."

"What the hell do you mean!" Inman bellowed.

"We got the pot," Jim said. "But they got your money and escaped into the woods. But it's OK because we've got the woods surrounded." Jim held the phone away from his ear while the D.A. screamed.

At the time, this was the largest drug bust in the history of Columbia County. I was elated. This life provided the excitement and change I felt I needed after my recently ended twelve-year marriage. In addition, it satisfied my still conservative nature.

Before long I was able to buy pills, such as amphetamines, cocaine, and other hard drugs. The first cocaine bust was something to write home about. I had heard rumors about a coke dealer in the northern part of the county. I began to frequent a disco bar that was wall-to-wall people on weekends. Although I didn't find the guy I had originally set out to find, I found a bigger catch.

One night a girl asked me if she could borrow some money to buy coke. "Sure, if you can get me in on it," I told her. That's how I met "The Golden Swan." The moniker aptly described the light-skinned, golden complexioned black man. He neatly printed "The Golden Swan" on each packet of coke, and drew his logo—a picture of what looked to me like a duck. He was a real charmer. I learned that he came over from Massachusetts and was the source of all the coke in the State Line Bar. Years ago, the old State Line Bar was right on the state line. There was a white line painted on the floor, so when the bars closed at night in Massachusetts the patrons moved over to the other end of the bar which was in New York, where they were allowed to keep later hours. The new building that now housed the State Line Bar was well over on the New York side.

I made several coke buys from The Golden Swan and had them tested at the State Police lab in Albany. The stuff was pure, and of high quality. Bertram, a meticulous planner who eventually became sheriff after Proper retired, DeRuzzio, and I planned the bust. Our greatest fear was that we'd cause a riot. On weekends, the racially mixed crowd packed the building beyond its legal capacity. If that crowd got out of hand, it would be disastrous.

We decided that I would attempt to buy more than the dealer normally stocked; then he would make an appointment with me on a designated night. I could meet him outside and avoid the crowd, but we'd have to keep everyone inside when it all came down.

He fell right into it. Everyone was in place on the night of the big bust. Our black windowless van was parked in the east lot; Jim, the undersheriff, and three of his deputies were inside armed to the teeth. Another four deputies waited a mile down the road in two marked patrol cars. Bobby DeRuzzio wandered around the parking lot posing as a drunk. I sat on the hood of my car in front of the nightclub and nursed a twelve-ounce bottle of Budweiser for two hours. Everyone except me wore bulletproof vests; on me its bulk might have been too obvious.

We almost called the whole thing off when a fight inside spilled out of the bar. One man ran to his car and came back with a baseball bat. He was out for blood. Fortunately, he was disarmed by other patrons and sent on his way. Jim figured there were some lives at stake and almost intervened.

Finally, our subject arrived in a long white Buick. He parked on the west side of the bar. I tossed my empty Bud bottle toward the van to get my cohorts' attention. Bobby saw me throw it and moved into position. The van proceeded slowly around the back of the club. I sauntered over to the Buick.

"How's my man?" The Golden Swan said through the rolled-down window. We engaged in some small talk for a minute. Then we got down to business. He had my coke order ready, so I paid him and shoved the package into a jacket pocket.

A raised arm, like a stretch, was my prearranged signal for Bobby and the rest of the squad to move in. Timing was crucial. Nonchalantly, I began my stretch. My eye caught Bobby as he stood by a tree about ten yards away—urinating.

Nature's call didn't impede him, though. Before I could pull my own revolver he rushed over with his drawn pistol and shouted, "Freeze, or I'll blow your fuckin' head off!"

The Golden Swan looked up at the weapon in wide-eyed surprise. Then he looked down in disbelief. Bobby's penis hung out through his open fly. "Hold this," Bobby ordered while he handed me his gun and put his penis away.

By this time the van had pulled in and Jim radioed the cruisers. A couple of patrons who witnessed the action ran into the club. Then the cruisers arrived, and four of the department's burliest deputies guarded the doors to keep everyone in. Jim and his team assisted with the arrest and searched the perpetrator. Later, the sheriff announced that The Golden Swan had $50,000 worth of cocaine in his possession that night. Another Columbia County record had been set.

Our arrests continued to make front page headlines, and became the lead stories on the 6 o'clock TV news. Reference was always made to "an undercover officer," without revealing my identification.

After Sheriff Proper handily won his reelection bid, he offered me a full-time position with the Sheriff's Office, but I declined, preferring to work on special assignment.

When reporting to Sheriff Proper one day, he gave me my next assignment. "You'll have to go to school," he began.

"Fine," I replied. Maybe I'd get a college education after all, I reasoned, but that wasn't what he meant.

The county's only college, Columbia-Greene Community College, a two-year school that is part of the State University of New York system, had experienced a rash of suspicious fires. The suspected arsonist, a student, was the son of a highly placed state government official. To nail him and make the charges stick, the sheriff wanted me to catch him in the act.

I checked the young man's school schedule and found that he spent much of his time in rehearsals for a play. School officials introduced me to the college's theater director, Barbara Simon. She was told that I was in a graduate course at Albany's College of St. Rose, and was assigned to write a paper on the production of a play.

Day after day I attended the rehearsals for Barbara's production of *You Can't Take It With You*. Grandpa, one of the main characters, was played by boxer/trainer Kevin Rooney. A fine actor, Barbara had cast him once before as Stanley Kowalski in *A Streetcar Named Desire*. Kevin worked with the famous trainer Cus D'Amato. He told me about a young fighter named Mike Tyson whom they had brought up to Catskill from Brooklyn.

"He's gonna be heavyweight champ of the world someday," Kevin said.

Sure, I thought. I admired his ambition. Kevin didn't know I was a Word of Life boxing champ, nor was I inclined to tell him.

One scene in *You Can't Take It With You* involved blintzes. Almost no one in the cast had ever heard of this food, so Barbara held a blintz party at her apartment. She invited me, too, since I was the "production observer."

The supply of white wine went dry, so Gina, one of the cast members, went out to buy some more. On the way out the door Gina asked Barbara if she could get anything else.

Barbara responded, "Find me a boyfriend!"

Gina nodded her head toward me, "What about him?"

"Him?" Barbara said.

"Sure," Gina said. "Do you know he's been to a Seder?"

Gina reasoned that because I knew something about Judaism, and Barbara was Jewish, we might hit it off. I knew Gina from her job at the probation office—I sent a few clients her way. One time we discussed my participation in "Christian Seders," an aberration of the Jewish Passover celebration.

Until then my relationship with Barbara was strictly professional; soon, though, we began to date.

The arson suspect displayed bizarre behavior from time to time, but I never caught him trying to burn down the school. He left Columbia-Greene soon after the final performance of the play. The case was closed.

Barbara imagined that our relationship would be a "run-of-the-play" one. Well, it wasn't.

As an undercover cop, I met some pretty decent people who were part of the drug scene. Sometimes I felt sympathy for those who we arrested. Sure, some were scum, creeps who threatened my life, and frightened my family. But except for them, and the dealers in hard drugs who preyed on the misery of other human beings, many of the people with whom I dealt were normal, middle-class Americans who unwittingly got involved in something over their heads. Some just grew small amounts of marijuana for their own use, so they could occasionally smoke a joint. No big deal, really.

I came to realize that as long as the demand was there, all the law enforcement in the world would not solve the problem. While the demand remains, someone is going to figure out how to make a profit by meeting that demand. And the demand is there, by and large, because people are unproductive and unhappy, so drugs—including the legal drug, alcohol—too often fill the gap in their lives. It's a societal matter, which should involve education and health more than law enforcement.

After my divorce from Linda—and after the hula dancer—Linda and I became friendly enough to share a four-bedroom house with our children. We each had our own room. Meanwhile, my relationship with Barbara grew and became serious. So, with some apprehension because of the possible affect on the chidren, I moved to Hudson to live with her.

While I performed many tasks at the newspaper, I excelled at selling advertising. After all, I'd been selling Jesus for years, so selling newspaper ads was a cinch.

I left the *Independent* and became the advertising sales director of a new, experimental paper called *The Intermountain Express*. I was there for a year.

During that time, an event in Guyana, South America, shocked the world. At a place called Jonestown, almost a thousand people—all followers of the Reverend Jim Jones, a Pentecostal minister from California—committed mass suicide. I shuddered when I learned of the terrible incident. Although Jonestown was a different group, it reminded me of Sam Fife's end-timers who also went to the jungles of South America. And it brought to my awareness that more Jonestowns might be just a few years down the road.

The experimental paper folded, and I went into radio advertising at WSBS in Great Barrington, Massachusetts. At this point, I stopped taking any more assignments from Sheriff Proper. Soon afterwards, he retired.

One day in April, a real-estate agent gave me her radio advertising copy for some new listings. One house in particular sounded so appealing that I took a look at it. When I brought Barbara over to see it, we determined that, somehow, we would buy it. In August, by selling everything of value we had, and borrowing some money from family members, we finally closed on the little house in the Berkshire hills. By this time, my lawyer had located Maile in Hawaii, and finalized our divorce. At the same time, some Christians told Barbara that they were still asking God to put Linda and me back together, and by doing so they demonstrated a total lack of sensitivity.

Eventually, I went from WSBS to WUPE/WUHN in Pittsfield. While I was there I became acquainted with someone who was about to make a bid for a state-representative seat.

Publicly, this fellow claimed to be a conservative, but pro-choice, Republican. I liked the guy, and volunteered to help him get elected. He had everything going for him, and should have won, but he blew it and lost.

After the election, Barbara and I left our jobs and started a small advertising agency. Out of it evolved an idea to publish a county-wide phone directory, combining three existing directories. With the potential sales of yellow page advertising from the whole county being substantial, we expected to make quite a bit of money. Because we had no money for start-up costs, we involved my friend whose political campaign I managed. He put up some money, and we were off and running.

Meantime, Barbara and I got married by a Justice of the Peace under the willow tree in our front yard. My three children, my parents, my sister Linda and her family, Barbara's mother, and a few friends attended the wedding. As a wedding gift, Barbara's father, involved in an educational project in Africa, sent us plane tickets to visit him in Botswana.

So, as our first phone book rolled off the presses, we left the States for the Dark Continent. Our month-long stay in Africa was a pure delight. We drove by car from Cape Town, South Africa, all the way up to Victoria Falls, in Zimbabwe, covering thousands of miles in between. One of the highlights of the trip came during a photographic safari of the Chobe National Park, along the Zambezi River. We spent a day tracking and photographing elephants. At the end of the day, we observed and photographed scores of elephants as they watered at the river.

The striking scene carried a strong resemblance to a mental picture I once had of Linda and me and the Durfields. In that imaginary scene, the four of us sat on a riverbank deep in the African bush, watching the sun set after a hard day of missionary work. Ah, but that was just a dream; this was real.

A very unpleasant surprise awaited Barbara and me shortly after we returned to the States. While we were in Africa, my partner figured out a way to wrench the company away for himself. An ensuing legal battle threatened to ruin the company, leaving all of us with nothing. Finally, our lawyers reached a settlement, and we came away without incurring much direct loss, except for the potential of what we could have made had the other party been ethical.

After that, we went back to our advertising and promotion work, and at the same time we decided it might be worthwhile to tell my story in a book.

17

Jesus Doesn't Live Here Anymore

As I put my story on paper, a startling picture emerged. Religion had played a very detrimental role in my life, so much so that I wanted to forget about it, but I couldn't. I had to go back and look at it squarely in the eye. I felt like I'd been had, duped.

Years after I walked away from religion I was still bothered by guilt and fear, the two unmistakable building blocks of fundamentalist Christianity. Sometimes I even felt a twinge of guilt because I didn't feel guilty about anything! In born-again Christianity, not feeling guilty about *something* is abnormal. A common phrase for the guilt that accompanies the Fundamentalist mind-set is used by many born-againers. It is "being under conviction."

By now, prayer had long since ceased being a part of my life. Through the use of visualization, hard work, and chance, all the things for which I had formerly prayed came to pass without having to beg God.

Does the prayer of faith work? Yes, because prayer is a great self-motivator, and through it you can convince yourself that what you hope for will actually come to pass, thus giving you peace about the matter. So, at the very least, you can receive some amount of self-assurance through prayer. In many cases, people will work for what they pray for, thus producing the answer themselves. The old adage is true, "God helps those who help themselves." That's similar to a "fortune" I recently pulled out of a fortune cookie: "Pray for what you want, but work for the things you need."

Public prayer can impart confidence to others, and it can also be used to broadcast a need to which others will respond. I have often seen this happen in prayer meetings.

So when I say I stopped praying, I mean that I found other ways to meet my inner and physical needs. Rather than talking to myself, which is what prayer is, I visualized—I formed a mental picture—that would meet my needs. It's almost the same thing as praying, except I no longer bothered God about things.

I began to realize that I had been self-deceived for most of my life. Even the signs, wonders, and miracles that are part of the Pentecostal/Charismatic belief system could easily be explained. For instance, the demon I saw in Pasadena. That experience came after fasting for several days—I'd fasted up to seven days on just water, without any food whatsoever. Now, the human body has its own amazing survival mechanisms. As I fasted, my glands released powerful mind-altering, euphoric-producing chemicals into my system. As a result, my perception of reality changed; thus, I could see demons and other imaginary things, much as one would from LSD, or too much alcohol.

A couple of years ago, Studs Terkel, the author, interviewed me. Upon learning that I knew how to speak in tongues, he asked me to speak a few words for his tape recorder. I refused, because I felt embarrassed about my many years of gullibility. As a believer, I frequently spoke in tongues, and believed it to be the supernatural evidence of the baptism in the Holy Spirit. Since then I've learned that this gibberish—sometimes called glossolalia—can be taught to anyone. It is not really a language at all, as I was led to believe.

According to an article by Martin Gardner in *Free Inquiry*, linguists are in agreement that tongues are not languages. "Glossolalia has no discernible grammatical structure. The tongues have nothing in common except a vague overall resemblance to the sounds and cadences of a natural language," he said. He noted, "Sid Caesar and other comics are experts in rattling off gibberish that sounds exactly like German, Japanese, or some other foreign tongue."

Gardner added, "Tongues speakers who lose their Pentecostal faith invariably retain the ability to glossolate. Some have said they enjoy glossolating during orgasms."

True Fundamentalists, however, don't glossolate during orgasms, or at any other time, because they believe the so-called "gifts of the

Spirit" ended when the Bible was completed. Having the Bible, they feel no need for any other heavenly tools.

Every healing I witnessed over the years was either intentionally fraudulent, or had perfectly rational explanations.

Leg lengthening is popular in many healing meetings. The healing evangelist calls out for a person with a back problem to come forward—in every crowd there is someone with a backache. After the person comes up and is seated, the evangelist lifts the subject's feet to show the audience that the legs are of different lengths. Many people's limbs are not exactly the same length, and that's normal. The difference in length may also be due to the way a person is sitting—a slight body shift makes a major difference. And that's the key. As the evangelist prays, he gently pulls on the shorter leg and pushes the longer one, until both are of equal length. Sometimes, the person being "healed" subconsciously shifts their legs just enough so they look perfectly even. After the legs are evenly matched, the evangelist pronounces the person healed, and everyone is amazed and praises the Lord.

Doctors tell us that upwards of fifty percent of our illnesses may be psychosomatic, that is, in our minds. So, if a malady is imaginary, it is simple to imagine that it's cured. And it is.

When I mentioned some of the processes that occur when a person fasts, I alluded to the body's defense mechanisms and its ability to heal itself. With a positive mental attitude, including a good sense of humor, the body is often able to heal itself, sometimes even when doctors say there is no hope. For example, there is no known cure for the common cold, so how are we healed when our nose runs and our chest is congested? The body's immune system fights it off until complete healing occurs.

I'm the first to admit that people are sometimes healed as a result of prayer. The *reason* they are cured is that the prayer of faith convinced them of their healing. Their mind is changed from a negative mode, "I'm sick," to a positive one, "I'm healed." This allows the body to release whatever processes it uses to affect the healing.

Here's another thought on divine healing for Charismatics and Pentecostals. The Bible is replete with tales of lepers being healed through the prayer of faith. Believers are told that they "shall lay hands on the sick, and they shall recover." (Mark 16:18) Today, evangelists claim to heal diseases of all sorts "in the name of Jesus."

It could be said that the modern-day counterpart of the dreaded disease of leprosy is AIDS. In the Bible, the prayer of faith healed leprosy. If the prayer of faith can heal anything at all, it can heal AIDS, too. Although we have accounts of evangelists praying for AIDS victims, not one has been healed. Why? I think it shows that the dynamics that activate a healing are human in origin. And, while positive thinking and other human devices have been shown to have some effect in slowing down the development of full-blown AIDS in some people who have the HIV-virus, it is not sufficient to actually heal anyone with AIDS. If God, or the prayer of faith, really can heal, why hasn't it happened with these unfortunate victims?

One other thing concerning the gift of healing: As a Pentecostal, I followed a number of healing evangelists; and, of course, I was amazed by their apparent gift. I always wondered, though, why didn't they just drop by their nearest hospital and clean it out?

My final step in deliverance from oppressive religion came when I looked objectively at the Bible. There are many good books available on the subject for those who are willing to read them with an open mind. Here I'll just highlight some of my discoveries.

Christianity is based upon the New Testament record of Jesus, yet there is no account of a single word written by him. We have only the words of others who claim to tell us what Jesus said. These writers, with a few exceptions, never knew him. What they put into writing, as much as ninety years after his death, was hearsay. The Gospel writers don't even agree on Jesus's genealogy, or exactly what he said, or the details of his life, leaving us with a record replete with inconsistencies and contradictions.

I recognize the fact that some liberal Christian denominations follow the words of Jesus, as we have them, and have developed a humanistic type of Christianity based upon those words. The theologians in those churches are more honest in their approach to the Scriptures.

For example, in the spring of 1991, a 200-member group called The Jesus Seminar, composed of Bible scholars, ministers, and lay people, wrapped up a six-year study of the Gospels. They concluded that no more than 20 percent of the sayings attributed to Jesus were actually said by him.

Many of the supposed sayings of Jesus were actually made up by his followers. One example cited: "I am the way, the truth, and the life: no man cometh unto the Father, but by me." The group also rejected the Gospel accounts of Jesus's announcements that he would return again in glory amid earthly tribulations.

Most of the New Testament is a collection of Saul/Paul's letters. Paul was a sexist, racist (he endorsed slavery), bigoted zealot, yet his carefully crafted monographs succeeded in creating a major religion out of the life of an obscure Jew. The fruit of Paul's letters has been the root of more than three hundred Christian denominations and sects, most of which were formed as a result of disagreement over the correct meaning of Paul's words.

I came to realize that a simple three-letter word perpetuates the entire born-again industry: "sin."

No one is perfect. Everyone occasionally makes poor choices, and sometimes acts maliciously, but no one "sins." "Sin" is nothing more than a theological concept which has no basis in reality. Sin sells religion. No one is going to be punished by God for sins. I firmly believe that, and when I finally accepted the truth, it set me free.

Writing my story helped me to see the big picture; it enabled me to sort these things out. I didn't however, escape unscathed. Occasionally, I still have unpleasant dreams about the things I experienced as a fundamentalist Christian. At the age of eleven, I invited Jesus to live in my heart. Full of faith, I said, "Jesus, I invite you to live in my heart." And, in my mind, he lived in my heart for many years. Now, without a shred of guilt or fear, I can say, "Jesus doesn't live here anymore."

The Rapture and other end-time theology really took Barbara by surprise. Not only did she have difficulty understanding how anyone could believe that stuff, she was further stunned to learn that the President of the United States believed it as well.

Around the same time I started writing my story, a published interview with President Reagan quoted him as saying: "Never . . . has there been a time in which so many of the prophecies are coming together." He continued, "There have been times in the past when people thought the end of the world was coming, and so forth, but never anything like this." Ronald Reagan concluded, "I turn back to your ancient prophets in the Old Testament and the signs foretelling Armageddon, and I find myself wondering if, if we're the generation that's going to see that come about."

We wondered how people could vote for a man who believed this nonsense. So, for the time being, we laid my story aside and tried to interest a publisher in a book about the President's end-time mentality. Through it, perhaps, we could convince Americans that Ronald Reagan was not a responsible choice for the presidency.

Then on Saturday, May 5, 1984, the Republicans of western Massachusetts selected their delegates for the National Republican Convention in Dallas. The national convention was scheduled for August. Because Republicans hadn't been a big factor in Massachusetts politics, these events generally didn't produce any surprises. Normally, this caucus would have gone practically unnoticed. However, this year a bomb was dropped.

A local businesswoman and political unknown, Lilliane Schmid, took complete charge of the caucus, and, as a result, was the top vote-getter for a delegate spot. Her friend, Thomas A. Toole, took the second highest number of votes.

The caucus was held to elect three delegates, and three alternate delegates, from the 1st Congressional District. It was open to all 40,000 enrolled Republicans in the district, but only 202 participated. Of those 202, Lilliane Schmid controlled 150 votes. Many of these voters had enrolled as Republicans just a few days prior to the caucus.

Lilliane Schmid and her husband, Gerhard—an internationally famous chef—operated an inn and restaurant in the town of Lenox. Although she was virtually unknown to local Republicans, she was active in the sprawling Lenox-based fundamentalist ministry called The Bible Speaks.

In 1982, Schmid heard Democrats claim on television that they would have the women's vote in the 1984 elections. "Over my dead body!" she declared, and she decided that that would not happen.

Schmid, an ultra-conservative, organized a Christian political action committee called Task Force '84, "to point out the vast differences between Republicans and Democrats." When I read about this in *The Berkshire Eagle*, it was the first time I had heard of Christianity being equated with the Republican party.

Lilliane Schmid became an instant celebrity, of sorts. The local Republican leadership kissed her feet. Some people suggested that she run for an office, such as state representative. Speculation over her ambition was rife.

When I learned about President Reagan's belief in Bible prophecy, and then saw these events unfold in Massachusetts, I became concerned because I could see clearly what was about to happen—across the land, a sleeping giant was beginning to awaken.

One day in August, Barbara arrived home infuriated. "I just heard the most terrible, obnoxious, arrogant woman I've ever heard!" Barbara screamed. "I am so angry; we've got to do something!"

She had been listening to a program called "Mid-day Magazine," on WAMC, a public radio station in Albany. They interviewed a delegate to the National Republican Convention in Dallas.

"I heard this voice," Barbara told me. "It was a woman's voice. The woman's voice irritated me. But more than her voice, her message irritated me. She was talking about when her family came to this country from Europe," Barbara continued, "how they pulled themselves up by their own boot straps. They went to work, they all worked hard every day, as if to imply that none of us in America worked hard anymore. This woman continued, 'We worked hard for every penny we ever earned. We all woke up early and worked hard and saved our pennies, and that's how we've gotten where we are today. I'm sick and tired of people who think the world owes them a living. The only thing the world owes them is a right to life!'"

"When I heard these words," Barbara said, "I immediately sensed who was speaking. I just knew who it was by her manner and attitude. It could be only one—Lilliane Schmid! I was angry! I didn't like her message; I didn't like her attitude—which said, in effect, 'the only reason you peons don't make money is because you don't work hard!' And I didn't like her no-choice point of view!"

"You're right," I said. "We'll do something about this. We've been silent long enough."

Immediately, I called WAMC's news department. "We heard your interview with Lilliane Schimd, and we want equal time to present a different point of view," I demanded.

I was told that the interview was a legitimate news story, because Schmid was a convention delegate. Therefore, they wouldn't give us equal time, but they offered to let us share our viewpoints on "Northeast Dateline," a program which aired in the afternoon.

A week later the taped interview was conducted by telephone. I explained how my world view had changed—from that of a Fundamentalist minister to a secular humanist. Barbara talked about her views as a modern Jewish woman in America, and what threats she saw from the likes of Lilliane Schmid.

We never heard the interview. The day it aired, we were on our way to London to spend a week with Barbara's father. Early that morning we took a bus from Great Barrington to Port Authority, where we picked up a shuttle to Newark International Airport. The *New York Times* helped us pass the time on the three-hour bus trip from the Berkshire Hills to the Big Apple. One article practically jumped off the page. It disclosed the phenomenal influence that Christian Fundamentalist factions exerted at the Republican National Convention in Dallas. The story "made my blood boil," to borrow a typical religious right-wing expression.

The *New York Times* article mentioned people very familiar to me, such as the Rev. Jerry Falwell, and the Rev. Tim LaHaye. LaHaye's book, *The Battle For The Mind*, published four years earlier, viciously attacked secular humanism. LaHaye wrote, "No humanist is qualified to hold any governmental office in America—United States senator, congressman, cabinet member, State Department employee, or any other position that requires him to think in the best interest of America." He added, "A humanist is just not qualified to be elected to public office by patriotic, America-loving citizens."

The fact that the Rev. Tim LaHaye has labeled humanism "the world's most dangerous religion" proves he is a bigot, and un-American. Although some humanists consider themselves religious humanists, to secular humanists, humanism is not a religion. Even if it were, humanists, Christians, or anyone else has a right to hold any office in America. It made me angry to think that Tim LaHaye had influence in the Republican party.

After our return from Great Britain we learned that a reporter from *The Berkshire Eagle* had heard Barbara and me on WAMC, and wanted to interview us. The timing was perfect. While we were in England we reached a decision to speak out for the separation of church and state.

On August 18, 1984, *The Berkshire Eagle* published a half-page story, replete with a photo of Barbara and me, which described our proposed mission. The headline proclaimed, "Ex-born-againer and wife to fight religious 'conspiracy'." It described our backgrounds, including my participation with Pat Boone and Dean Jones in "God and Country" rallies designed to "put God's leaders into government, and to replace ungodly leaders with Christian leaders."

The article mentioned a recent development from The Bible Speaks, and Lilliane Schmid's Task Force '84. Schmid's friend and Republican co-delegate, Tom Toole, had announced his intention to run for state representative.

Barbara and I, of course, opposed his candidacy on church/state grounds. Toole had said, if elected, he would "act on his moral and religious beliefs in carrying out his duties as a public official." He believed that the constitutional separation of church and state was simply "to keep the state out of the church." He added, "Obviously they [the authors of the Constitution] wanted the offices to be filled with godly people. This is a nation under God," Toole said. "If they didn't want it that way, they would have left out all that God language." For the record, there is absolutely no "God language" in the Constitution. It was obvious to me that he had never read the document.

The next day, the director of community activities for Simon's Rock of Bard College called. He asked me and Barbara to speak at the school in September. Because of my Fundamentalist background, we decided I would give the talk.

The Thursday-evening lecture was well-publicized by Simon's Rock. I was anxious because I hadn't spoken in public in seven years, and I hoped for a small audience.

When Barbara and I entered the hall, I was relieved to see that only two dozen chairs had been set up in the large room. As I laid out my notes on the lectern, the hall filled up rapidly. Soon, those in charge of the event had to bring in more chairs. When all the chairs were taken, people sat on the floor. The large room was packed full.

My lecture was billed as "an insider's view of the evangelical movement, and a discussion of the political and social issues raised by the movement's activities in the United States." When I finished my talk, I entertained questions from the audience. The ignorance of many of those in attendance surprised me. They expressed the sentiment that this is a Christian nation, and had no concept of the purpose and value of the separation of church and state. Later, I learned that students had been bused in from The Bible Speaks, and the Berkshire Christian College. No wonder they were so ill-informed.

Overall, Barbara and I were pleased with the evening's outcome. We met some fine people who would support our work in the years to follow, and the press had been there, too.

The next morning we were stunned when we opened up *The Berkshire Eagle* and read its front-page headline, "Alleged conspiracy is debated." The article related the events of the night before. Soon, we received calls from other newspapers; radio stations called with invitations to appear on talk shows.

Meanwhile, Thomas Toole had no trouble winning the Republican nomination. Of nineteen towns, Lenox alone provided 57 percent of his votes. Obviously, The Bible Speaks easily had enough votes to control the town of Lenox.

All Toole had to do now was to mail an all-important acceptance-of-nomination letter to the State Elections Division in Boston, a letter he sent by certified mail. Meanwhile, Toole had six weeks left to campaign. It looked like the incumbent, Christopher Hodgkins, had some serious competition for his seat.

Then, the unexpected happened. The October-1 deadline to file nomination papers arrived, but Toole's letter had not. The state notified him that his name would not appear on the ballot. Toole's candidacy was doomed. The postal service was first blamed, then the State Elections Division.

Finally, eight days after the deadline, Toole's letter arrived. He had used the wrong ZIP code on his letter. With that, Representative Chris Hodgkins remarked, "I seriously question his qualification to do the job."

Without missing a beat, Schmid went on to her next campaign. This time it was over fluoridation.

Dr. Robert K. Brown, chairman of the Lenox Board of Health, fully expected the town's voters to approve fluoride treatment of their water. Yet, when the votes were counted, fluoridation was defeated by just twenty-eight votes. Dr. Brown declared, "The Bible Speaks has spoken."

Between the climate engendered by the newly emerged religious right, and a President who saw Armageddon around the corner, our mission became clearer: we had to get the word out.

After several futile attempts to publish a book, we decided to publish a newsletter to promote the separation of church and state. Fortunately, our credit at a local printer was good, because the balance in our checking account was down to about $10.

Our first press run of 100 copies came out in September 1984. It was difficult to choose a clever name for our newsletter, so we called it *Control Q*. The name came from a command on our Epson QX-10 computer which brought a "quirk menu" to the screen. Since our campaign focused on quirky people and ideas, this seemed like a reasonable name. We knew, however, that before long we'd have to decide on a better name, because *Control Q* sounded too conspiratorial.

After three monthly issues we learned about two other organizations involved in the fight to preserve the separation of church and state, both of which were located in the Washington, D.C. area. They were People For the American Way, founded by television producer Norman Lear—and formed as a reaction to Falwell's Moral Majority—and Americans United for the Separation of Church and State. The latter group was founded in 1947 to combat the Roman Catholic church's violations of church/state separation in America.

As soon as we became aware of these groups, we contacted them in order to learn more about their place in the scheme of things. Had we known of them earlier, our efforts might have gone in a different direction.

About mid-December, we received a call from a producer of "People Are Talking," a popular talk show on Boston's WBZ-TV. He asked if I could come into Boston to debate a Fundamentalist. I had never been on television and was quite unsure about doing such a show, but I believed in our work. "Sure," I replied. "Who do you have in mind for me to debate?"

"Jerry Falwell," the producer replied.

Scheduled to appear a week before Christmas, I only had a few days to prepare. Actually, I thought a month wouldn't be enough time to prepare to debate Falwell, being aware that Falwell did this every day. He could debate in his sleep.

A friend of ours from New York had a friend, Mary Jo Slater, who taught acting classes for television actors. He asked her to coach me. She offered to give me some free lessons before a video camera. Barbara and I went to Mary Jo's apartment on New York's West Side, which she shared with her young son, Christian, an up-and-coming child actor.

Mary Jo urged me to act impassioned about my political position. She reminded me to look into the TV camera which displayed the red light; the red light indicated which of the several cameras was currently operative. My performance was poor.

On the way to Boston, Barbara helped me rehearse my opening statement: "I was part of the Christian conspiracy to take control of America through the political process." It went on for several more lines. I figured that if I memorized my opening, the rest of my thoughts would flow easily. Instead, I came across as stilted. Also, I was unable to locate which camera displayed the red light. Apparently, the producers deliberately covered the red lights so that participants would be unable to create their own camera head shots. When I decided just to be myself and get on with the debate, I came alive, so all was not lost.

Rev. Falwell—who appeared from Lynchburg, Virginia via satellite—attempted to avoid the issues and attacked my morality—or lack of morality, as he saw it. He was difficult to pin down, because he deflected questions by simply ignoring them. Instead, he continued to tout his Moral Majority's political agenda.

When I criticized his narrow viewpoints, Falwell countered with claims that he was popular with many groups, including Catholics and Jews. He referred to a forum in which he had recently participated in New York. "There were two thousand Jews present," he bragged.

I had just read about the symposium in the *New York Times* and I shot back, "You know as well as I do that those two thousand Jews weren't supporting you! Fifty of them had to be carried out!"

"They were gays, sir, carrying signs!" Falwell quipped.

He later denied that he told his followers how to vote. He said, "We shared with them, as other groups do, what we believe to be an agenda that is important."

I asked Falwell to respond to a quote from his 1979 book, *America Can Be Saved*: "I hope I live to see the day when, as in the early days of our country, we won't have any public schools. The churches will have taken them all over again and Christians will be running them. What a happy day that will be!"

"I never wrote that!" Falwell said. He was right, he didn't *write* it; the statement was transcribed from a sermon he had *preached*. He didn't write it, he spoke it.

Another opponent on the "People Are Talking" show was the Rev. John Martelli, a graduate of Falwell's Liberty Baptist College. Martelli carried and presented a book called *The Hebrew Republic*. I don't know who the author was, except that Martelli said that it was "written by an unbiased person—a Presbyterian." He said the book "documents [that] the government—the judiciary branch, the legislative branch, the executive branch—represents God the Father, God the Son, and God the Holy Spirit." Martelli added, "It's right here in this book."

Dan Rea, the moderator, was astounded. "Run that by me again?" he asked.

Martelli repeated what he had said, and added, "It's all documented through Scripture. It's no accident that we have a system of checks and balances."

Dan interjected, "We're speaking metaphorically, not literally?"

"No," the Rev. Martelli insisted.

Martelli took away any points that Falwell may have scored for the Moral Majority. I think Falwell's former student embarrassed him.

About a week later, I received a letter from the Rev. Harold Crowell, then president of the Massachusetts Moral Majority. He wrote, "You have nothing to fear from us, unless you're a baby killer, moral pervert, etc. The only intolerance we possess is INTOLERANCE OF MORAL EVIL."

In February of 1985, Barbara and I drove to Washington for scheduled appointments with Anthony Podesta, president of People For the American Way, and Robert Maddox, executive director of Americans United for the Separation of Church and State.

Tony Podesta was friendly. "So, you're freedom fighters?" he said. The three of us agreed that we certainly all were in a fight for American freedoms. We explained our mission to Tony and even volunteered to work for his organization. He declined our offer, but encouraged us to continue what we had started, because he realized we could reach people he was unable to reach. He offered to share some video resources with us.

Our next meeting that day was in Silver Spring, Maryland, a suburb of Washington. After Joe Conn, the editor of *Church and State* magazine by Americans United, gave us a tour of their facility, we went out for lunch. Besides Barbara and me, Bob Maddox, Joe Conn, and writer-researcher Al Menendez attended.

We had a delightful time and, again, offered our services, but got a response similar to the one from Podesta. Nonetheless, we received encouragement from these two groups. We had hoped to work with them or perhaps receive some financial assistance for our newsletter. Now we knew that we had to forge a path of our own.

The next morning we headed home. One thought was on our minds. What should we rename our newsletter? We knew that an appropriate name would give us vitality.

Over coffee at a diner where we had stopped for breakfast, we stared blankly at each other, both of us trying to come up with a name. Suddenly, a broad smile appeared on Barbara's face. "Let's call it *The Freedom Writer*."

18

The Tupelo Ayatollah

Under normal circumstances Route 78 from Memphis, Tennessee to Tupelo, Mississippi is a good highway. In the fall of 1986, on the day I made the ninety-mile trip to Elvis Presley's hometown, I encountered torrential rains. At one point visibility was so poor that several vehicles just stopped right in the middle of the road and waited.

To psyche myself up for my mission I tuned into a local gospel station—pretty easy to find on the dial in that part of the country. There were plenty of programs from which to choose. As I approached Tupelo, "The Don Wildmon Report" began. Good golly Miss Molly!

My purpose in going to Tupelo was to learn more about the operation of the National Federation for Decency (NFD—now called the American Family Association, AFA). The Rev. Donald Wildmon founded the organization in 1977. I had been reading some of Rev. Wildmon's literature, and I sensed that he would become a major player in the battle for church/state separation, but at that time his name was not widely known. The man's determination, however, told me that he posed a threat to First Amendment freedoms.

Wildmon bills his group as "a Christian organization promoting the Biblical ethic of decency in American society with primary emphasis on TV and other media." I had two problems with this statement. First, the "biblical ethic of decency" applies only to the church, not to the state. If he wanted to promote that ideal in his own church, the United Methodist Church, or in Christianity in general, fine, but

America is officially a secular nation, not a Christian nation. Secondly, Wildmon says his primary emphasis is on "TV and *other media.*" That is so broad that it could include everything that we hear, read, and see. It covers radio, television, movies, recordings, and newspapers. The only way Wildmon can achieve his goal to affect the media through his so-called "Biblical ethic of decency" is through censorship.

Six months earlier I called NFD headquarters to have my name placed on their mailing list. The woman who answered the phone turned my call over to Allen Wildmon, Donald Wildmon's older brother. Allen serves as the NFD/AFA's director of public relations.

Before adding my name to the mailing list, Allen interrogated me. Initially, I had decided to use an assumed name, Rev. Charles Porter. The "Reverend" apparently encouraged Allen to delve into my background and current position. Finding myself on the spot, I improvised.

Before we concluded our conversation, Allen asked me to consider organizing an NFD chapter in Great Barrington. Choosing the correct buzz words, I said, we'd "pray about it." "We" referred to the "Great Barrington Christian Fellowship" I'd created moments earlier.

A few days later I received a package from the NFD. Included were Donald Wildmon's book, *The Case Against Pornography*, a videotape by a Dr. Holland about child porn, and a packet of materials with which to start an NFD chapter.

I filled out the forms, enclosed a check for $25, and within a month had a bona fide NFD chapter. The following month the NFD asked us to picket our local Cumberland Farms convenience store. Cumberland Farms stores were selected because they sell *Playboy* and *Penthouse* magazines. In order to appear cooperative, we fabricated a newspaper story about the Great Barrington NFD's picketing activities and sent it to, as "Brother Don" likes to put it, the "home office," in Tupelo. To my amazement, the story was published in the November *NFD Chapter Newsletter.*

During the six months The Freedom Writer organization operated our NFD chapter we received reams of materials from Tupelo. On one occasion I wrote to Don Wildmon and enclosed a stamped, self-addressed envelope in order to encourage a personal response. In the letter I asked Don if he thought pornography could lead to demon possession. He replied, "Concerning pornography leading to demon possession, this could might [sic] well be true since porn is the work of the devil."

About the only remaining opportunity to gather information about the workings of the NFD was an in-person visit. Don was expecting me. When I made the appointment, I neglected to ask for directions, and the only address I had was a post-office box. From our files I had a newspaper photo which showed Don at NFD headquarters in a storefront on Main Street in Tupelo. After driving up and down Main Street, I couldn't locate any storefront NFD headquarters, so I parked the rental car and telephoned.

Don's secretary informed me that the NFD had moved about two miles outside the center of town. Within minutes I drove into their parking lot.

Located on a side street, the new NFD headquarters was a big step up from the storefront operation. Built especially for the NFD, the new building is a contemporary one-story office building. The NFD logo and name were emblazoned on the front of the building.

After entering the building I was struck by the bevy of young beauties in Wildmon's employ. At least four of the young women seated at desks were a prime sampling of the South's delectable belles. I realize the danger of sounding sexist here, but what I'm saying is that I carried a preconceived notion of women with their hair tied up in buns. One young lady arose from her desk and brought me to the desk of Forrest Ann Daniels, Wildmon's executive secretary, and an NFD board member. Forrest Ann is very charming. She introduced me to Allen Wildmon, who later introduced me to Don.

Allen was quite cordial, and he proceeded to give me a tour of the NFD facility. I was impressed.

Whether at a desk or working with specialized equipment, everyone was busy at some project. About a dozen people performed various tasks.

"There are a lot of people out there. Are they volunteers?" I asked Allen.

"No," he replied, "all of 'em are on salary."

Allen proudly showed me their IBM mainframe computer, which keeps their mailing list. He told me they mail out 320,000 *NFD Journals* a month at a cost of $56,000. This was in 1986. Typesetting of the *Journal* and other literature is performed on their own computerized Varityper typesetting equipment. Small printing jobs are done in-house on an AB Dick offset printing press. They even have an envelope-stuffing machine, which was out of order at the time.

Allen told me that Richard Viguerie does the direct mail fund-raising for them, although Don writes most of the fund-raising letters. With laughter, Allen remarked that Viguerie was good at bringing in the dough. He also commented that Don likes to pay cash for everything.

One room contained four television sets with corresponding VCRs. This equipment is used to monitor prime-time television. Shows are rated according to their sexual content, profanity, violence, and "anti-Christian bias."

After retiring from the insurance business in 1979, Allen began working with his brother at the NFD. His first responsibility was to total the column inches of advertising each month in *Playboy* and *Penthouse*. Armed with that information, he formed a hit list of national advertisers.

As we toured the building, I mentioned their victory in getting the Southland Corporation, the 7-Eleven franchiser, to stop carrying *Playboy* and *Penthouse*. Allen's response intrigued me.

"Yeah, we were real pleased with that. We got word of it about three days before it happened," he said.

"You mean that they were going to stop the sale of the magazines?" I said.

"Yeah," he said, lowering his voice. "The reason on that occasion is you got Christians on the inside. They will call you. For instance, at the FCC [Federal Communications Commission] we had a lady that would call. She was way up, right close to the head, the head one, Mark Fowler. And she would call us at home, at night, and say, 'Look, you're doin' good, you've got his attention. . . .' The same way at the Justice Department. We even got the magazines out of the Federal prison system, forty-two of them. We had a person on the inside up there that volunteered to call, and says, 'If you keep goin' they're gonna pull them! Just need to hold on!' "

"Every time," Allen Wildmon continued, "it just seems like there's somebody—like with the Holiday Inn [For years, Wildmon has led boycotts against Holiday Inn because they show pay-per-view R-rated adult movies]—we've got somebody at the Holiday Inn who calls Don, 'Look, this is what's happening in the front office. Just want you to know what they're thinking up here and. . . ,' you know."

After the tour of NFD headquarters, we took seats in a small reception room and waited for Don. Memorabilia from the NFD's war against porn covered one wall. In the center was a photo of Don shaking hands with President Reagan. I later learned that the picture was taken while Don was at the White House with a group of other ministers. Each of the ministers was allowed to have his photo taken individually with the president. The wall collection included framed magazine covers featuring Don Wildmon. Don's face on the cover of *The Conservative Digest* still stands out in my mind. There were also plaques from Morality In Media—for "victory in the Southland battle," from Jerry Falwell's Liberty Broadcasting System, and from Oklahomans Against Pornography.

Soon, Don arrived, and during the half-hour which followed he did most of the talking. In his rambling discourse, Don said, "There'd be no X-rated bookstores open if *Playboy* hadn't been on the stands." He continued, "We're fighting *Playboy* and *Penthouse* on an economic basis."

In reference to then-Attorney General Ed Meese, Don said, "I don't think he's going to try to prosecute *Playboy* or *Penthouse*, of course. What they're [the magazines] afraid of, and what we can do, is in the wave of prosecuting the obscenity and pornography, you can pile in *Playboy* and *Penthouse* with the same. I mean, what you're doing is changing public acception. This is what you're doing when you're out picketing the stores—raising community standards, and also in the same process the community is saying, 'We don't want that garbage, but we don't want *Playboy* or *Penthouse* either.' You may not be able to get *Playboy* or *Penthouse* legally, but you get 'em economically. You can go picket a store."

Wildmon continued, "They're hurtin', *Playboy* and *Penthouse*, hurtin'. I think the tide's going our way, and what we need to do is just keep picketing pretty regular. You won't think it's doin' any good, but it's hurtin' 'em. It's having an effect on 'em, 'cause it's bringing 'em to their knees. We're letting the community know, 'this store's selling porn,' and they got a lot of business at stake, and they [the customers] won't go. They [the stores] won't ever tell you; it embarrasses them. That's the reason Southland pulled it—because of economics, not because of the Porn Commission report or anything else, pure economics."

After a while, Don excused himself, saying he had work to do. I continued talking with Allen for another hour. While we talked about a number of related topics, I'll just mention a few of his comments.

I commented to Allen about the fact that his brother seemed to be a Fundamentalist, yet he's an ordained Methodist minister. I said that most of the Methodists I knew didn't really preach the gospel.

"They don't down here either, in Tupelo, Mississippi, or anywhere else." Allen said it was his personal belief that Don would have given up the Methodists a long time ago, except that he's trying to turn that church around. Don attends the Methodist church, Allen said, so "he can appeal to the so-called moderates or liberals, maybe have some influence in turning their thinking around."

"You know you're doing some good when the opposition starts screaming," Allen said. "*Playboy*, the recent issue, called Don the Tupelo Ayatollah. But that ain't bad."

He summarized the NFD opposition to erotica in these words: "It doesn't take a person with a doctoral degree to figure out if a dog gets stimulated sexually he's going to look for a female dog. I think humans, they've got sexuality the same as other animals, you know. And if you stimulate them enough, they're going to seek a sexual object."

This comment surprised me for two reasons. First, most Christian Fundamentalists never equate humans with animals, because that indicates some acceptance of the theory of evolution. Secondly, humans can exercise the normal, safe option of masturbation as a way to release sexual urges.

The next morning Allen made a comment which confirmed an attitude I thought I also observed in Don. "This is a business, just like any other business," he said. Our most recent figures indicate that their "business" takes in $5 million a year.

I'm glad he said that, for it was not only a revealing statement, but it was the last thing of any use I got from the Wildmons that day. While we sat in the room, the door opened and six other men entered. The party included reporters from the *Jackson Clarion Ledger*, the *Northeast Mississippi Daily Journal*, a detective from the Tupelo Police Department, Don and his son Tim, and another NFD employee.

Apparently all my questioning tipped them off that I was not who I said I was. I learned that the night before they did some checking up on me. They found out that the Cumberland Farms store in Great

Barrington hadn't been picketed. And, an Assemblies of God minister in Great Barrington told them that I was "on some sort of crusade against what 'he calls the extreme right.'" He was correct.

Having noticed that I took some pictures inside their building, they insisted on having the film. After exposing the film to the light, I handed it over. Allen gave me ten dollars for it. They wanted to know who I was, and who sent me. I refused to answer any questions and said, "I guess our meeting is through," and got up and walked out.

Outside, two patrolmen stood by a cruiser, so I got in the rental car and drove away, nice and slowly.

A blurb about the encounter appeared in the local Mississippi papers. The article noted that I had done nothing illegal, so no charges were pressed. Wildmon also wrote about the incident in his *NFD Journal*. My sources tell me that Wildmon loves to tell this story to his friends in Tupelo.

What motivates Don Wildmon? "If you took off all the sex and violence on television, it would still bother me," Wildmon told a reporter in 1986. He said that for a long time he couldn't put a finger on what bothered him about network television. Then, like a light out of heaven, it came to him!

"Clearly, the networks are intentionally pushing a particular value system," Wildmon said. "That value system is secular humanism. That was what had been disturbing me."

In his book, *The Home Invaders*, Wildmon wrote, "We're not engaged in a war against dirty words and dirty pictures." In effect, he said that *Playboy* or *Penthouse* photo features aren't dangerous. "The danger lies not in the vulgar and obscene pictures which grace the pornographic magazines and films or explicit television programs," Wildmon continued. "The danger is the philosophy behind those pictures. That philosophy, the one which the leaders of the media are pushing on the American public, is humanism."

In Wildmon's writings and speeches he constantly attacks secular humanism. He contends that America was founded upon "the Christian view of man," and that there is some sort of diabolical plot to replace "the Christian view of man" with "the religion of secular humanism."

According to *Christianity and Humanism*, a study guide published by Wildmon, "Humanists believe that man is basically good, and if given the right environment and social context, by reason and intelligence can formulate laws which are in his own best interest." In Wildmon's eyes, the philosophy is evil—from the devil.

Wildmon's "Christian view of man" is in sharp contrast with the "evils" of humanism:

> [B]asic to Christian beliefs: is the fallen nature of man. He is *not* inherently good . . . his nature is flawed by sin. Not only does he need the atonement of Christ, but also he needs the absolutes of the Bible to give order and direction to his life. Man is a sinful creature, and therefore cannot be his own lawgiver and judge. Law must come from God. . . . Scripture ["God's law"] teaches that sex outside of marriage is wrong, sinful and destructive.

In this battle of ideologies, Wildmon perceives, "The struggle will determine whether the Christian view of man will continue to serve as the foundation of our society." Or, will we be a secular nation that will employ reason and logic to serve the needs of our society?

Donald E. Wildmon may be sincere, but he is undeniably misguided. Secular (which means "not religious") humanism is not a religion, but a term used by the radical religious right to label anything with which they disagree.

As leaders of the radical religious right cleverly focus national and local attention on such topics as "pornography" and the "evils of secular humanism," their real line of attack is on something else—our distinctly democratic values of diversity, dissent, and debate.

19

Why Wasn't Jimmy Carter Reelected?

The evening was warm, but not uncomfortable. An orange sun slipped silently behind a few wispy clouds on the western horizon. The ocean was out of view, but the smell of the sea hung in the air, reminding us that it was nearby. A stroll on the beach would have been enjoyable, but, as happens frequently, our work came first.

Barbara and I had not planned on attending a Holy Roller meeting that night. The hand-drawn, photocopied flyers distributed around the seaside village of Madison, Connecticut were devoid of any religious overtones. They read:

> HELP SAVE OUR CHILDREN
> Anti-pornography Meeting
> Guest Speakers:
> Joan Bershefski & Antonia Sequeira
> Co-Chairwomen of
> Stratford Coalition Against Pornography
> June 13, 1986   7:30 P.M.
> GRANGE HALL, MADISON, CT.
> For more Info. Call . . .

Barbara and I ascended the three wooden steps at the entrance of the small white building. The sign above the entryway read, "Grange Hall, Madison, Connecticut."

We stepped inside and looked around. After our eyes adjusted to the glare of the fluorescent lights, we saw a large, carefully lettered sign leaning against the wall near the front door. The sign read "Rock Church," and informed us that the church was led by Pastor Ryan Young, with services and Bible classes on Sunday mornings, and prayer meetings on Sunday and Wednesday evenings. Since it was Friday, I guessed that the church rented the building and put the sign out on weekends.

A group of people hovered over a pile of magazines on a long folding table. It appeared as if someone had gone on a hard-core pornography shopping spree at New York's Times Square. Several men and women eagerly thumbed through the magazines.

A smaller table on the opposite side of the room displayed anti-pornographic literature from Rev. Wildmon's National Federation For Decency, and another group, Morality In Media. There was no danger of paper cuts here, because there was no one at this table.

Barbara loaded up on the anti-porn literature before taking a seat next to me. After settling down on the folding metal chairs we observed the front of the meeting hall. We faced an altar rail. On the other side of the altar rail sat a large, boxy, plywood pulpit. To the right of the pulpit stood a small upright piano, covered by a white sheet. Next to the piano was a set of metallic blue drums, partially visible under another sheet. With the drums and pianos inactive, I took solace in knowing there wouldn't be any dancing in the aisles.

A heavyset woman huddled around the pulpit, in conference with three other women. We heard her tell the others, "I preach under the anointing." She was saying that the Holy Spirit told her what to say, enabling her to speak publicly without the aid of notes. Often, "preaching under the anointing" means that the talk is too long, and incomprehensible.

Our attendance at this meeting wasn't by chance. A reader of *The Freedom Writer* who lives in Connecticut called to tell us about this event. He expressed concern that a witch-hunt was about to take place in Madison, similar to the one that had taken place just up the coast in Salem many years earlier. In this case, though, it might be magazines that were burned. At issue were First Amendment rights. Censorship, once permitted, knows no bounds. In fact, this meeting represented a problem much larger than the issue of pornography. At stake was whether Americans were going to permit a minority of religious zealots to dictate governmental policy based upon their narrow interpretation of the Bible—or any other interpretation of the Bible.

By a quarter-to-eight, anyone planning to attend the meeting was already there. It wasn't a sell-out crowd. Sixteen adults were in attendance, including the guest speakers, a video-camera person, Barbara, and myself.

A young Biblical-looking character stood before the group and introduced himself as Andrew. Smiling, he told the gathering that he was going to pray for the Lord's presence to be made known in the meeting. That meant he was inviting the unexpected. I made a mental note of it. The bearded man bowed his head and began praying.

While he prayed, we looked around the room. Everyone else's heads were obediently bowed and their eyes were closed. Even before entering the building, we suspected that Christian Fundamentalists were sponsoring the meeting, but we were still surprised by their blatant openness about it. Usually, at public meetings like this, these groups hide their overt religious practices in order to trap the unwary, and to avoid being accused of forcing their religion upon others—which is exactly what they intended to do.

Andrew finished his prayer, and introduced the guest speakers, "Sister" Joan Bershefski and "Sister" Tiny Sequeria. After the introduction, Andrew sat down.

Bershefski and Sequeira, looking a bit like Laurel and Hardy, remained seated as they told the audience about their qualifications for addressing the issue of pornography. Their credentials were based upon the number of years each had been married, the number of children they had borne, their number of grandchildren, and the fact that they were both excellent Christians.

Then, Sister Joan, the big one, stood to speak. Tiny, the tiny one, remained silent throughout the rest of the evening.

"It is perfectly proper to open a public meeting with the Word of God," Bershefski said. She opened her thick referenced edition of the King James version of the Bible and read aloud from Isaiah 58, which says in part, "when thou seest the naked, that thou cover him." Evidently, she interpreted this passage to mean that God wants us to clothe the naked men and women in adult magazines. I find it interesting that many conservative Christians are more upset over pictures of naked people in magazines than they are about the tens of thousands of hungry, homeless people in threadbare clothing who live on the streets of America.

Bershefski claimed to have a God-appointed mission to rid the nations's store shelves of erotic material. As she loosened up, "God's anointing" fell on her and she launched into a diatribe against the evils of humanistic philosophy. Furiously, Barbara and I scribbled notes as Bershefski rambled on.

"The word on the streets is . . . ," she said frequently. This oft-quoted phrase of Bershefski's made her audience think that she had first-hand experience in dealing with the underworld. I thought to myself, The returning warrior has just come back from wallowing in the filth and squalor of street life, with its hookers, pimps, drug dealers, and child molesters.

"Pornography is sin!" Bershefski proclaimed, waving her arms through the air.

"If you play with a snake, you're gonna get bit! This material is addictive," she said. She confessed to the audience that she had to "pray in the spirit" every time she looked at pornography, so she wouldn't get hooked.

"Ninety percent of porn is controlled by the Mafia," she claimed. Because of that, when starting her car in the morning, she never knew whether or not a bomb would go off, sending her to heaven.

"Are we going to live by what God has set down for this nation, or by what the ACLU says?" she asked the audience, while pounding her Bible with a fat fist.

"Because there are so many homosexuals working in government, AIDS is the first disease that has ever been protected politically. The AIDS virus can be transmitted by mosquitoes," she stated authoritatively.

"Why wasn't Jimmy Carter reelected?" she asked rhetorically. "Because he gave an interview to a porno magazine [*Playboy*]. God wasn't going to honor that kind of compromise.

"Unless we band together we are going to be taken captive by the enemy." She explained how her group rid the stores in Stratford, Connecticut of naughty magazines. According to Bershefski, it started when she walked into a Cumberland Farms convenience store and purchased a *Stag* magazine. Then, with her dirty magazine under her arm, she charged into the police station and filed a complaint against the clerk who sold her the magazine. Quoting the obscenity law from the Connecticut General Statutes, she demanded that the police go to the convenience store and arrest a horrified fifty-seven-year-old woman for promoting obscene material.

"It only takes a few people to get the ball rolling. Our commanding officer is the Lord! We are only his foot soldiers." Excitement swept through the small audience. I fully expected someone to burst forth with "Onward, Christian Soldiers!"

"In heaven, would you stand before Jesus Christ with this material?" she inquired, indicating that that was her standard for judging obscene material.

After an hour of ranting and raving, Bershefski's Holy Ghost anointing apparently lifted. Now, composed again, she entertained questions from the audience. After several people asked questions, Barbara raised her hand.

"I have two questions," Barbara said. "First, in your talk you referred to a pornographic school textbook. You said it depicted children and adults performing obscene sexual acts. What is the name of that book?"

"The book's title is *Where Did I Come From?*" Bershefski answered.

Barbara, having worked for Family Planning, recognized the title. It is a highly respected volume on sex education for children, and not at all the pornographic book described by Bershefski.

"Sexual abuse is a serious problem," Barbara continued. "Is it possible, though, that pornography is merely a symptom of the problem, and not its cause?"

"It is both," Bershefski replied authoritatively.

Next, Bershefski acknowledged my raised my hand. I stood, with a copy of *The Living Bible* under my arm, and introduced myself.

"My name is Porteous, Reverend Charles Porteous." Smiling, I said, "I feel like I'm in a Women's Aglow Fellowship meeting tonight." Bershefski, and several ladies in the audience smiled back.

"I was saved when I was eleven years-old. In the two summers that followed my conversion I attended the fundamentalist Word of Life camp, in Schroon Lake, New York. The second summer, Pat Robertson and his wife Dede attended the same camp.

"As you know," I continued, "Pat founded CBN, the Christian Broadcasting Network. His ministry has been of great interest to me for many years. Robertson said the greatest revelation of God's vision came to CBN in May of 1968 when God spoke through a word of prophecy and said, 'I have chosen you to usher in the coming of my Son.' " More smiles and nodding of heads followed.

"In 1975 and 1976 I was the New York state coordinator for the If My People movement. If My People was the first national attempt to bring America back to God." Several people nodded approvingly, apparently recognizing the movement.

"I worked with Dean Jones, the Disney actor, and Pat Boone, the singer, in an effort to involve Christians in the political process. I organized a God and Country rally in Albany, New York, which was attended by 2,800 born-again Christians. Dean Jones addressed the gathering. It was our hope that these people would register to vote and help make this the Christian nation God intended." Agreement registered on the audience's faces.

"That year, 1976, we elected the first president to proclaim himself a born-again Christian. As you know, Jimmy Carter was a disappointment because he didn't push to make the Bible the law of the land." The audience nodded sympathetically.

As I continued, the audience listened eagerly to what the stranger in their midst had to say. By now, I had them in my hand. Now, to drop the bomb.

"I, too, feel that it is appropriate to read a Bible passage in this meeting." Bershefski nodded approvingly. Knowing what I was about to do, my voice quavered a bit as I continued.

I opened my Bible to the nineteenth chapter of Genesis and read the story of Lot and his two young daughters. In the story, Lot offered his virgin daughters to a mob of homosexual rapists, "to do with them as they please." Later, on two successive evenings, the daughters managed to get their father drunk, and then seduced him. Each daughter committed incest with their father and became pregnant by him.

"For some unknown reason," I added, "the New Testament writer, Peter, calls this man Lot, 'a just man.' "

"Now, my point is," I said, gathering strength, "if you censor magazines which some people consider pornographic, what will you do if others turn around and forbid the sale of the Bible because it contains pornographic stories such as the one I just read?"

The audience looked bewildered. Bershefski and her silent partner, Tiny, stared at one another, puzzled.

"Before coming here tonight," I continued, "we stopped at the book store on Main Street. After careful inspection, we found *Playboy* and *Penthouse,* and even *The Living Bible.* We did not, however, see any of the type of material displayed here tonight. Madison, Connecticut is not Times Square."

"How can you deprive people of their right to choose their reading material? The Constitution's First Amendment guarantees freedom of speech and freedom of the press. And, besides," I added quickly, "we are talking about two different things—erotica and porn. There is a difference." Now, all hell broke loose. As people shouted at me, I continued, raising my voice.

"Not one shred of scientific evidence was presented tonight. It was all hearsay and anecdotes. You certainly have the right to believe as you do, but by the size of this audience, you obviously don't have the support of the community." With that, I took my seat.

Now in an uproar, members of the audience shouted absurd statements and questions. One lady even wept. The Biblical-looking Andrew jumped up, and within moments brought things under control.

Sister Joan's broad smile had long-since disappeared; her countenance turned pale. After Andrew restored order, Bershefski stood, and while leaning against the pulpit, she addressed the audience in an attempt to counter my statements. Without her previous momentum, she lost control of the gathering, and the meeting just fizzled out. It was about quarter after ten.

Barbara and I arose and started for the door. She slipped out without being accosted, but I, having paused to pick up my Bible and notes, got intercepted by about seven people. They blocked my exit and fired hostile questions at me.

"Are you a Christian?"

"If you are, how can you defend this stuff!"

"Are you saved?"

"Where did you come from?"

"What are you trying to do?"

"What kind of a minister are you, anyway?"

"Listen," I responded, "in defending the First Amendment, I'm defending your rights, too!"

"Answer this," a man demanded. "Do you believe that Jesus Christ is come in the flesh?"

I recognized this as the Pentecostal method of testing spirits. Derived from 1 John 4, it's used by some born-againers to determine whether a person is from God or is a false prophet. They believe that a false or lying spirit cannot answer the question affirmatively.

"Of course I believe Jesus Christ is come in the flesh," I said, looking the man straight in the eye. "Isn't that what the Bible says?"

Smiling, I turned and walked through an opening in the small band of fanatics. Barbara was waiting for me in the parking lot.

She expressed her surprise that the people didn't follow me out of the building.

"They think the devil was in their midst tonight," I said. "They'll probably hold an all-night prayer meeting, now."

We drove back to Massachusetts.

From what I understand, *Playboy, Penthouse,* and *The Living Bible* are still available in Madison, Connecticut.

20

Meet the Media

Since its inception, *The Freedom Writer* has taken an activist position on the separation between church and state. While I recognize that religious fanatics have certain rights, after my experience with Christian fundamentalism, I never, ever, want to see them control our country. And while, in a sense, Jesus may be alive and well in the United States, he is not the head of the household.

For the record, let me offer a brief explanation of the separation of church and state. The words "a wall of separation between church and state" are not found in the Constitution. They are the words of Thomas Jefferson. The First Amendment to the Constitution reads: "Congress shall make no law respecting an establishment of religion [governmental neutrality toward religion], or prohibiting the free exercise thereof [religious freedom]." The Fourteenth Amendment extended this requirement beyond the federal government to all the state governments.

In *Reynolds* v. *United States* (1878), the Supreme Court said, "In the words of Jefferson, the clause against establishment of religion by law was intended to erect 'a wall of separation between church and state.' " This was further emphasized in *Everson* v. *Board of Education* (1947), as expressed in the opinion for the majority written by Associate Justice Hugo Black, who said, "The First Amendment has erected a wall between church and state. That wall must be kept high and impregnable. We could not approve the slightest breach."

In *Lemon* v. *Kurtzman* (1971), the Court established a three-prong test to determine if a governmental action is neutral toward religion. First, government institutions or legislation must have a secular purpose; second, the primary effect must be one that neither advances nor inhibits religion; and third, there must not be an excessive government entanglement with religion. This principle was further clarified by Associate Justice Sandra Day O'Connor in *Lynch* v. *Donnelly* (1984). She said, "What is crucial is that a governmental practice not have the effect of communicating a message of government endorsement or disapproval of religion."

Our dedication to the First Amendment is such that we've never permitted our lack of money to hinder our activities. At one point Barbara and I took a second mortgage on our home so we would have funds to work with. Never, since 1984, have we had any abundance of resources. Barbara's excellent, conservative financial management abilities have enabled our work to continue.

Today *The Freedom Writer* has readers in every state and in several foreign countries. It continues to grow as more people recognize the need for such a publication.

The Institute for First Amendment Studies, Inc.—our incorporated name—is an educational organization. Our main method of operation is to gather intelligence, and then to disseminate that information through our newsletters and the national media. The material we supply to the media reaches far more people than do our own newsletters. Over a dozen national magazines, a number of newspapers, the wire services, and four television networks have used our research materials. Individual journalists and authors call us regularly for information on the radical religious right.

Although *The Freedom Writer,* or the Institute for First Amendment Studies, usually receives no credit for the material we provide, our mission is still accomplished. What's important is that the information we uncover—threats to First Amendment freedoms, and violations of church/state separation—reaches the public. An informed public is a responsible public.

Our readers are usually the ones to alert us to various incursions in the wall of separation between church and state. For instance, a reader alerted us to the activities of Mayor Donald Kainrad of Ravenna, Ohio. Until we opposed him, Kainrad regularly used his official position, including city stationery and secretarial services, to advance his born-again religious beliefs. (See Appendix A.)

In Alexandria, Louisiana, a reader called and told us about the Bible-distribution program in that city's schools. For some forty years, The Gideons distributed Bibles there. In less than two weeks, our efforts in Louisiana brought an end to the practice.

With the headline "Ex-Fundamentalist Fights Church Influence," an article in the *Washington Post* (3 February 1990) said, "Porteous has been out in front of more established organizations such as the American Civil Liberties Union and Americans United for the Separation of Church and State in campaigns such as those in Ohio and Louisiana." I was proud of that, because it indicated that some of the harm I've done over the years through my previous religious fanaticism is being reversed.

While *The Freedom Writer* focuses on First Amendment issues, particularly defense of the separation of church and state, we developed another newsletter called *Walk Away,* which deals specifically with Christian fundamentalism. The radical religious right recruits its troops through evangelism, and while we must defend their right to evangelize, nothing prohibits us from critically examining fundamental Christianity.

Walk Away carries testimonies of those, like myself, who have walked away from destructive Bible-based religious groups. We strongly encourage others to tell their stories. Just getting one's personal walk-away episode down on paper is a big step in the healing process, and publishing it helps others who need the courage to walk away, or have done so already and need reinforcement.

Walk Away regularly publishes information on dangerous groups; helpful tips about religious addiction; undoing the results of mind-control; and warnings concerning things to look for before joining a group. It also reports on religious news of particular interest to our readers.

Radio and television has played a large part in the success of the work of *The Freedom Writer* and *Walk Away.* After that first radio interview on WAMC, the public radio station in Albany, New York, when Barbara and I first started to speak out, several people besides *The Berkshire Eagle* reporter called us. About the same time, someone at WWCN, another Albany station, heard about what we were doing and scheduled me for an on-the-air-debate with a Bible Speaks minister who pastored a church in Albany. That is when I began to realize that radio would be a good way to reach people with our message.

Those two interviews were more or less by chance; I had no idea then how to get on the radio talk-show circuit. Then I saw an ad in the *New York Times* which promised to get authors and other interesting people on radio talk shows. After a call to Rex Communications in New York City, I learned that, for $50 a pop, they could book me on shows around the country.

Contrary to widespread belief, persons appearing on radio or television talk shows receive no compensation for their appearances. Some television programs, though, will pay their guests' travel expenses and sometimes put them up in a hotel.

Even though it would cost no mean sum, Barbara and I agreed that the expense would be a worthwhile investment for *The Freedom Writer*. The beauty of it was that I could conduct all the interviews right from our home office in Massachusetts. I purchased two pieces of equipment at the local Radio Shack; one allows me to connect a microphone-equipped headset to the telephone—leaving my hands free, and the other turns on a cassette recorder whenever that phone line is in use. That way I'm able to record each show. To complete my "studio," I mounted a large, wall-sized map of the United States, replete with four quartz clocks, one above each time zone. Thus, whatever city I'm being aired in, I can look at the map and have a real sense of where I am. Psychologically, that's quite beneficial.

We contracted with Rex for twenty initial bookings. In March 1986, I appeared on WCKY in Cincinnati, and KING in Seattle. The switchboards at both stations were flooded with calls. The excited callers added drama to the programs. From the very beginning of the radio campaign, I offered free copies of *The Freedom Writer* to listeners who wrote to us. Immediately, the mail poured in from Cincinnati and Seattle. I knew we were on the right track.

Then, on the evening of March 29, I did an hour show on KNUS in Denver. The host knew precious little about the separation of church and state, so I just pressed forward in my assault on the religious right. The station's toll-free number was announced several times, but no one called. Now this was Denver, no small city. I couldn't believe that no one was calling, until I realized that it was Good Friday, just two days before Easter. After that agonizing hour I never did another show within a week before a major religious holiday.

Another of my earlier interviews was on WTNS in Coshocton, Ohio.

During the interview I compared some of the leaders of the religious right to the late, right-wing Senator Joseph McCarthy. Agitated listeners called the station to blast me for my statement, adding, "What's wrong with Senator McCarthy? He was a great American!" Ohio, with its rabid conservative element, served as a reminder to me about how far I'd come since leaving radical Fundamentalism. "I was once like some of these people," I thought to myself. The thought was frightening.

The pace picked up during the following month, when I went from three interviews to ten. During one day alone I did shows in South Bend, Indiana; Birmingham, Alabama; Baltimore, Maryland; and San Antonio, Texas.

In successive months, I conducted several more interviews in San Antonio. Then I was set up. Out of courtesy, producers usually—especially if you ask—inform their guests about what to generally expect from each show. For instance, whether the show will be live or taped, and whether or not phone calls from listeners will be accepted. Also, they'll say whether someone with an opposing point of view has been invited—and if that person is in the studio or on the phone—which makes a difference. Almost all of my shows are live, with phone calls from listeners encouraged. About a quarter of the producers or hosts invite someone with an opposing point of view. And, if you don't already know, the producer will tell you whether the host of the show is liberal or conservative. This is usually good to know before you go on the air.

So, once again, I went on WOAI, in San Antonio, with Carl Wigglesworth as the host. Right after we started getting into the thick of things, he introduced the radio audience—and me—to a fundamentalist minister who was sitting with him there in the studio. I recovered from this surprise move after a few moments, and the show went well. Wigglesworth tried the same tactic a second time, but the next time I was mentally prepared for such a possibility. I mention this because, even today, I usually become apprehensive before doing a talk show. It's always more comforting to have a good idea about what to expect.

In that regard, one of the most relaxing shows I've been on is Teddy Bart's "Beyond Reason," on WSIX in Nashville. Teddy's one-hour interviews are really laid-back. The show is taped for later broadcast, and no calls are taken. Teddy Bart gives you a chance to explore issues in depth, which is difficult to do on many talk shows. I've been on "Beyond Reason" several times and always receive positive letters from its listeners.

One of the few other times I was tricked by a radio station was by WLW in Cincinnati. A strict anti-porn ordinance had just been passed in that city, and WLW called *Penthouse* to see if the magazine cared to respond to the new law. Because *Penthouse* had just published an article of mine called "Loony Bin," a satire on the religious right, they asked me if I'd speak on censorship and free speech. So, while in no way an official representative of *Penthouse,* I agreed to do the show.

Two of the local anti-porn crusaders were in the Cincinnati studio, and because of the passage of the new law, they were ecstatic. I mean, they were so beside themselves that I wondered if they were drunk, they were so giddy. The worst was yet to follow. They brought a stack of the now-illegal magazines—including *Penthouse, New Look, Playboy,* and *Hustler*—with them to the studio. Then, on the air, they proceeded to describe some of the magazine's various photo layouts and cartoons.

From my position, looking at a wall map in Massachusetts, I could hardly counter the claims these men made while they drooled over the magazines. In one instance, they described a photo that appeared with an article in *New Look* magazine about New Age religions in Southern California. They told the radio audience that the photo showed a young man standing over a bare-breasted woman, and that her skirt was pulled up over her hips. They said, in his hand he held the bloodied knife that he had just used to kill the young woman—as a human sacrifice for Satan. The photo, they said, clearly showed the woman's slit throat. The host of the show agreed that his guests accurately described the *New Look* photo.

So, here I am, speaking out against censorship, and these pro-censorship guys are describing this kind of stuff on the radio. Of course, they, and the entire radio audience, condemned me and the magazines for supporting such sexual depictions and graphic, wanton violence.

Several days after that show, I obtained a copy of *New Look* magazine. It came as no surprise to see that the photo that was described in such detail on the radio was not at all like the religious fanatics said it was. You see, I've learned that these people will lie and use all sorts of deceptive tactics to sway public opinion.

Across America, callers to talk shows ask me the same tired and worn questions. Additionally, they continue to present the same half-truths and outright lies that I accepted for so long. For the most part, these people refuse to really look at their beliefs with an open mind, and thus they remain enslaved to them.

Often they attempt to defend the myth that this is a Christian nation. I usually reply, "America is a great nation, but it is open to people of all religions, or none at all, not just Christians." Without a doubt, the question I'm asked most often on the air is why I left the ministry and am no longer a Bible-believing Christian. That, of course, is difficult to answer in twenty seconds. Maxx Hackett, of WGOW, in Chattanooga, Tennessee, was the first talk-show host to suggest that I put my story in a book.

In the first five months after going on the air I conducted a whopping 185 radio interviews. Pretty soon I figured out how to get the bookings myself, and since then, that's what I have done. While the pace has let up some, as of this writing I've done more than 500 shows in the past five years in the United States and Canada. And yes, I still get anxious before an interview.

Some of the shows were nationally syndicated, so our message has effectively reached every state. Once, I did an interview in Adelaide, Australia, and because of the International Dateline, I appeared on Australian radio a day ahead of the date here.

Some stations, especially smaller ones, tape the radio interviews and play them again and again. KDSU, in Fargo, North Dakota does this. Every time I receive a bunch of letters from North Dakota and northwestern Minnesota, I know KDSU replayed my interview again.

Not every interview produces the results one might expect. I looked forward to being on the air with two of New York's most well-known talk-show hosts. When I did a short interview with Bob Grant on WABC, he spent most of the time making fun of my name "Skipp." "What kind of a grown man would have a name like 'Skipp'?" he said repeatedly. He allowed me, though, to explain my views on the separation of church and state without interruption. All I can suppose is that he agreed with my point of view. I received just a handful of letters from that interview.

The other New York talk-show host was the venerable Barry Farber. Farber is multilingual and quite brilliant in many ways. For instance, watching Farber do a restaurant commercial is fascinating. He simply pulls out his address book to ascertain the address of the restaurant scheduled on his radio log and ad-libs the whole damn commercial. He's so good that when he's finished, you're ready to hop in your car to go down and enjoy a sumptuous dinner at that particular restaurant.

Barbara and I journeyed to the Big Apple where I appeared on Barry Farber's late-night program. What a big disappointment. Farber apparently hadn't been briefed on who I was or what I was there to talk about. After we finally got into a discussion on the separation of church and state, he kept talking about how much he liked Jerry Falwell. Then, three of the phone callers, obvious set-ups, promoted some guy's book, which had nothing to do with the evening's subject matter. Farber let them get away with it. And Farber rambled on, enjoying what he had to say. I didn't receive a single letter from the hour interview.

One of my most outstanding shows was with Al Rantel, when he was on Miami's WNWS. That lively show went on for an hour and a half, and Rantel promoted *The Freedom Writer* at the beginning of each segment. In the days that followed, the mail poured in, to the tune of over 100 letters. Many of these fine people have become avid *Freedom Writer* supporters.

Miami's radio market is extremely competitive. I've had producers in Miami book me only if I promised their station an exclusive interview.

Neil Rogers, on WINZ at the time, and I were strangely in tune. The two times Neil's producer called me to book a show, Barbara and I had plans to be in Miami at that exact date. So, I did those shows in the studio with Neil. Neil Rogers is totally irreverent, and a lot of fun.

One event earned me my Andy Warhol fifteen minutes of fame award. As a sort of tongue-in-check response over the brouhaha concerning the U.S. Supreme Court's decision allowing flag burning, I developed a fire-retardant flag. That got more press than I thought was possible, and I used it to point out that freedom in America is so great that we can even burn the very symbol of our freedom, if we wish. The best reason not to burn the flag is because we can.

After I introduced my flame-retardant flag, just prior to the July 4 weekend in 1989, I conducted over fifty interviews in three days, thirty-six of them on the first day alone. Of the thirty-six interviews, twenty-eight were with either individual radio or television stations, or networks; the rest were with newspaper reporters. I was tethered to the phone for a tedious 15 hours that day. In order to go to the bathroom, I had to take the phone off the hook. In that three-day period I spoke to virtually every radio and TV network in the United States, including the wire service's radio news bureaus.

The *New York Times,* in their "Topics of The Times" on the editorial page, wrote:

> The Supreme Court's decision that the Constitution protects flag-burning has evoked an extraordinary number of responses—no one of which is as peculiarly American as that of Skipp Porteous of Great Barrington, Mass.
>
> Mr. Porteous, a man who knows a market opportunity when he sees one, bought a batch of flags from a Boston manufacturer and treated them with a fire-retardant. Now he's selling them for $10 apiece, and says the proceeds will go toward a commemoration of the ratification of the Bill of Rights he's planning for later this year.
>
> In producing a flag that defies ignition, Mr. Porteous displays a grand old trait: Yankee ingenuity. He displays something else, too. In contrast to those now spouting heated nonsense in Congress, he seems the epitome of cool common sense.

Congress went ahead and passed a law outlawing flag-burning. However, the U.S. Supreme Court struck down the law as unconstitutional.

Over the past five years I've debated a number of religious-right leaders on the radio. They've included Donald Wildmon and his son Tim; Mel Gabler, the Texas textbook censor; Tim LaHaye; and a host of others who are perhaps less well known to the average person.

Television has been another story. While, as I mentioned previously, I've done "People Are Talking" on WBZ in Boston, and "9BP" [Nine Broadcast Plaza] on WWOR, and a few other local and national shows, the most interesting has been "The Morton Downey, Jr., Show." I'll elaborate on this in the next chapter.

Now, as far as really getting a point across, television is often futile. On the other hand, to receive recognition while shopping in the supermarket, TV is great. After doing four "Morton Downey, Jr., Shows," complete strangers come up to me and say, "Excuse me, but weren't you on television?" I'm convinced that not one of them had any idea of why I was there or what position I took on anything.

While I still do radio interviews on a regular basis, *The Freedom Writer* has been focusing on print media for the past year or so; however, I prefer the immediacy of radio. For instance, when Pat Robertson was running for President, we obtained his campaign schedule and followed him around the country, from city to city. Whenever I could, I scheduled interviews in cities at the same time Robertson was there campaigning. Of course as a non-profit, tax-exempt organization, we aren't allowed to oppose or endorse candidates. So, I simply told radio audiences—in his own words—where Robertson stood on various issues. (We have a massive collection of original Robertson material, including video tapes of hundreds of his "700 Club" shows, audio tapes, and written material. So, we know where he really stands on just about everything.)

When Robertson arrived in New York, WABC taped an interview with him. Then they called me and told me when the tape was to be aired so that I could listen and respond. Then they interviewed me and aired my response the next morning.

In Boston, WRKO's Jerry Williams invited Robertson to his studio for a live interview. At the same time, he invited me to come out and appear with Robertson. I went to Boston, but, unfortunately, Robertson refused to come on the air with me.

The other aspect of the immediacy of radio is that I often respond to late-breaking stories. We have CNN on in our office all day long. If the Supreme Court, for instance, hands down a decision on a church/state case, I know about it right away. I'll then pull our files on the case, or whatever matter or person the story might be about, and just wait for the phone to ring. Invariably, some radio station will call for my comments about the late-breaking news. During the televangelist scandals, I received quite a few calls. In fact, CNN called me for information about Jimmy Swaggart the night before the story broke.

Until now, all the radio stations I've mentioned were secular. By and large, the media tends to be liberal, which, of course, has been to our advantage. Now and then, though, I have to tangle with an ultra-right-wing talk-show host.

One popular fundamentalist radio program interviewed me after the *Washington Post* published a story on *The Freedom Writer*. The program was Dr. James Dobson's "Family News in Focus." It was a straight-forward, nonconfrontational interview, which I enjoyed doing. The program is aired on hundreds of stations, and I welcomed the opportunity to speak frankly to the people I once sided with.

A later chapter consists entirely of a typical, fast-paced, radio interview. While most shows are just an hour, this one lasted two hours, and could have gone on longer had I not had other commitments. Once, on WBAL in Baltimore, because of the number of callers, I did three straight hours.

Radio has been the greatest tool for building our mailing list and worth every penny of our initial investment in the medium. Word-of-mouth advertising is a close second, followed by print media. Television is in a category of its own. In the next chapter we get into the medium that has been dubbed "a vast wasteland."

21

Meet Morton Downey, Jr.

While my television experience is limited, it has certainly offered some worthwhile highlights. By the beginning of 1988, I had been on television only a few times. And although I didn't particularly care about doing television, I knew it was a good way to reach a lot of people. So, I started watching TV talk shows. Several times a week I watched Oprah, Donahue, Geraldo, and Sally. One night I turned on the TV (which was unusual, because other than the news, I hardly ever watch television) and saw a ranting, raving maniac. I watched this guy work his audience into a frenzy, then literally throw his guests off the show. I couldn't believe it. I learned that his name was Morton Downey, Jr. With flashing teeth, a cigarette in his hand, and a loud mouth, the ultraconservative Downey castigated guest after guest. Well, I decided his was one show I definitely did not want to be on.

Then, early in April, a producer from WWOR, Downey's station, called and asked if I could come down to New Jersey to debate Jerry Falwell on "The Morton Downey, Jr." Show. I couldn't resist tangling with Falwell again, so without a second thought I said yes. As usual, Falwell would appear via a satellite linkup with his Lynchburg, Virginia headquarters.

In the green room (where people wait before appearing on TV, and called that regardless of the color of the room) I met two other allies who would appear with me. They were Sharon Churcher and Dr. Edmund Cohen. Sharon writes a column called "USA Confidential" for *Penthouse*. I'd talked to Sharon on the phone on several occasions, relative to the material which we regularly give to the media, including *Penthouse*. Edmund Cohen is the author of *The Mind of the Bible Believer*. Ed is a lawyer and psychologist, and though he has a Jewish background, he was a born-again Christian for a short while.

After a producer briefed us about the show's "no holds barred" format, the three of us took turns in the makeup room. Then, moments before air-time, we passed through a metal detector which scanned each guest and member of the audience for weapons.

As the show kicked off, Mort dashed into the studio, greeted by the kind of macho cheers usually reserved for football games or wrestling matches. While his shows were often male-dominated, this night's audience looked more balanced.

Pathetically, Falwell was allowed to pontificate for the entire first half of the program. I suspect this was because WWOR paid for the satellite linkup—which costs big bucks, and they felt they should avail themselves of Falwell's presence—and his ability to draw an audience. Meanwhile, we (the other guests) and the audience sat there bored out of our minds.

When the second half of the hour show finally began, Mort said, "Let me introduce Skipp Porteous—a former Pentecostal minister, a practicing fundamentalist for twenty-two years, a minister for ten of those years, a former radio evangelist, and a self-appointed expert on the religious right movement."

From here, I'll relate my portion of the segment as it happened. As we go along, my commentary about the dialogue appears in brackets. Ellipses (. . .) indicate either a pause, an interruption, or a change in the conversation's direction, not any omission of dialogue.

MORT: Now, as a former Pentecostal minister, you are very critical, I understand . . . what has turned you away from the movement?

SKIPP: A lot of things, Mort. And as I look back now, I feel like I've abandoned a sinking ship. I'm glad I left the movement.

MORT: You thought you could improve the movement away from it rather than from inside it?

SKIPP: I thought they'd do fine without me . . . And I guess they have. When you look at the Bakkers, and Swaggart, I think TV evangelism, at this point, is totally discredited because of the things that have happened. And I'm really glad I left it.

I saw child abuse in the name of Biblical discipline. I was in a Charismatic branch of loonies, where I saw exorcisms and phony healings, and these kinds of things.

MORT: What child abuse did you see?

SKIPP: I saw children beaten in the name of Biblical discipline, where scriptures were quoted . . .

MORT: Is this while you were in the Moonie movement?

SKIPP: No, I wasn't involved with the Moonies. I went to LIFE Bible College, which is Aimee Semple McPherson's school, and I became a Pentecostal. I believed in healing, exorcism . . . and I have to laugh now when I hear Swaggart say a demon attacked him—the spirit of lust. It's so ridiculous. Since I left, I've been able to get my mind back again—reason and logic, which I really lost for a long time, Mort.

MORT: How about it, Rev. Falwell? Did you hear what Skipp had to say? Is Skipp just another person who . . .

FALWELL: I find myself agreeing with a good bit of what I just heard. I have not lived in that segment of the evangelical society—the Pentecostal segment.

I don't think it's fair to broad brush all of Pentecostalism for the misconduct of a few, because, while I'm not a Pentecostal, I know many Pentecostals who are very, very wonderful people. But, I would comment on the statement that television evangelism is totally discredited because of the misconduct of Bakker and Swaggart. I disagree with that. I don't think that we . . . certainly Watergate, Chappaquiddick, Iran-Contra . . . these things certainly hurt politics, but we don't for a moment think that the White House, the Congress, the Judiciary, are relegated out of existence or discredited. We think they are damaged for a brief time, and likewise more recently in the world of business . . .

MORT: We're saying then, Reverend . . .

FALWELL: The cause of Christ is always injured when those who in the name of Jesus act differently than what they teach and preach . . .

SKIPP: Mort, I've got to disagree with that, because he is comparing TV evangelists—who claim they've got the unlimited power of God on their side—with politicians and Wall Street people. There's no comparison at all. These people, like Swaggart, claim the power of the Holy Ghost to keep you free from sin and immorality.

I read an article that Swaggart wrote recently on masturbation. He said the only way . . .

MORT: He probably would have been a lot better off if he . . . [laughter and applause from audience]

SKIPP: I agree, I agree. He claimed that through prayer and fasting and seeking God, he could cure these things, but look what it did to him. It didn't help him at all.

FALWELL: I don't disagree with you at all on the fact that the calling to the Gospel ministry should be, by far, the highest, the most accountable, because those who preach the Gospel—and there are four hundred thousand of them—should be held to a higher level of accountability, morally, and in every way.

[I wasn't referring to accountability, because they are only accountable if they preach against something, and then do it themselves. Fundamentalists tend to inextricably link morality with sex, while morality is so much broader. I was referring to the alleged spiritual power which Christians claim to have over "sin," while in reality they are just as vulnerable as the next person. Yet they won't admit it. When they "fall," they blame the devil.] But, what I'm saying, it is not fair to broad brush all four hundred thousand of these preachers of the Gospel with the misconduct of a few, any more than it would be fair to say that because Janet Cook won a Pulitzer Prize with the *Washington Post* that all journalists are bad. I think that's the point I'm trying to make.

MORT: Let me ask you Skipp. The Rev. Falwell tried to defend his reputation in his libel suit against Larry Flynt. I understand you supported the Supreme Court's decision. Now, how do you defend that kind of filth? C'mon, pal.

SKIPP: It's easy. Take the Bible, for instance, that Jerry likes to quote all the time. You have a story in Genesis . . . Genesis is used in every Sunday school in the nation. There is a story in Genesis 19 about a guy called Lot. The Bible calls Lot a "just" man. That means that Lot was a good man. Lot offered his two virgin daughters to a group of homosexual rapists. Well, the same . . .

MORT: If they were homosexual rapists, they obviously wouldn't want his daughters . . .

SKIPP: They wanted two [male] visitors that were in Lot's home. But, the point is, later on, Lot got so drunk that he had incest with his two virgin daughters . . . got them both pregnant, and yet the Bible calls Lot a "just" man. My problem with Jerry Falwell and the whole movement is that . . . now, I defend Jerry's right to use the book of Genesis, and the story of Lot—this pornographic story in his Sunday school . . .

MORT: You don't believe the Bible, do you?

SKIPP: No, I don't believe the Bible at all. Now I defend his right to use a pornographic book in his Sunday school, but why can't he defend my right to go to the corner convenience store to buy *Playboy*, *Penthouse*, or even *Hustler* if I want to? He doesn't defend that right.

FALWELL: Oh, I do! Yes, I defend your right to do that. I think you have the right to read anything you wish. My complaint is not with you, or any readers of pornography. My complaint is with persons who make a living, for example, Mr. Flynt, who make a living exploiting, for commerce, the bodies of women. And not only exploiting them and using them for commerce, but hurting families with the very obscene and vulgar product of their vain imaginations. I think that we have the right in this country to walk with our family into a grocery store and buy our groceries without having that kind of filth at the eye level of our five-year-old child.

SKIPP: You know, in my ministry I've seen more families broken up over fundamentalism . . .

MORT: Skipp, why do you refer to your past ministry when you don't even believe in the Bible. . .

FALWELL: Let me ask you . . .

SKIPP: The point I'm making . . . wait! The point is important! I've seen more families broken up over fundamentalism than from these erotic magazines that Jerry's talking about.

FALWELL: Were you ever a pastor or evangelist?

SKIPP: Yes, both.

FALWELL: How long ago did you stop, quit?

SKIPP: A good ten years ago.

FALWELL: At that time, did something bad happen? Did you lose your family or go through some terrible experience that caused you to be so bitter?

SKIPP: I went through a lot of experiences over twenty-two years. You know Word of Life ranch, Jerry. I started up there in 1956, the same year Pat Robertson was there. I was a Word of Life boxing champ.

It started there where I couldn't play ping pong on Sunday. I saw child abuse later on. I saw spiritual anti-Semitism . . . later on in the ministry. I mean, it was one thing after another.

MORT: You saw all these things, and yet you decided to become a minister?

FALWELL: What I'm hearing . . . I counsel a lot of former pastors, former evangelists . . .

SKIPP: I hope you don't try to counsel me, because I'm really not interested!

FALWELL: Well, I'd like to. I really think that your problem is not that God is bad or the Bible is bad, but you had some bad personal experiences. Maybe some people have hurt you, who were Christians. I don't know what happened, but I can tell you that if you really knew the Lord [Fundamentalists typically say that those who abandon born-again Christianity never knew God in the first place], and when you went to—I don't know LIFE [Bible] College, but if you really. . . . Now, I think you know the Bible. I've been hearing some things from you that are very accurate and well-discerned . . .

SKIPP: Like the pornographic Bible stories . . .

FALWELL: I don't think it's pornographic at all that God tells the truth. By the way, Lot who was—the word "just" means "justified"—he, like Mr. Swaggart, began, allegedly, a very sincere person. Later, God killed his [Lot's] wife, in judgment for the kind of sin he lived in. [It makes no sense for God to kill Lot's wife for something that Lot did. If God killed anybody, he should have killed Lot. Anyway, Falwell erred, because Lot's wife died in a hail of fire and brimstone before, not after, Lot's incestuous affair with his daughters.] But, what I'm trying to say to you is that I have to believe that if you really were in the faith, I can't believe you're very happy now fighting against what you once believed in. [Don't kid yourself, Jerry.]

MORT: Skipp, what are you doing now?

SKIPP: I'm doing this, right here . . .

MORT: You go around the country . . .

SKIPP: We produce a national newsletter called *The Freedom Writer*, which has members in all fifty states, and we expose, in their own words, people like Jerry Falwell, Pat Robertson, and all the. . . . You know, I didn't leave angry. I left the movement happy, but when I got away from it and started to look back, and saw some of the movements that I was involved with in the early 70s, with Dean Jones and Pat Boone, to try to take over America for the Lord . . .

MORT: Those guys are bad, too? Dean Jones, Pat Boone?

SKIPP: I'm not saying they're "bad." I'm not saying anyone's "bad." I practiced the credo, "Serve the Lord by running for public office." In 1984, I saw the Republican Convention practically taken over by fundamentalists and evangelicals, and I felt that I had a responsibility to share what I know from the inside . . .

FALWELL: Do you have a wife and children?

SKIPP: Yes.

FALWELL: Have you been married more than once?

SKIPP: Yes.

FALWELL: Was that first breakup of your marriage . . . I just . . . I'm a counselor . . . did you leave your wife for somebody else, then, leave the ministry at the same time?

SKIPP: [laughing]: Wait a minute! Wait a minute! Jerry, I'm not looking for a counselor, and I don't know what your fees are . . .

FALWELL: It's all free . . .

SKIPP: Free! Hey! The last thing I got free from Falwell was my Moral Majority membership card! [Which came unsolicited in the mail.]

FALWELL: I'm just trying to tell you, I think the problem is not that the Lord failed you. I think you failed him back there somewhere . . . [The audience, seeing through Falwell's shallowness, loudly booed him at this point. I've never claimed that God failed me. Nobody ever failed anybody. Since walking away, I've experienced growth and satisfaction, not failure. As a fundamentalist Christian, I was taught —and I taught it to others—that one should grow into maturity. And this is where maturity has brought me. Perhaps those Christians who can't accept this suffer from pangs of jealousy, because by finding my way out, I found what they still seek.] I think if you're checking the background of others, I think that maybe somebody needs to check yours a little.

If you wanted to start, for example, Roman Catholics Anonymous, you would find a lot of disenchanted former Catholics. Phil Donahue would probably be the president of it for you, who would start a chapter in every state. But, that doesn't mean the Roman Catholic church is all bad, or that the priests are all bad. It means that maybe there were some bad experiences. You could start a Judaism

Anonymous . . .

MORT: Skipp, during the break I'll take you back in my room and give you a little counseling. [With that, we took a break. When we came back, Sharon Churcher and Edmund Cohen participated in the program. Just before the program concluded, Downey turned to me again.]

MORT: Skipp, on an average hour-long religious television show, how much of that show is with the message of God, and how much is for the message of the pocketbook?

SKIPP: Well, we tape all these shows every Sunday, Swaggart and Falwell and so forth . . .

MORT: How much time?

SKIPP: Jerry Falwell spends 45 percent, or twenty-six minutes of every hour pitching for funds.

MORT: Was that on one particular show, or on an average?

SKIPP: This was the whole summer, last summer.

MORT: How about the others?

SKIPP: Well, we gave Jerry the Panhandler of the Month award last summer because he spent 45 percent, and Oral Roberts spent 15 percent, and Jimmy Swaggart spent 9 percent . . .

FALWELL: I'd like to respond to that. We make about three hundred television programs a year. The only day we're not making a one-hour television program is on Saturday, and for the past year we averaged five minutes and thirteen seconds, out of sixty minutes, in fund raising, which is about the amount dedicated to that in the average one-hour Sunday morning, 11 A.M. church service. We try to keep compatible with the local church service. [Almost everyone, including Jerry Falwell, knows that an "hour" television program actually ranges from fifty-four minutes to fifty-eight minutes. After taping ten weeks of several evangelists' TV programs, and timing their fund raising appeals with a stop watch, we stand by our figures.]

In closing, Mort gave Rev. Falwell thirty seconds for a concluding statement, which time Falwell used well to preach his fundamentalist's beliefs. Then, Mort told his audience, "There's nothing religious about me, but I like that man Falwell."

This was typical Morton Downey, Jr. rhetoric. Unknown to the national television audience, during one of the breaks, Mort positioned his backside before the TV monitor on which Falwell appeared from Lynchburg, and playing up to his studio audience, urged Falwell to kiss his ass. Of course, Falwell was unaware of Mort's antics.

After that show, I really didn't expect to be on Mort's show again, but I was invited back three more times. The next time was after WWOR producers decided to take "The Morton Downey, Jr. Show" on the road. Instead of Secaucus, New Jersey, my next show would be taped at Harlem's venerable Apollo Theater. After a stretch limo picked us up at my mother-in-law's in New York, and took her, Barbara, my youngest daughter, and a friend up to Harlem, I was escorted to the dressing rooms. The peach-colored walls of my dressing room were decorated with framed photographs of some of the performers I had seen at the Apollo twenty-five years earlier. How strange and wonderful it felt to be there.

Around this time, we had been opposing the fundamentalist's national hysteria about the movie *The Last Temptation of Christ*. We saw the elaborate campaign against this movie, along with the typical fundamentalist lies, as a fund-raising ploy by the religious right. So, this Downey show would ostensibly explore all sides of this issue.

Over a thousand people, mostly black, packed the Apollo for the taping of two of Mort's shows that night. Mort was equipped with material disseminated by the Rev. Donald Wildmon. He read from this material in an attempt to convince the audience that the *The Last Temptation of Christ* was blasphemous. [Actually, anyone who bothered to find out what the movie was really about discovered a beautiful, touching story.] Well, Mort—even though I correctly insisted that the things he was reading were not in the film—convinced the audience that the movie was bad, and that I was there as the devil's emissary.

Mort accused me of lying about the contents of the movie. He said that he knew I wasn't telling the truth, because "I saw it," he claimed. I didn't believe for a second that he saw it, because he was giving out Wildmon's inaccurate information.

Appearing with me was Rob Sherman, national spokesperson for Madalyn Murray O'Hair's American Atheists. While Rob was, of course, on my side in defense of the film, I felt somewhat uncomfortable with his tactics. For instance, he displayed a cartoon of Santa Claus and two elves hanging on crosses. While this might be humorous in some settings, I didn't think it was funny on the stage of the Apollo, before

1,000 agitated spectators.

During a break, Mort, who had an empty coffee cup in his hand, approached Rob, who was sitting next to me. He asked Rob for his permission to pour a cup of water on his head during the next segment. Rob readily agreed to go along with the stunt.

Because of the presence of us infidels, Mort easily played upon the outrage of his audience. While he worked the crowd, he moved about the stage with the coffee cup in his hand—which was now filled with water.

"Do you want me to make a Christian out of this atheist Jew?" he barked to the audience, in reference to Rob Sherman. The audience went wild as Downey approached Sherman.

"I baptize you in the name of the Father, the Son, and the Holy Ghost," Mort pronounced as he poured the water on Sherman's head. Of course, Rob squirmed around and pretended to cover his head from the assault.

Not long after this pitiful scene, a fight broke out in the audience, right behind where my family and friend were sitting. A dozen burly security personnel descended on the area of the fight, with Mort and a cameraman in pursuit. For a moment, I prepared to bring my family up on the stage with me. The perpetrators, though, were quickly hauled off.

After the show ended, and the "techies" were taking our microphones off, Mort stood at the edge of the stage promoting the next show, which was to feature two opposing black civil-rights leaders.

"If you think this show was hot," Mort thundered, "wait until you see the next show! We've got the Rev. Al Sharpton and Roy Innes. So, stick around folks, it's gonna be hot!"

As I started for the stage door, Roy Innes pushed through. "Hi, Roy," I said, and pumped his hand.

The next day, the New York tabloids showed front-page pictures of Roy Innes decking Al Sharpton on "The Morton Downey, Jr. Show." I wasn't surprised to see the photos of Sharpton going over backwards, as Innes stood before him with his arms outstretched. After all, Mort said it was going to be a hot show.

About two weeks later, a Downey producer called me again and said that my defense of *The Last Temptation of Christ* had been justified, and that Mort was wrong. Would I come back again to defend the film? Well, of course, I would, because I knew I was right. I also knew, however, that "The Morton Downey, Jr. Show" was owned by MCA, producers of *The Last Temptation of Christ*. Without a doubt, someone from Hollywood called Secaucus to find out what Mort was up to. Nevertheless, truth is truth, and I didn't care who owned what. By now, I had seen the film at a special showing in New York, where I had the opportunity to greet the film's director, Martin Scorsese. Seeing the film confirmed to me that it was definitely not what its detractors said it was.

Back in WWOR's green room, I was met by "The Morton Downey, Jr. Show" producer, Bill Boggs. He told me that he and Mort had just returned from seeing *The Last Temptation of Christ*, and that they were both favorably impressed with the movie. While I was glad to hear this, it confirmed my hunch that Mort had lied to me at the Apollo when he said he saw the movie (which was why he agreed with Rev. Wildmon's assessment of the film.)

On the air, Mort talked about the program we taped at the Apollo, and before his national television audience, he said that he'd been wrong about the film, while Skipp Porteous correctly defended it. He told the audience that he just saw *The Last Temptation of Christ*, and as a result, he had "a new love for Jesus."

My last show with Mort concerned child evangelists. I appeared to maintain that these young people are exploited by their parents. One of the Strode children—the kids who were booted out of public school for preaching loudly on the school grounds—and their father also appeared on that show. As usual, the show was lively, but by now Mort's ratings were slipping.

Soon, though, Morton Downey, Jr. was back in the headlines. During a visit to San Francisco, he claimed that some skinheads attacked him in the airport men's room. Appearing before the cameras disfigured, he said the attackers chopped his hair with scissors, and drew swastikas on his face and clothes. No skinheads were seen by anyone else, and no charges were ever pressed against anyone for the alleged assault. By now, Mort's credibility and ratings had slipped so low that his national program was cancelled.

At times, Mort played the obnoxious showman; nevertheless, I liked the man. Although he usually was my antagonist on the air, he greeted me with an embrace in the studio dressing room. While at the height of his fame, he wrote an autobiography called *Mort! Mort! Mort!*, which outlined his conservative beliefs. Mort signed a copy for me. In it he wrote, "Skipp, Kick ass, pal! Mort, Jr."

OK, Mort.

22

Sound Off

On Friday evening, January 4, 1991, I appeared as a guest on "Sound Off," with Paul Gonzales on WSB, Atlanta, Georgia. The reason for the interview was to discuss a story published in the December 1990 issue of *The Freedom Writer*. The story, called "The New Radical Religious Right," was based on some of the material in the first chapter of this book.

While the bantering on this show is typical of the hundreds of radio interviews I've conducted in the past few years, the content of this particular program is especially significant. And, as a surprise twist, the wrap-up was particularly satisfying.

The dialogue is unedited, except in the rare instances where clarification is necessary. Of course, the commercials, news, and weather have been deleted.

OFF THE AIR, JUST PRIOR TO AIR TIME

>PAUL: Hold on and I'll be right with you . . .
>SKIPP: How long do you figure this'll be?
>PAUL: Well, would you go at least an hour?
>SKIPP: Oh yeah. Sure.
>PAUL: And maybe even more?
>SKIPP: Maybe more.

PAUL: Let's go, because if we get cookin', this'll be a hot show. Atmospheric conditions have been real good, too. I've been getting calls from Canada lately. So, hold on . . .

PAUL: Well good evening America, from Florida all the way on up to Canada, and all of the Free World, and all of the nine planets of the universe, this is "Sound Off," on the 50,000-watt, clear-channel voice of the South.

We have a hot show to get into tonight. As a matter of fact, in a moment we're going to tell you about a religious group that advocates for homosexuals, abortionists, and adulterers, all to be executed —not necessarily in that order.

We do have a delay system here. I'm actually speaking to you seven seconds behind time. So, if people think they can call in to say dirty words, you know, like "doo-doo" and stuff like that, you can't do that.

Right now, I'd like to welcome back a very interesting guest, not only on this show, but he appears on radio talk shows throughout the United States, one of the favored guests . . . look at that, they're already calling in!

I'd like to welcome back to our WSB program, Skipp Porteous. Skipp is the editor of *The Freedom Writer* newsletter, the national newsletter that defends the separation of church and state. I just got the latest issue in the mail a couple of days ago, and there's a story in there about a group called the Reconstructionists. As I mentioned before, these people want homosexuals and people like this put to death, and they're serious. And, Skipp, I'd like to welcome you to AM 750 WSB in Atlanta, tonight. Skipp, how are ya?

SKIPP: I'm fine, Paul, and it's good to be with you.

PAUL: Tell people about what you do, for those who haven't heard you on the radio before.

SKIPP: We do a number of things. Primarily, we monitor the activities of the religious right. We have one of the biggest, most active services in the country for monitoring the religious right. That's how we come up with these kinds of stories we're talking about tonight— Reconstructionism. And, we defend the separation of church and state. We've been involved in some legal battles where there were prayers or Bible-reading in schools, or other things that were truly illegal. We try to let the media know about the information we uncover. And our research is first-hand. Everything in this article we're speaking about was researched by our group here, first-hand. We interviewed the people we're speaking about, the people who want to execute gays and abortionists. So it's not just something we've gotten in the mail or heard from somebody else. This is right from the horse's mouth. It's really scary, you know.

We started in 1984, around the time the Moral Majority was really coming on the scene. And most people thought that when the Moral Majority rose and fell, and then the TV evangelists fell—and Swaggart fell from Grace, or whatever her name was—they thought it was over. It's not. The religious right has quietly been born again. It's more frightening than ever.

PAUL: Well, who started this so-called Reconstructionist movement?

SKIPP: A fellow named R. J. Rushdoony is considered the father of Reconstructionism; he's a former Presbyterian minister. And since 1964 this fellow, who's seventy-four years old now, has been laboring quietly writing documents and greatly influencing the church. People don't realize this, but many of the books on Christian activism found in Christian bookstores are written by Reconstructionists, like John Whitehead, Donald Wildmon, Franky Schaeffer, D. James Kennedy, Tim and Beverly LaHaye. These people are prolific writers. They have a great influence on American Christianity and they are all members of this group called the Coalition On Revival, which is a Reconstructionist front.

PAUL: I mentioned that these people [Reconstructionists] want to execute homosexuals, and even people who play around on their husbands and wives; now, they actually came out and said this?

SKIPP: Absolutely. And, you know, that would be a disaster for Pentecostal churches. I've pastored Pentecostal churches, and been a member of a number of them, and in almost every one, in the music department, or the choir, or the band, or at the piano, there were many gays. Even though Pentecostal ministers will rail against them, and preach sermons against homosexuality, they know very well that in their own churches there are many gays, because the ones that are there just happen to be very talented in music and what-not. So, if they were going around executing homosexuals, it would go right into the church.

Yes, they come right out and say this. I spoke to a Reverend Leonard Coppes in Denver, Colorado. He's part of a group of one hundred and eighty Presbyterian churches, and he said, "It's not what we think"

—I'm paraphrasing what he said—"but it's the Bible. The Bible says that homosexuals, if they don't repent, should be put to death." He said, "It's a matter of what God says."

This is what I find often, Paul; I found it when I was a minister myself, that we're unwilling to take responsibility for our own prejudices, so we quote the Bible. That's what they're doing. They quote the Bible because they're bigoted; they're prejudiced against gays or other types of people. And they use the Bible as their shield, as their weapon, instead of coming right out and saying, "I'm a bigot."

PAUL: Let me ask you this: you mention this guy Coppes, who has one hundred and eighty Presbyterian churches?

SKIPP: Yes, it's a sect of Presbyterian churches called the Orthodox Presbyterian church. Now, you have D. James Kennedy in Florida, who's a Presbyterian. He's a member of this organization called COR, the Coalition On Revival. Now, I don't say that every single person who's a member of this group believes that gays should be executed, but they all run together and believe that the Bible should be the law of the land. They're very clear about that. They say that the Bible should rule the church and the state.

PAUL: Wait a minute, now. How can these people consider themselves to be Americans and want, what this sounds like you're saying here, a theocracy?

SKIPP: Well, I hate to say it, Paul, but many Christians, Bible-believing Christians, really do not believe in the Bill of Rights. They put the Bible above the Bill of Rights, and they see the Bible as the supreme law of the land. And believe me, if they could do away with the Bill of Rights, they would. I mean our Bill of Rights is in danger by these groups.

What's scary about this, Paul, is that these people are in it for the long haul. It's something they don't plan to achieve overnight. As you may have read in the [*Freedom Writer*] article, one of their goals is to Christianize the state of California. And they've targeted two counties, one in northern, and one in southern California, to start. And beyond that, the article didn't mention it, but they also have sixty major cities in America, including Atlanta, in which they want to take over the city government, the city council, and the county government.

PAUL: You're kidding!

SKIPP: This would include the sheriff's offices, and they believe in not only state militias, but county militias to help give their government, the Christian government, a government with force. Now, this is what they told me, I'm not making this up. And so they want to elect their own representatives in the city councils. Now, in the last election they won several seats in northern California, just as they had planned to do. They're extremely well organized.

Collectively, the people we're speaking about represent literally millions of American Christians. Now, I would say that most Christians do not know a thing about what I am talking about. They're just not aware of these Christian leaders' plans.

PAUL: I know, people have been calling the station all day, wanting to know if I was joking when I did my promotional announcement today about this.

SKIPP: Yeah, I would suggest that any of your listeners write to us for this copy of *The Freedom Writer*. There are one hundred and thirty-five major Christian activists who signed a document committing themselves—"until the day we die," they said—toward these goals. And we listed twenty or so of them. We have the whole list here.

PAUL: We're gonna tell people how to get that newsletter in just a moment . . . and, my goodness, we must have hit some buttons, because I haven't, you noticed, asked for any phone calls, and yet, every single line in Atlanta and all over the country is tied up. So, if you want to get through, you'll probably have to wait ten or fifteen minutes. But those of you on the lines, we're going to get to you . . . Robert, Ed, Zack, Ken, Chris, the rest of you, stand by.

Our guest is speaking to us live from chilly Massachusetts, and he is Skipp Porteous of *The Freedom Writer*, the national newsletter defending the separation of church and state.

This is Paul Gonzales, always trying to find something new, that you haven't heard about, and present it to you.

COMMERCIAL BREAK

AM 750 WSB, and we're talking about a real fun topic here for a Friday night, the execution of homosexuals, adulterers, fornicators, and people who have abortions. And our guest to tell us about the so-called Reconstructionist movement is Skipp Porteous.

Skipp, I understand, and I mentioned this to you off the air, that one of the members of this so-called Reconstructionist movement will be calling us later on from right here in Atlanta. So, you're right, this movement is alive and well here in Atlanta, Georgia.

SKIPP: Great, I can hardly wait.

PAUL: I was just sitting here thinking about the percentages if these people could get what they want. I would say that probably in this country 50 percent of the people have had sex outside of marriage. So we're talking, let's just say 50 million people. And then 10 percent, from what the experts say, of the population in America is homosexual. So we're talking, what, another 20 million. How many people commit adultery? Well, let's just round it off and say 50 million. Here, we've got 120 million people. Now, Adolf Hitler executed 6 million Jews, as well as other groups of people. If you think about it, these people want to kill more people than Hitler.

SKIPP: It's really incredible. It's really hard to imagine. I think they would be going after the hard-core crop first. But when you look at countries like Iran, Iraq, or even Saudi Arabia, Saudi Arabia has no religious freedom at all, and they execute people over there without a second thought, for religious reasons, for using drugs, for fornicating, for committing adultery. It's second nature to them, it seems. And they are a theocracy. That's what this country could become if we allow it to happen. It's just beyond my imagination, but when I see groups that are so well-organized, and they have groups in every single state, and they are planning to do this, then I'm appalled. Yet, I've done this research and I know others who are researching these things, and it's true. We, as Americans who love our pluralistic society, who are tolerant of other faiths, need to stand up against this and say, "This is enough. This group is going too far."

PAUL: Let's start racing through the calls here. Robert in midtown is gonna be first. Robert, you're on AM 750 WSB.

CALLER: Yeah, hello Paul. I usually call most of your UFO shows.

PAUL: Well, these people are kind of alien, too, when you get right down to it.

CALLER: Definitely.

PAUL: So, what do you think about this, Robert? Have you ever heard of such a thing?

CALLER: I haven't heard of these groups specifically, but I kind of knew they were out there. It's kind of scary when you think about it. Skipp, I think you were sort of saying this, too: fundamentalism in any guise is probably dangerous, be it Christian or Muslim or Sikh.

PAUL: Bob, in Clinton, Tennessee, you're on AM 750 WSB.

CALLER: Yeah, I had a question for Skipp, there. The question is: I understand that you get funded by *Playboy*. Is that true?

SKIPP: We received a grant several years ago of five hundred bucks from *Playboy*. Since then I've asked for a lot more and haven't gotten it, and I wish I could.

CALLER: OK, and also, the last time you were on the show you were kind of taking a lambaste at the American Family Association. Isn't it true that they almost had you arrested for false credentials when you went down there and presented yourself in a false image to those people?

SKIPP: No, they didn't have any . . . [interrupted]

CALLER: In fact, the second day you were there they had local police authorities there?

SKIPP: Yeah, but they didn't arrest me, did they?

CALLER: No, they didn't arrest you, but you certainly got caught in your little act there. And the names you mentioned—you mentioned Doctor James Kennedy and you mentioned some other names, the LaHayes—and I would venture to say if they found out that you were propagating the idea that they were saying that they wanted to see homosexuals executed, and people who were acting out of marriage executed, they would be very upset because that's a bald-faced lie. I read their materials, and they have never, ever, advocated any such practice.

SKIPP: Have you ever heard of the Coalition On Revival?

CALLER: I sure have!

SKIPP: All right. Are they members of this?

CALLER: Apparently, you say they are.

SKIPP: Do you know the Coalition On Revival advocates the things I've been saying?

CALLER: Well, what I'm saying is the names you mentioned, those people do not specifically advocate, nor have they ever advocated that. And I'm not totally convinced you've got the proper context of what the Coalition On Revival is saying.

SKIPP: Well, I talked to . . . [interrupted]

CALLER: You use these names and slander them; it's just ridiculous.

SKIPP: Everything I'm saying tonight I got from the horse's mouth, from Jay Grimstead, Doctor Jay Grimstead, who is the head of the Coalition On Revival. He told me these things. Now, maybe Kennedy, maybe the LaHayes, maybe Rev. Wildmon do not advocate these things. I don't know what they advocate for they won't talk to me, of course. [I made seven unsuccessful attempts to talk to Rev. Donald Wildmon specifically about these things. Once, when his brother, Allen, came on the phone and found out it was me, he hung up on me.] But they belong to this organization that does advocate these things. Now, if you were a member of the Nazi party, people would say that you believe in killing Jews, wouldn't they?

CALLER: I think that when you start mentioning names and assuming that they are going along with this advocacy, which is, once again, I think taken out of context by yourself, I would really consider that you think out before you start slandering these names on nation-wide radio.

SKIPP: I'm telling you what this organization believes, and I'm telling you who belongs. Now, if they don't believe these things . . . [interrupted]

CALLER: You're leading us to assume that these people support that stand . . . [interrupted]

SKIPP: . . . then they should quit it, if they don't.

CALLER: Well, once again, I'm saying you don't have the right to try and make the American public believe that these people . . . [interrupted]

SKIPP: You mean you're denying my freedom of speech?

CALLER: Pardon?

SKIPP: You're denying my freedom of speech?

CALLER: No, I'm just saying that you need to weigh your words and present them in a way, and say specifically, that you don't know whether or not.

SKIPP: I know what the Coalition on Revival believes, and what they advocate. They told me.

CALLER: Well, that's like saying that a member of a state government which believes in capital punishment—if a state government approves of capital punishment—that means that every legislator, because he's a member of that governmental body, supports capital punishment. That's not valid.

SKIPP: Well, state government gets paid . . . I wouldn't belong to an organization that advocated these things. I would quit immediately, as soon as I found out.

PAUL: And ding, that's the end of round one. And we'll be back with our second round in just a moment. Those of you waiting patiently on the lines, we will get to you, but I want to remind you, you've got to get to your point. Now, that guy there did a nice job of debating. If you do as well as he did, I'll give you a couple of minutes, but you've gotta get right to the point. Quick question or quick comment, because we've got a terrible backup already. Backup's already thirty minutes. Number in Atlanta is 872-0750. Outside the area 1-800-WSB-TALK.

[off the air] That was good, that was real good. Hold on, I'll be right back.

"This is your chance to sound off, with Paul Gonzales. To be part of our show, call . . . [number] Now, here's Paul Gonzales."

PAUL: And my guest is Skipp Porteous, and he is the editor of *The Freedom Writer* newsletter, the national newsletter that defends the separation of church and state. We're going to tell you how you can get yourself a copy of this a little later on, and you can read more about the Reconstructionist movement. And there's a list of these folks who belong to this COR organization, the Coalition On Revival. And our guest was very careful in saying just because these people are members does not necessarily mean that they do want to execute gays. But he also said that if you join the Nazi party, it's assumed that you, at least in some way, support not liking Jews.

And our next call is gonna be Will, in Loren Heights. Hello Will, you're on AM 750 WSB.

CALLER: Hey Paul, great show!

PAUL: Thank you, Will.

CALLER: Skipp, Porteous is a real old American name, isn't it?

SKIPP: Yeah, it goes back to England, actually, but we've been around for a while.

CALLER: I agree with a lot of what you are saying, but I think it's improper to put Wildmon in the category of being some sort of religious scholar. I'm interested in hearing what your understanding is of the Knights of Malta having the United States divided up into three colonies? You know, it's not just the Protestant religious right . . .

[interrupted]

SKIPP: Yeah, I'm a former fundamentalist. I was a Pentecostal minister for ten years, and I specialize in the Protestant religious right. There is a whole other aspect as to what the Catholic church is doing, and I don't get into that too much, but I follow what you're saying.

PAUL: Thank you, Will. Skipp, now you're obviously no longer a member of the Pentecostal religion, but are you still a member of the Christian faith?

SKIPP: No, I would say, Paul, that you've got a bona fide secular humanist on this show tonight.

PAUL: OK. Of course, you're in the company of a lot of well-liked people.

SKIPP: Tim LaHaye said that we're not fit to hold office. He said that no secular humanist should hold any office in America.

PAUL: There are some famous secular humanists. I believe Carl Sagan is one.

SKIPP: Sure, we're not devilish people out to subvert the minds of our young people, in any sense. We just want tolerance. We want to try to get people to use reason, logic, to think. I'm all for religious freedom, even though I'm not a holy roller Pentecostal anymore, tongues speaking and all that. If people want to do that, that's fine, but don't put your laws on my body. Do it in your churches, but keep it out of government; keep it out of the law of the land.

PAUL: Next call is Ed, in southwest Atlanta. You're on AM 750 WSB.

CALLER: Good evening Paul and Skipp. I have a question and a statement. Do the Reconstructionists believe that those who cheat the public in the name of religion should also be executed?

SKIPP: They haven't made a statement on that one yet.

CALLER: I would think not. I don't think they would advocate killing their own. They would only kill those who do not agree with their philosophy. And what you said about them getting elected, they can't get there unless we pull the switch for them.

SKIPP: A good point.

CALLER: If they don't convince me that they need to be in office, then I don't push the button.

SKIPP: We need to be involved in local politics, because this is where it's happening now. They've taken the emphasis off national politics and they're focusing on the states, counties, and cities.

CALLER: What I'm saying, though, is that they still have to come out and campaign, and you can tell if a person is a religious fanatic or not, based upon what they say, their political record.

PAUL: But sometimes you don't know about these people running for office. One time I had a guy on a show—it wasn't here, it was in another state—he was wanting to be elected to the school board. I gave all the school-board candidates a chance to speak, and somehow or another, a reliable source told me that this fellow was getting money from, and being supported by, Pat Robertson. And he was rolling along on the air talking about all the things he wanted to do, and I stopped him and I said, "Are you getting your money from Pat Robertson?" And his face turned white, and he got very nervous and started sweating, and he beat around the bush, and he finally admitted that he was getting his money, and he was, basically, being a puppet of Pat Robertson. And he wanted to get on that school board so he could censor books.

CALLER: That's what recalls are for. When someone gets on there, and it's decided they didn't tell the truth, then you have a recall, you take them out, and you don't let them back in again.

SKIPP: We have to try to get them before they get elected, though.

PAUL: Hey, Ed, thank you for calling. Jonathan in Atlanta, you're on AM 750 WSB.

CALLER: Good evening, Paul, and good evening to your guest. I'm in underground Altanta, so I'm not able to hear everything that's going on, but I do want to make a comment, and I hope I don't sound stupid here because I can't hear everything that's going on. These people that I heard on your promo when you were announcing tonight's show, they call themselves "Christian." Is that correct?

PAUL: Yeah, that's right.

CALLER: OK. I find that a little hard to believe if you understand the Christian faith, based on the fact that we believe Christ is the savior. He said, "Forgive your enemies." "Love those who persecute you." He's already done . . . we don't need to, quote, "punish" people for sins of the flesh, fornication, adultery, stealing, those type of things. We can punish them by our laws, but Christ never intended for anyone to be killed. It seems to me there's a story in the Bible where a young woman was about to be stoned for committing adultery . . .

PAUL: Yeah, the Mary Magdalen story, where Jesus said, "Let those without sin cast the first stone."

CALLER: So, how can they call themselves "Christian?"

PAUL: That's a good point. That's a good question.

SKIPP: There are three hundred Christian denominations in the United States, and the reason for that is they all have different interpretations of the Bible, especially Paul's writings. Paul was a bigot, he was anti-just-about-everything, it seems, pro-slavery, even. So, we have all these different divisions. This group happens to believe in the Old and New Testament, and they believe in Old and New Testament punishments for people's sins or for their crimes. I agree, Jesus said "Forgive them," but there are many people who are not willing to forgive.

PAUL: Yeah, and these people who are . . . by the way, thank you for your call, Jonathan, we'll talk again . . . these people, though, are right in saying that this stuff is in the Bible, because death is prescribed as a punishment for adultery in the Old Testament.

SKIPP: Yeah, Jay Grimstead, the head of COR, says, "The Bible has something like eleven reasons for capital punishment. Murder was one. Homosexuality, rape, kidnapping were some of the others." And he said, "The actual punishments we don't have agreement on, but we think that homosexuality, and abortion, and pornography should be outlawed."

PAUL: Oh boy! Short break, then we'll be back. We'll talk to Bill, and Bob. Still no lines in Atlanta, but if you want to get us from out of state, you can call us toll-free at 1-800-WSB-TALK. Our guest is Skipp Porteous, and he is with *The Freedom Writer* newsletter. And we're going to tell you how you can get a copy of this particular issue, talking about this new radical religious right, here in just a few minutes, so get a pencil and paper ready.

[off the air]

PAUL: I stole that stuff about adding up the people who were gonna be killed, and compared them with Hitler, from Steve Allen's book [*Steve Allen on the Bible, Religion, and Morality,* Prometheus Books]. You probably noticed that. It's from the forward of his book. He's very eloquent, you know.

SKIPP: He's amazing. You know, people think he's just a comedian, but I think he's written thirty-five books.

PAUL: Yeah, thirty-five books, and like two thousand songs.

SKIPP: Smart guy.

PAUL: Yeah, smart guy. Did you read the part of his critique about the story of Noah? You'll love that. He talks about what kind of God would get mad at the people, and then kill all the animals? There's a lot of humor in it. Once you start reading that book you won't be able to put it down. Here we go . . .

AM 750 WSB. . . . Just when you think you've heard it all, you tune into the Paul Gonzales show and you find out there's a group of Christian people, these people that call themselves Christians, who advocate the execution of homosexuals, adulterers, fornicators, and I guess, women who have abortions.

SKIPP: Yes, and the ones who perform the abortions.

PAUL: Oh boy! The next calls gonna be from D.B. in Cartersville. You're on AM 750 WSB.

CALLER: Hello, how you doing? I'm calling about the adultery business. In the old days they stoned them when they committed adultery, right?

PAUL: Right.

CALLER: Today they get married again, and maybe the first wife kills the husband or something like that.

SKIPP: Do you think adulterers should be killed?

CALLER: No, I don't think they should be killed. I think they should be departed from, until they can get right and live for God.

PAUL: I don't understand your point, D.B.

CALLER: I was thinking how people get divorced and remarried, but maybe they should leave their first husband or second wife, and just stay like normal.

PAUL: Right. Well, thank you, D.B. I appreciate your contribution to the show. How about Bob in Stockbridge. You're on AM 750 WSB.

CALLER: Yes, Paul, I'm a Christian myself, and I agree with your guest on the Reconstruction movement, that it's a very destructive movement, and I do not agree with any of their teachings, but I believe your guest has kind of lumped all Christians into one category.

SKIPP: And what category is that?

CALLER: For instance, you made a remark about Paul being a bigot.

PAUL: Not me, of course, because I'm no saint.

SKIPP: The Paul in the Bible was a bigot.
CALLER: Excuse me?
SKIPP: I'm talking about Paul in the Bible.
CALLER: Right, that's what I'm saying. You said that he's a bigot?
SKIPP: Yes.
CALLER: Well, I think your interpretation of slavery, and the way that you read the Bible, is totally inaccurate.
SKIPP: He said slaves should honor their masters.
CALLER: That is not referring to the way you think it is, though. Paul was definitely not a bigot. Paul was a follower of Christ. Christ was the full expression . . .
SKIPP: Paul didn't even know Christ! He came years later; he came years after Jesus died. He didn't know anything about him! Paul started his own religion.
CALLER: You're talking about the Apostle Paul?
SKIPP: Yeah, the Apostle Paul.
CALLER: The Apostle Paul . . .
SKIPP: He did not know Jesus . . .
CALLER: The Apostle Paul met Christ on the way to Damascus.
SKIPP: No, he had sunstroke. C'mon, he was in the desert.
CALLER: Paul, this is showing your intelligent listeners, whether they're Christian or not, what this man is.
PAUL: You know, there's only one problem here. You have believed what you have heard. This man that we have on the air, Bob, knows the Bible from cover to cover, used to be a minister, and if you want to get some facts about that and some of the other stuff about the Bible, pick up Steve Allen's new book, a critique of the Bible, an historical analysis of it. There's a lot of stuff in the Bible that's there, and people have never read it. I don't know about the story of Paul; I was always taught in Catholic school that Paul was one of the Apostles. The writings of Paul were how far after Christ was crucified?
SKIPP: Oh, goodness, it was ninety, a hundred years later when Paul came along and wrote these things, and most of the gospels were [written later]. [Actually, I missed the mark here. Paul converted to Christianity at least five years after Jesus died and never knew Christ. It wasn't until another fifteen years later that he began to write his letters, called epistles, to various Christian groups. In contrast, John's writings came along between 90 A.D. and 100 A.D., which is where my

mind was when I made the statement on the air.] What we have in the Bible is replete with errors, hearsay, stories that were told from one generation to another. You know, it's not accurate. If you want to build a humanistic religion on it, fine. "Love thy neighbor" and all that, but to take it word-for-word, literally, you just miss the whole point.

PAUL: Bob, are you also aware that the story of the Flood and Noah was taken from the Babylonian religion? It was just a rewrite of a pagan legend from Babylon. Thank you, Bob. The number in Atlanta is 872-0750, and outside of the area, 1-800-WSB-TALK. And now we're going out to Longview, Texas. And Richard, you're on AM 750 WSB.

CALLER: Hello, how are you tonight, Paul? Say, I just tuned you in a little while ago, and I heard this gentleman talking, and I heard some of the names he mentioned, and this new group he's talking about; I guess it's a new religion he's talking about. And he also said these men were wanting to get rid of people, you know, sinners, and this and that. Now, some of the men he mentioned are some of the men I hear trying to save some of these children from being aborted. Now, I don't quite buy his story. I'm no Hebrew scholar, Greek scholar, or anything like that, but I know what the man says, and what he says is contradictory. These men are trying to save these kids from being aborted.

SKIPP: You mean trying to protect fetuses in wombs?

CALLER: That's right.

SKIPP: The Coalition On Revival advocates that abortionists be executed. This is what they believe. It's a Reconstructionist Christian viewpoint that abortionists be executed, along with homosexuals and other people. I'm not making these words up; this is what they're saying. And I listed some of the people who belong to this organization. Whether they believe that or not I don't know, but the organization is espousing these views.

PAUL: Hey, Richard, I gotta run and take a break. Thanks for calling AM 750 WSB. And don't forget, those of you who are on Bell South Mobility, you can call our talk shows for free. The number is 872-0750. That'll be a free call on your Bell South Mobility phone. My guest is Skipp Porteous.

[break]

PAUL: AM 750 WSB. Our guest is Skipp Porteous. I know that the lines are tied up and some of you think, "Uh, oh, it's almost news time and I'm not gonna get on." Our guest will stay with us into the next hour. And Skipp, a lot of people have been asking how they can get your newsletter. I promised them we could give them that information a couple of times. Why don't we do one right now?

SKIPP: Sure, the address is really easy. It's *The Freedom Writer*, with a "W." Just write to *The Freedom Writer,* Great Barrington, Massachusetts, which is M-A. The ZIP is 0-1-2-3-0. [repeats a couple of times] Just write to *The Freedom Writer,* and we'll send you a free copy of this issue we're talking about.

PAUL: They can get a free introductory issue; then if they want to join and get the whole nine yards, it's twenty-five bucks a year, right?

SKIPP: That's right.

PAUL: You aren't getting rich with this, are you?

SKIPP: Hardly, but I wish.

PAUL: The next call is Brad on the car phone. Brad, you're on AM 750 WSB.

CALLER: Hello Paul, I've always admired you a lot. I've always thought you had intelligent guests and everything. I thought the last caller made some pretty good points.

PAUL: Yes, he did, thank you. The next call will be Bill, in Cummen. You're on AM 750 WSB.

CALLER: Hi, Paul, it's good to be on with you. I've listened to a lot of discussions like this on WSB that center around religious controversy, but there always seems to be something missing out of the conversation.

PAUL: Like what?

CALLER: It seems to me that anybody, that as soon as he gets out of bed and his feet hit the floor, he goes through the day making decisions and operating from what I would term to be on the basis of presupposition, or faith, or truths that he takes for himself that he cannot prove. He takes them by faith, and whether you're a Christian or not, it seems to me that whoever you are, you take your basis for operating in the world as it is, on faith.

PAUL: Now what does that have to do with what we're talking about?

CALLER: What it has to do with is this: you seem to be all for religious freedom except for that which is effective.

PAUL: Bill, listen! Why don't you speak in English, besides trying to speak in big words? Just boil it down in plain English and tell me what's on your mind, OK?

CALLER: Well, what bothers me is that you can come on the show and talk about Christians as if they shouldn't have any effect in the world in which they live.

PAUL: You know, we're not talking about the vast majority of Christian people. We're talking about a small group of Christian fanatics. I have had fundamentalist preachers on this show, probably more Christian people and Christian ministers on this show than any talk show in Atlanta [he lists some]. Man, if you don't think the Christian point of view gets a good airing on this show, you ain't listening! Either that, or you're stupid.

Our next call is Don in Atlanta. You're on AM 750 WSB. Oh, the radio's on there, Don. Stephanie in Swanee, you're on AM 750 WSB.

CALLER: Hi Paul. I've been listening to you quite often and finally got through this time. I was just sitting here and found myself getting angrier and angrier listening about these Reconstructionists. I want to ask Skipp just about how many he thought there were? What percentage?

SKIPP: Well, they represent the largest body of Christians . . . these well-known Christian leaders in the Reconstructionist movement, in the Coalition On Revival, actually represent millions of American Christians. For instance, Beverly LaHaye, who is the head of the Concerned Women for America, is on the Steering Committee of COR, the Coalition On Revival, this Reconstructionist group. She claims six hundred thousand members in her group alone. Then you've got a number of other groups that have many members. So, they represent millions of Christians. And I would say that the Christians are being represented without their knowledge or their will. They're supporting this ministry and they don't really know what these ministries stand for.

PAUL: I think we ought to underline the fact, Skipp, even though we're talking about hundreds of thousands of people who may be members of these groups, this is still a very small percentage of the Christian community in this country.

SKIPP: Oh yeah, according to Gallup, there are sixty to seventy million born-again Christians in America. And most Christians, 99 percent of them, do not believe that [Reconstructionist doctrine]. Unfortunately, the top, some of these national Christian leaders, are members of the Coalition On Revival, the group that's advocating these things. Millions of Christians support them, not knowing what they're really supporting, what they're trying to bring on into America. And they should really know about this.

PAUL: But the point I'm trying to make, especially for that caller who somehow or another thought this was a Christian-bashing show, I would think that probably mainstream major denominations of Christianity would be just as upset about this as you are.

SKIPP: Well, they should be. Look at the Southern Baptist Convention, the largest Protestant body in America. They have, for years, maintained a strong separation of church and state. And I give them credit for that. You know, we need to keep these two separate, so we can have political freedom and religious freedom.

PAUL: Yeah, the Baptists are considered by a lot of people to be conservative, but the Baptists have been victims of discrimination and have learned a lesson, and are certainly champions of freedom of religion here in this country. So, we're not talking about Baptists, not talking about mainline Presbyterians, and Catholics and Episcopalians. We're talking about Reconstructionists—a dangerous group in this country today.

Our guest is Skipp Porteous, and we'll be back here to our phones in just a moment.

[news break]

PAUL: AM 750 WSB, and we're talking to Skipp Porteous, who identifies himself as a secular humanist. And he used to be a Pentecostal minister, and now he's the editor of *The Freedom Writer,* the national newsletter that defends the separation of church and state. And this organization will go to a lot of trouble to find out about what's going on when it has to do with the separation of church and state.

And it is true, as we touched on in the last hour, that you went down to Tupelo, Mississippi, and infiltrated Don Wildmon's organization, but you didn't do anything wrong and you didn't go to jail, Skipp.

SKIPP: No, but he didn't like it.

PAUL: No, he didn't. You and him are not friends any more.

SKIPP: No. You mentioned that I went from a Pentecostal to a secular humanist. You've heard of "back sliding?" Well, I "front slid."

PAUL [laughing]: OK! Don, in Atlanta, you're on AM 750 WSB.

CALLER: Hey, Paul.

PAUL: Hey, Don.

CALLER: The subject tonight is Christians wantin' to kill homosexuals and all that?

PAUL: Well, that's part of it.

CALLER: I heard a joke like that the other day. The only question I've got . . .

PAUL: There's a joke about Christians killing homosexuals?

CALLER: Well, it's a joke to me because it's not real. A joke to me is something that's not real. I don't understand how they can call themselves a Christian. It sounds to me like what Christ said. He said, "Satan comes to steal, kill and destroy."

PAUL: Christians have, from time to time, done some very strange things. From my understanding, about half of the Christian ministers were, initially, supportive of slavery.

SKIPP: Yes, and Christianity is based on the Bible, and the Old Testament is very clear about who should be executed. And even the Apostle Paul said that homosexuals are "worthy of death."

CALLER: Yeah, the Apostle Paul was there when they stoned Timothy to death, as a follower of Christ. Yeah, but the Apostle Paul was changed on the road to Damascus. He became one of the best servants of Christ. He's one of my favorites in the Bible.

SKIPP: Yeah, mine, too.

CALLER: He suffered so much, I mean this guy, he had to look death in the face every day. He was in prison. He was even stoned to death and brought back to life. You know what he said, "Oh, these light afflictions." He had the power of Christ in him. I have a five-year-old nephew who accepted Christ. He knows more about Jesus Christ than most grown people do. You know, Christ's message . . .

SKIPP: That's because he hasn't learned a lot yet.

PAUL: OK. We appreciate your testimony there, Don. And our next call is Debbie in Barnesville. You're on AM 750 WSB.

CALLER: Paul, thank you so much for letting me have the opportunity to make a comment. If I could say something to Skipp.

SKIPP: You can.

CALLER: I'm a supporter of Beverly LaHaye and the Concerned Women for America, and Doctor Kennedy, and like a couple of earlier callers, it's very hard for me to believe that they support these things, but I plan to, and would urge others of their supporters, to write them and find out what their stand is.

SKIPP: Amen, I would agree with that. Why don't you write to Kennedy and to Beverly, and say, "If you're a member of COR, this Coalition On Revival that advocates the death penalty for homosexuals, and abortionists and so forth, I won't support your ministries"? Why don't you be that honest and brave and tell them that?

CALLER: Oh, I wouldn't have a problem in the world with that, but I'm just about 99.99 percent sure that they do not support that. I wonder if you might be operating under the theory that if A equals B and B equals C, then A equals C. I think that's maybe what's happening.

SKIPP: Why would they belong to such an organization? Why do you think?

CALLER: I find it difficult to believe, Skipp, I really do, but I have supported them and believed all the things they have supported to this day. So, I would like to get to the bottom of it, because I do send my money to both organizations. And I'm definitely a fundamentalist Christian, I suppose.

SKIPP: Well, you have the right to send your money to whoever you want.

PAUL: Debbie, let me ask you, repeating Skipp's question. Why do you suppose that Tim and Bev [LaHaye] would be members of this organization?

CALLER: I really . . . I just have to say, I find it difficult to believe . . .

PAUL: I wonder if this organization [COR] has a letterhead or anything like that with their names on it, Skipp?

SKIPP: Oh yeah, it does. I have a whole file on the Coalition On Revival, all their members, who signed this statement that they would live for these principles [COR Manifesto] until they die. Beverly LaHaye is a Steering Committee member, and I believe D. James Kennedy is also on the Steering Committee, but they're both members. And Jay Grimstead, the head of COR, Doctor Jay Grimstead, told me himself about the death penalty for homosexuals and so forth.

CALLER: I don't know anything about Mr. Grimstead. I've never heard of him. I just know these two people, and I know, up to now I've supported everything they've promoted. I will be writing them, and would like to go on record, I do not believe they promote these things. I would like to find out.

PAUL: What if you find out, Debbie, that Tim and Bev belong to the Coalition On Revival?

CALLER: If I found out that they promoted the death penalty for homosexuals . . .

PAUL: They probably don't, OK? Tim and Beverly probably don't. They're very nice people on the air. I've had them both on the air. In fact, do you know, Beverly has a Christian sex manual out? It's really interesting. Boy, for those people who like to get some real erotic stuff in the Christian book store, get Beverly LaHaye's Christian sex manual. Oh, it is . . .

CALLER: No, no, no, no, no . . . no, I can't listen to that. That is distorting things. I don't want to tie up the line, all I have to say is that I would just like for the record, because these people I think so highly of, I would just say that anyone that questions them, that is a supporter of theirs, just find out, rather than cut off support for them based on the conversations tonight. Write them and find out! And I do appreciate the chance to make a comment.

SKIPP: Support them, but tell them to leave COR.

PAUL: Find out if they belong to that organization, and find out why. That's a very simple, fair question, OK? Gary, you're on a car phone on AM 750 WSB.

CALLER: Yeah, thanks a lot. I have a question for Skipp. I'm a new Christian myself, and I've always wondered, how did you leave the church?

SKIPP: I just walked out the door.

CALLER: I mean, what happened in your life for something like that to take place, especially being a man of God like you were?

SKIPP: Well, something did happen. It's too long to get into now . . . my book is coming out later this year . . . but something did shock me awake, and I did stop to reason and think, and I looked at the whole thing, everything I was involved in, everything I believed. I looked at the Bible from a very objective point of view, and I decided that I was living in a dream world, and it was not what I wanted to do.

CALLER: Did you not see significant changes in your life when you became a Christian?

SKIPP: People become more of what they already are. If you're a fanatic when you start as a Christian, you'll be a fanatic Christian. If you have a lot of love and compassion in you as a non-Christian, you'll have more as a Christian. I've seen this so many times in new converts. You don't really change. Somehow you just emphasize some of your better aspects.

CALLER: Hmmm. I strongly disagree with you, but I wanted to better understand where you're coming from.

SKIPP: My book is called *Jesus Doesn't Live Here Anymore,* and that'll be out later in the year. Look for it. The whole story's in there, and I think it'll help you.

CALLER: I'll probably pass on it, but I appreciate your comments.

PAUL: Well, thank you very much for your call. The next one will be Dick in Norcross. You're on AM 750 WSB.

CALLER: Yeah, it was just commented earlier that he would like to have all religious principles removed from our law system. Well . . .

SKIPP: No, I didn't say that at all.

CALLER: Well, what did you say?

SKIPP: I said that . . .

CALLER: You said you didn't want Biblical law placed on your body, right?

SKIPP: I said that Christians or any other religious groups should not impose their religious beliefs as the law of the land.

CALLER: Let me ask you, how do you account for the fact that the Ten Commandments is embodied in the laws against murder and . . .

PAUL: That's not just Christianity. Almost every culture in the world has that. Those are just basic laws of right and wrong that people don't kill each other and steal from each other.

SKIPP: Soviet, atheistic Russia for years embraced the same things.

CALLER: My question is, why are those innate? With what law system would you replace with the current Judeo-Christian system?

SKIPP: Well, we don't have a Judeo-Christian law system. We have laws that aim to be of the best benefit for mankind. You could really say that the laws we have today are humanistic laws. They're not Judeo-Christian laws.

PAUL: And, when you really get right down to it, the Ten Commandments were very good rules to live by.

SKIPP: According to the Old Testament, if you broke them you had to pay the penalty. This is where Reconstruction comes in because they want to go back to Old Testament Biblical law and have a true Judeo-Christian law system. That's what we're trying to avoid.

CALLER: If I may make two quick final comments—number one, there are very few death-bed conversion accounts to atheism; and the second, I'm just delighted, as a Reconstructionist myself, to see you folks in full cry. We really must have your attention. [HANGS UP]

SKIPP: You do . . .

PAUL: Wait a minute! Uh oh, now you see there . . .

SKIPP: Yep, he fell back from the front lines when he had his chance.

PAUL: Hey Dick, call me back. What's the matter with you? Are you a chicken? Now, you just said that you were a member of this group, and you didn't even give me a chance to ask you if you advocated the death penalty for homosexuals.

SKIPP: Boy, there are a lot of questions we'd like to ask Dick.

PAUL: Dick, we want you back on the phone, Dick. I'll tell you what, if you call that number, 1-800-WSB-TALK, if you have the courage to . . . in fact, we'll open up a special "Dick line." And that number is 741-0750. Of course, you can call that number collect, because you're calling from outside the toll-free Atlanta area. We do want to talk to you, Dick.

It's 9:18, and this is AM 750 WSB.

[break]

PAUL: [off the air] Our producer knows him. He used to be a bigoted talk-show host in Atlanta.

SKIPP: A talk-show host! Well, I hope he calls the Dick line.

PAUL: He's back! I've got him on the Dick line!

SKIPP: That's great!

PAUL: That's perfect double entendre, isn't it?

[laughter]

PAUL: Hold on . . .

PAUL [on the air]: At the WSB weather center it's one hundred degrees here in the studio and on our phone lines. Our guest is Skipp

Porteous, and he is the editor of *The Freedom Writer,* the national newsletter that defends the separation of church and state. And by gosh, guess what? That caller took our challenge. He said that he's one of these Reconstructionists, and he actually had the nerve to call us back, and Dick, I'm so glad you called us back on the show, because I didn't want you to hang up like you did.

CALLER: Well, I probably will regret this on the basis that you will always have the final word—you and the guest. And it's two against one, so have at it.

SKIPP: Hey Dick, why don't you tell us what Reconstructionists believe.

CALLER: Christian Reconstructionists is basically, and I'm not a member of this group, I'm a member of a church which is nominally attached to the Rushdoony group, the Chalcedon Foundation. I've read Rushdoony, I've read Whitehead, I've met them. So, I know these folks, and I do not believe for example that they in good conscience would espouse the killing of homosexuals or adulterers, because the Christianity that I embody and embrace, and the group around me embraces, is to hate the sin, but love the sinner.

SKIPP: What does that mean?

CALLER: It means that those who repent of sinful behavior are to be welcomed back into the Christian community.

SKIPP: Suppose a homosexual does not repent of his homosexuality?

CALLER: Well, it looks to me, Skipp, as though the homosexuals are in the process of executing themselves, what with AIDS and all.

PAUL: That didn't answer the question.

CALLER: Well, no, it doesn't answer the question, but I would not favor executing homosexuals, to put it in a word.

SKIPP: Do you know of any Reconstructionists who would be?

CALLER: No, I do not know of any.

SKIPP: Do you know Doctor Jay Grimstead?

CALLER: I do not know Doctor Grimstead.

SKIPP: Do you know who he is?

CALLER: I know who he is.

SKIPP: All right. I'm telling you what he told me. Of course, you know that Rushdoony has advocated the return to Biblical law, which includes the death penalty for some of these things, don't you?

CALLER: Yes, I do.

SKIPP: All right.

CALLER: And I would ask you a question. Has Western society improved or degraded in the two hundred years, in America's case, the two hundred and twenty years since it was founded? Have we become a better people, have we become a more righteous people, or have we become something less than that?

SKIPP: Well, you said this was a Judeo-Christian nation, that our laws are based on Judeo-Christianity. So, if that's true, then it's your fault . . .

CALLER: It began on that basis, but it's become so diluted and so watered-down. I remind you that it was Karl Marx himself, and I know that you're going to invoke the fact that Marxist philosophy has been discredited. Marx himself said, Marxism is humanism and humanism is Marxism. And there are many of us out here who have embraced the Christian Reconstruction movement, and after doing so found that the folks on the other side, and I don't know if you're one of them or not, but I suppose you are at this point, really have some sort of agenda, a little hidden agenda for America that you're not really articulating, and won't do so until you have sufficient numbers to implement it.

PAUL: What do you think that agenda might be?

CALLER: I think that agenda may be a totally socialistic system.

SKIPP: Dick, what is your agenda as a Reconstructionist?

CALLER: My agenda is to return to the principles of basic Christianity, the Golden Rule.

SKIPP: I have no problem with the Golden Rule. I'd join you there.

CALLER: And I have no problem with . . . do you have a problem with the Decalogue [Ten Commandments] and its embodiment in our law system?

SKIPP: Yeah, I do.

CALLER: Well, what system would you replace with . . .

SKIPP: If you're talking about the Ten Commandments your talking about . . .

CALLER: What system would you replace that with, Skipp?

SKIPP: It's not a system that we need . . .

CALLER: We have to have a system of ethics. We have to have a system, as the word Bill used earlier—unfortunately he didn't articulate it as well as he could have—the presuppositional basis for your system.

SKIPP: We have the system already; we don't need a new system. It's there.

CALLER: Which is what? The jungle?

SKIPP: It's the law of the land: we have the Constitution; we have the First Amendment.

CALLER: Are you aware that the Constitution itself refers to Christ, and refers to Christians?

SKIPP: Name it. Give me one verse in the Constitution that . . .

CALLER: How about at the end of the Constitution, "In the year of our Lord, 1787." To what Lord did Mr. Madison refer? Why is it . . .

PAUL: Awww, this is the way people gave dates in those days!

CALLER: It's a custom, OK. Then, let's assume the Sabbath is to be a protected day in Christian custom. Then, why is it embodied in the Constitution that the President may not sign bills on a Sunday?

SKIPP: Hey, wait a minute! Sunday is not the Sabbath, Dick. You know that. Saturday is the Sabbath, if you want to go by that.

CALLER: Well, there's a thirty or forty minute argument there.

PAUL: And I don't want to get into it, but I want to ask you some more straightforward questions here. You're telling me that the members of the Reconstructionist movement don't favor any penalties for homosexuality . . .

CALLER: I can't say that, Paul, because as you know, there's a bell-shaped distribution curve in any group.

PAUL: So, OK. How about you? Would you favor any penalties, any legal penalties for homosexuals?

CALLER: For homosexuals, legal penalties?

PAUL: Yeah.

CALLER: I don't necessarily favor legal penalties as long as their homosexuality is not, I mean, let's face it, Paul, homosexuality today is not striving for equal rights. Their driving for superior rights. They want to force their system on the rest of us. They want the right to do what heterosexuals have been traditionally arrested for doing in public.

PAUL: But be honest with me now, Dick. If indeed you were in power, what would you do with . . .

CALLER: I would attempt to convert them. The scripture commands me to try to do that.

PAUL: And what if they said, "No, I don't want to convert . . ."

CALLER: If they didn't convert? I don't think I'd execute them, but I certainly wouldn't welcome them into my family.

PAUL: Well, OK. How about, let's say, people who perform abortions—what would you do with them?

CALLER: I think God has plans for those folks. I think it's his judgment that ultimately will prevail on those folks, as it will with homosexuals.

PAUL: How about pornographers?

CALLER: I feel much the same way, although how do you explain the fact, you and Skipp, that we have constant drives by certain members of the legal profession to keep this stuff out of the public view, out of children's hands. Do you believe in pornography for children?

PAUL: Oh, come on man!

SKIPP: What use would a child have for pornography? Adults are attracted to pornography. It's probably a good thing; it's a good, safe release.

PAUL: One final question here that I want to ask you, Dick. Would you admit that maybe some of the members of the Reconstructionist movement might advocate legal penalties for people who are homosexuals, adulterers, and fornicators?

CALLER: I would say that's entirely possible, just as it is possible for those on Skipp's side of the spectrum to carry their philosophy to an extreme, and that is a totally Marxist-Socialist law system in this country.

PAUL: So, what do you say, Skipp?

SKIPP: No, I'm happy with the law system the way it is. We're trying to maintain the status quo. We have no agenda. It's hard enough just to fight back at this Coalition On Revival and all the other groups that want to push their religious viewpoints on everybody else and make them the law of the land.

PAUL: Dick, I've got to hand it to you, you did well.

CALLER: Well, listen, I just want to say to Skipp, I'm delighted that we have his folks in full cry. It means we're doing something right.

PAUL: OK. God bless you.

SKIPP: It doesn't mean they're doing something right, does it?

PAUL: I understand we have another Reconstructionist on the phone. We have Mr. Gary DeMar on the line, who we invited to join us, and he was kind enough to call us, and we'll talk with him in just a few minutes here on WSB.

Basically, if you're just tuning in, our guest is saying that there is a group of people here in this country known as Reconstructionists. And some of the people who are in this group advocate Old Testament punishment for homosexuals, adulterers, fornicators, and people like that. Of course, in the Old Testament the penalty for that kind of stuff was death by stoning. Of course, today we could do it with the electric chair, or the gas chamber, or some other means.

And we'll be back with our guest, and welcoming an additional guest on our line in just a moment on AM 750 WSB.

[break]

[off the air]

> PAUL: Are you having a good time?
> SKIPP: Yeah. Hey, where did you find Gary DeMar?
> PAUL: Do you know who he is?
> SKIPP: Yeah, he's on the COR Steering Committee.
> PAUL: Well, the ultra-conservative, right-wing talk-show host who works with me helps me out and I help him out.
> SKIPP: Yeah, he's listed on COR's letterhead. I have a picture of him here.
> PAUL: Have you ever talked to him?
> SKIPP: No, never have.
> PAUL: Oh, let me talk to him. I'll say "Hi" to him. Hold on.
> PAUL: Well, he's ready. This'll be fun, you'll enjoy this, won't you?
> SKIPP: This should be very interesting.
> PAUL: He says he's a writer.
> SKIPP: Well, he spoke at one of their [COR] conferences on "The Theology of Christian Activism."
> PAUL: Good, so you know a little bit about him. I wonder if he would say that homosexuals should be killed?
> PAUL [on the air]: AM 750 WSB, and our guest is Skipp Porteous, former Pentecostal minister, now editor of *The Freedom Writer* newsletter. And Skipp, we have somebody you've heard of before, and that is Gary DeMar, who is, among other things, a writer. Gary, we very much appreciate you joining us tonight on WSB.

GARY: Well, thanks for the opportunity. I appreciate it.
PAUL: How long have you been listening tonight, Gary?
GARY: Since the beginning.
PAUL: OK, what do you have to say to Skipp?
GARY: Well, I waited this long to see how many, I want to call them lies, but this is misinformation that Mr. Porteous has been sending out. He started off by saying the Coalition On Revival is a Reconstructionist organization. At first he said it was a "front" for Reconstructionism.

I've been involved with the Coalition On Revival since its inception. It is not, and I'm going to repeat, is not a Reconstructionist organization. It does not advocate the things that Mr. Porteous is saying. Mr. Porteous seems to be getting his information from a *Mother Jones* magazine article in the November/December [1990] issue. I should warn Mr. Porteous that Mr. Wildmon, Donald Wildmon, who was featured in that article, is suing a spokesperson for the National Endowment for the Arts, because she said the same thing about him. I believe he's suing this woman for close to a quarter of a million dollars for attributing these distinctions to Mr. Wildmon.

SKIPP: Well, Gary, I probably know more about that than you do. First of all, I have not said that Wildmon believes in the death penalty for homosexuals or any of these things that we're . . .

GARY: I think, Skipp—now I've listened to this from the beginning—that your listeners are getting that impression. Let's understand this, the Coalition On Revival is not a Reconstructionist organization, and it does not advocate the things you're specifying.

SKIPP: OK, you know who Doctor Jay Grimstead is . . .

GARY: Oh, sure. I spoke to him today.

SKIPP: All right. Is he a Reconstructionist?

GARY: No, he isn't.

SKIPP: All right. Well, listen; this is what he told me, and I quote him.

GARY: Let me get something straight. First of all, you have not defined Christian Reconstruction. You have defined certain distinctives that you say are Reconstructionist thinking. I have written a number of books setting forth detailed definitions of what Christian Reconstruction is. Even my Reconstructionist friends, and others who disagree with me, point to my books, *The Reduction of Christianity*, and another book I wrote called *The Debate Over Christian Reconstruction*, as primers as to what Christian Reconstruction is. I have not heard you give an accurate definition of Christian Reconstruction. And yet you've been on the air for an hour and thirty-five minutes.

PAUL: Why don't you give us a definition?

GARY: The definition of Christian Reconstruction is simply this: that the Bible applies to every facet of life. That means, not just the judicial aspects of life, civil government as one example, but self-government, family government, church government, business, economics, every facet of society. The Bible has something to say about each of those things. Now, most Christian Reconstructionists, especially those of us who write, are into the scholarly avenue of research. That is, we look at the Bible and we say, what does it say about this particular issue? And then we set forth what we feel the Bible says about that issue.

For example, the execution of homosexuals. We do not believe that homosexuals ought to be executed. The Bible doesn't say that homosexuals ought to be executed. Mr. Porteous claims to have been in the Pentecostal church and knows the Bible from cover to cover. The Bible doesn't say that.

PAUL: All right, let me get a comment from Skipp.

SKIPP: I'm wondering how many pages he's torn out of the Bible? Listen, this is what Doctor Jay Grimstead told me, and I quote him accurately and exactly. He said, "We believe that God has given the Bible as a rule book for all society, Christian and non-Christian alike." And, he added, "I concur with most of the Reconstructionist's matters. I am trying to help rebuild the society on the word of God, and loosely, that would be Reconstructionist orientation in anybody's book." Then, he also added, "The Bible had something like eleven reasons for capital punishment, and murder was one, and homosexuality and rape and kidnapping were some others."

That is what the leader of your group said, Gary.

GARY: Well first, he's not the leader of my group, and secondly, he's again, you . . .

SKIPP: What do you mean he's not the leader of your group! You say you're a member of COR. You're on the Steering Committee of the Coalition On Revival.

GARY: We're talking about Christian Reconstructionism. I'm a member of a number of different groups.

SKIPP: Well, you're on the Steering Committee of the Coalition On Revival. Jay Grimstead is the head of the group.

GARY: Let me explain. The Bible doesn't say that homosexuals should be executed. What it says is this: If two men lie together like a man and a woman lie together, they are to be put to death.

SKIPP: What the hell do you think that is!

GARY: Well, wait a minute. If a guy comes up to me and he says, "I'm a homosexual," that doesn't mean that he's to be executed. If you understand the Scriptures, it says very clearly, if a man comes up to you and says, "I've murdered somebody," that doesn't mean that person ought to be executed.

PAUL: Oh, so what you're saying, Gary, is if you catch homosexuals in the act, then the Bible says to execute them.

GARY: The Bible lays forth the severest penalty. The severest penalty would be capital punishment for two men who publicly engaged in sodomy. Which would mean, that if that law were on the books—which it has been on the books in many states, and probably still is in many states in the nation today.

PAUL: Does it say publicly in the Bible?

GARY: Oh, you've got to have two witnesses. So, you're going to have at least two witnesses who would come forth and testify against two people who engaged in sodomy. Now, Atlanta is a pretty populous city for homosexuality. I would imagine that most people in this city, probably 99 percent of them, have never seen two people engaged in sodomy. But, if it did happen, the severest punishment that could come from somebody would be capital punishment. It doesn't mean that has to be the punishment.

SKIPP: By capital punishment, you mean death.

GARY: Well, yes.

SKIPP: Now, there was a case a couple of years ago, and I believe it was Georgia, maybe it was another state . . .

GARY: It was Georgia.

SKIPP: Two men were seen by the police, because the police came in the house for a different reason, and saw them having sex, engaging in homosexual activity in bed.

GARY: Sodomy.

SKIPP: They were arrested. So, you're saying that these two men, according to the Bible, could receive the death penalty?

GARY: Well . . .

SKIPP: Is that what you're saying?

GARY: First of all, remember, the Supreme Court upheld Georgia's law. Secondly, yes.

SKIPP: Secondly, yes! The Bible advocates the death penalty for homosexuals.

GARY: No, it doesn't.

SKIPP: Homosexual activity, excuse me.

GARY: For example, if a guy raped a seven-year-old. He sodomized a seven-year-old boy—the seven-year-old boy is innocent.

SKIPP: No, no. You said "two men, lying together."

GARY: Right.

SKIPP: The Bible says they should be executed.

GARY: Right.

SKIPP: All right. So . . .

PAUL: Wait a minute, wait a minute. Would you condone that?

GARY: Condone what?

PAUL: If indeed this movement were to go right by the Bible as you just said a few moments ago, would you advocate two men being caught in a homosexual act being executed?

GARY: No. That's not what I'm saying. What I'm saying is that the severest penalty . . .

PAUL: Wait a minute, now! You said the Reconstructionist movement advocates the Bible being very much a part of every aspect of society and you mentioned government.

GARY: Right.

PAUL: So then, if you indeed believe that, then you would have to believe that people caught in homosexuality should be executed.

SKIPP: That's Biblical law.

GARY: They could be executed.

SKIPP: They could be.

PAUL: They could be.

GARY: Right.

PAUL: So, what are you saying here?

GARY: I just told you what I'm saying. That could be the severest penalty. Let me give you an example.

PAUL: Wait, before you get to that, now, you said—again, these are your very own words—you said, that this movement that you're involved with, advocates the Bible being used as a basis for everything in society, including . . .

GARY: Wait a minute . . .

PAUL: No, you wait a minute, please. If indeed that's the case, if you believe that, then you would be contradicting yourself if you wouldn't advocate homosexuals being executed for homosexual activity.

GARY: I want to make sure the listeners understand that when we talk about movement, are we talking about the Coalition On Revival, which is not a Reconstructionist movement, or are we talking about Christian Reconstruction itself? Which movement are you talking about?

SKIPP: Well, Jay Grimstead told me he's a Reconstructionist.

GARY: Jay Grimstead . . .

SKIPP: And he's the head of the Coalition On Revival.

GARY: You have to remember, you mentioned Donald Wildmon, who's not a Reconstructionist, John Whitehead, who's not a Reconstructionist, the LaHayes, who are not Reconstructionists, and D. James Kennedy, who's not a Reconstructionist.

PAUL: Yeah, but Gary, I'm understanding how you just very cleverly steered away from my point—that you would have to agree with the death penalty for people being caught in homosexuality.

GARY: Skipp, I already agreed with you that that could be the severest penalty. I mean, I don't know how many times I have to tell you. Yes, I agree that the Bible lays the death penalty for two men who are engaged in sodomy in public. Yes. I don't know how many times I have to tell you before it gets through your head!

SKIPP: Does the Bible allow the same punishment for an abortionist?

GARY: OK. Now, I assume, Paul, you're going to allow me to . . .

PAUL: Yeah, I'm going to give you plenty of time, but we do, as you know, have to take a break here. But, we'll be right back. And, boy, what a hot potato we have on tonight. We have secular humanist Skipp Porteous, and a member of, well, let's just put it this way, a fundamentalist religious organization; his name is Gary DeMar. He's written several books. In fact, we'll tell you the names of some of those books if you want to read them. And he's also a member, I understand, of the Coalition On Revival. And if you want to do a little more additional reading about this, Steve Allen has a new book out, and he talks a little bit about this Reconstruction movement.

[break]

PAUL: AM 750 WSB, and we have two guests with us. One's way up in Massachusetts, and one's with us right here in Atlanta. Skipp Porteous is in Great Barrington, Massachusetts, and he is the editor of *The Freedom Writer* newsletter, and we're also delighted to have Gary DeMar with us, who's right here in Atlanta.

Again, we invited you on the show, Gary, and I appreciate it, and with all my guests who I invite on the show, I like to give people an opportunity to be able to get a hold of their literature. I certainly don't mind if you'd like to tell me a couple of titles of your books, if people want to look more into this from your perspective.

GARY: I've written a three-volume set of books called *God in Government,* and *Ruler of the Nations,* and *The Reduction of Christianity.*

PAUL: OK, these are available nationwide?

GARY: Well, you could probably tell your bookstore. I've written twelve books. They could go to their local bookstores and ask for the titles and they could order them. I know that B. Dalton, Walden, and Cole's have carried my *Surviving College Successfully* and *The Reduction of Christianity.*

PAUL: OK, back to our little friendly debate here. You had a comment to make, and I promised you, Gary, that I'd give you that opportunity after the break and here we are.

GARY: Well, the abortion issue. If abortion were illegal, the question comes down to what punishment would there be for someone who performed an illegal abortion? Now, if the pro-life community is correct, which I believe it is, that a pre-born individual is in fact a human being, then the same rights are accorded to the pre-born child as a born child. Then the same punishment would occur for the doctor performing the abortion. So, the pre-born child is in fact a human being, and a born child is in fact a human being; therefore the same punishment prevails. That is, if capital punishment could be brought on someone who killed a one-day-old child, then the same punishment would occur with someone who killed a child in the womb.

PAUL: So Gary, you would agree that a doctor performing an abortion should receive capital punishment?

GARY: Obviously, if abortion were illegal, and he performed an illegal abortion and killed a pre-born baby, the same punishment would apply, and that would . . . and of course, we've got our own system today that very few people who commit murder actually suffer the death penalty. That could be the severest penalty, yes.

PAUL: So, now, what our guest was saying at the top of the show, that people who are Reconstructionist believe in this, you have told us that the death penalty could be given to people who perform abortions, and the death penalty—your word is "could"—be applied under a Christian nation for people who are caught in homosexual acts. How about, again, we all know the story about Mary Magdalene . . .

GARY: Well, it's not Mary Magdalene; it doesn't really give the name of the woman caught in adultery.

PAUL: OK, how about adulterers?

GARY: You can take two cases out of the New Testament. It's interesting, though, when people who don't believe the Bible, like Mr. Porteous, go to the Bible and takes cases out of it to support his position when it's convenient. And when it's not convenient he lays the Bible aside. But let's take two cases. The first case is Mary and Joseph. As we know, Mary was with child, but Joseph hadn't known a woman, hadn't known Mary. That is, he hadn't had sexual intercourse with her. Now, what was he to suspect? He was to suspect that she had committed adultery. Now, it says in Scriptures that he decided to put her away, quietly, or secretly. That is, he was to proceed with a divorce without making it part of the civil court. That is, not making a charge against her of adultery. Of course, an angel comes and explains to her that that which is conceived in her is not by man, but by the Holy Spirit.

Now, the law in Scriptures concerning adultery means that the innocent party has as [recourse] the toughest penalty that could be brought on the guilty party, the death penalty. So, for example, if a woman had a husband who was a constant womanizer, and he just would not stop, she could bring charges against her husband for adultery, and the severest penalty could be, according to Scripture, the death penalty. It wouldn't have to be, but it would be [I think he meant to say, "it could be," not "would be"]. Now, this would do a number of things. And again, I want to go back and underscore something. Most of the laws in the Bible were designed not so much to be implemented, but to keep people from practicing that particular behavior.

PAUL: Well, all laws are basically that way.

GARY: Right. Well, it was the same thing with homosexuality. When there were laws on the books that could punish homosexuality, it didn't do away with homosexuality per se, but it kept it hidden, kept it in the closet.

PAUL: And again, back with the same question again. You're using the word "could" be, and if indeed the Reconstructionist movement ever made it in America, would you advocate these Biblical principles being carried out, just like the execution of the adulterer, just like the execution of the abortionist, and just like the execution of the homosexual?

GARY: Well, I believe, like Mr. Porteous does, in the democratic process. Of course, these laws couldn't be brought into the legal system unless people actually wanted these laws.

PAUL: But, if indeed enough people who have your belief system get into that, and people vote for all of this, then you would go along with these strict penalties?

GARY: I'm saying that they could be implemented, yes.

SKIPP: You are working toward that goal, though, aren't you?

GARY: Not necessarily, no. This is what usually happens when you're researching in an area . . . Mr. Porteous has taken probably one-tenth of what we actually do, and he has blown it up like an inflated balloon and he says, "This is what Christian Reconstruction is."

PAUL: You know, what I'd like to find out is some more of the stuff you'd like to do, and we'll get into that in just a moment. And once again, our two guests, Skipp Porteous, Gary DeMar. We're talking about the Reconstructionist movement in America.

[break]

PAUL: [off the air] Boy, you know, we're getting this guy's true colors out here, aren't we?

SKIPP: Jeez, I know. He speaks with a forked tongue.

PAUL: I think I'm really nailing the hell out of him, don't you think?

SKIPP: It's amazing. He called me a liar in the beginning, but he's confirming everything I said. He's just putting his foot in his mouth the longer he talks.

PAUL: I know it; I love it. At least I gave him a plug for his book.

PAUL: AM 750 WSB, it's 9:52 and our guests are Skipp Porteous and Gary DeMar. What I'm going to do is give our two guests the final six minutes to debate a little bit, and all you people on the phones, I'll get to you to give your opinion. Skipp, anything you want to say to Gary?

SKIPP: Yeah, Gary, could you give us your viewpoint on the separation of church and state?

GARY: Well, first of all, the Constitution, including the Bill of Rights, says nothing about a separation of church and state. The First Amendment says, "Congress shall make no law respecting an establishment of religion, or prohibiting the free exercising thereof." Which simply means, that our national government cannot establish a national church. Typically, what's happened in our day, the courts, and other things, they have interpreted that to mean that nothing religious can be involved in any sort of civil decision. And I just think that that's just erroneous. Any fourth grader who knows anything about history knows as a fact that religion was always incorporated into decision-making policies. Prayer, Bible-reading, laws based upon Scripture principles have no violation under the First Amendment. At the time of the drafting of the First Amendment there were nine states that had established state religions. I'm not advocating that, but obviously the First Amendment does not mean what Mr. Porteous and other advocates of church-state separation . . .

SKIPP: Gary, Jay Grimstead told me that "the goal of a number of us is to try to Christianize the state of California." Then he said, "the church is not supposed to try to take over the government of San Jose. The people who take over the government of San Jose are American citizens who happen to be informed by the Bible on what is justice and what is injustice. The Bible controls both church and state." Would you agree with Doctor Grimstead on that statement?

GARY: That the Bible is a law book for both church and state? Yes, but that's different than saying that church and state are merged by the Bible. The Bible is very specific about a separation between church and state. And I recommend that you read my *Ruler of the Nations* to see how I've laid out, very specifically, in great detail, what the Bible and what the Constitution says about the principles. I'm getting the impression listening to you and debating this topic, and writing on this topic for over ten years now, that most of the critics of Christian Reconstruction haven't read what Reconstructionists have written. And Paul, to give you some idea, we have nearly one hundred books on the market right now, very easily available to anyone who wants them, to go in and look and see what we have to say. I'm amazed that Mr. Porteous misunderstands very clear statements in our books what we mean by separation of church and state.

SKIPP: Well, Gary, earlier you accused me of lying about many things I said tonight, but in the last twenty minutes or so, you've confirmed everything I've said.

GARY: No, because at the beginning of the show you claimed—and it was very clear what you were doing—the Coalition On Revival is a Reconstructionist movement, and then you said that these people, the LaHayes, Wildmon, and so forth, should leave this organization because this is a Reconstructionist organization, and it isn't. I've been on some of even the drafting documents, and anything that even hinted at Reconstructionist distinctives were left out because the people didn't agree with them. Now, how can you say it's a Reconstructionist movement when I was there? I've been there. I was in the drafting document on government. And there isn't anything about what you're saying about Christian Reconstructionist distinctives in that drafting document. So, to say then that the Coalition On Revival is a Reconstructionist organization, when its documents have none of the particulars of Christian Reconstruction in them, specifically the one on Civil Government, is a bald-faced lie.

SKIPP: Well, I happen to have some of those documents myself, and I'm also going by what your leader Jay Grimstead said, that he is a Reconstructionist and he agrees with most of the Reconstructionist doctrines.

GARY: OK . . .

PAUL: And wait, I've got to say something here so that we don't run out of time. You did say that our first guest, Skipp, mentioned that the Bible principles should be applied to society, in your viewpoint. And you did say that . . .

GARY: All Christians agree with that!

PAUL: Yeah, but most Christians don't think that capital punishment could be applied to people caught in homosexual acts, or could be for adulterers, or whatever.

GARY: Paul, this is one thing that I want to say . . .

PAUL: And that's what he said at the top of the show, for all intents and purposes. You agreed with that!

GARY: But see, Christian Reconstruct . . . what he's saying about Christian Reconstruction is one-tenth of one percent of Christian Reconstruction.

SKIPP: You know, the ovens in Germany . . .

GARY: Skipp, I mean, you know, I thought we had kind of a half and half thing here . . .

SKIPP: Hitler's ovens were one-tenth of what he did in Germany, too.

GARY: That's . . .

SKIPP: C'mon, the one-tenth I'm speaking about is the worst part of it.

GARY: Are you an atheist?

SKIPP: No, I'm not an atheist.

GARY: Do you lean toward atheism?

SKIPP: No, atheism doesn't appeal to me.

PAUL: Hey guys, I gotta go. I wish we had more time. Both of you could stay longer, but I know both of you have to go. I do appreciate very much both of you being on the show tonight.

We had some First Amendment here tonight, didn't we! Well, now the lines are totally packed. Boy, it's hot! I'm going to give you all a chance to respond to that fire you heard in the last two hours.

Epilogue

Since *The Freedom Writer,* and others, particularly Fred Clarkson, first wrote about the Coalition On Revival, several of its leading members have resigned because of the prominence of Christian Reconstructionists in the movement. However, as I indicated at the end of the first chapter, various radical Christian leaders will come and go, but there will always be others who will rise up to take their place. Whether or not the Coalition On Revival achieves its goals, or fizzles, the die has been cast; too many have been recruited who are committed to changing the course of the nation and the world. They are in it for the long haul. As we head into the next century, the war to preserve the separation of church and state, and individual freedoms, will be fierce.

Here is a brief update on some of the characters who have played a part in my story:

- Billy Graham finally received official recognition as a star, when, in 1989, his star became the 1,900th embedded in the cement of Hollywood's Walk of Fame.

   In November 1990, Graham, at seventy-two, utilizing satellite and video technology, held the largest crusade of his forty-year ministry. Organizers of Graham's Hong Kong crusade estimated that 100 million people in thirty-three countries heard each of Graham's five nightly sermons. So elated was Graham, that after the crusade he said, "In some ways, I feel that I am ready to

go to heaven now." He added, "I have seen the greatest crusade of my life, which I never dreamed I would at my age."
- A. A. Allen, the miracle-working healing evangelist, died on June 14, 1970, of liver failure brought on by acute alcoholism.
- Leroy Jenkins, another evangelist and faith healer, was released from prison in December 1982, after serving three years of a twelve-year prison term for conspiracy to commit arson—for hiring two men to burn down a South Carolina highway patrolman's house—and conspiracy to commit assault—for attempting to have a newspaper reporter beaten up. Jenkins has since founded "The Church of What's Happening Now," in Columbus, Ohio.
- William Brahnam, died on Christmas eve 1965, of injuries he suffered in an automobile accident—about two months after I first learned of this "prophet" from Ric Durfield.
- Demos Shakarian suffered a stroke, but continues to work with his Full Gospel Businessmen's Fellowship International, which has grown to 300,000 members with chapters in eighty-seven countries.
- Jack Hayford continues as senior pastor of the Church on the Way, which, under his leadership, grew from eighteen to over 6,000 members. Some of his 350-plus songs have won him awards, including one he made us learn at LIFE Bible College, "We Lift Our Voices Rejoicing." Hayford is a prominent leader in the Pentecostal-Charismatic movement.
- Kathryn Kuhlman died in 1976, at age sixty-nine. Her close friend, the Rev. Jamie Buckingham, noted: "She loved her expensive clothes, precious jewels, luxury hotels, and first-class travel."
- The Alamos—Susan Alamo died of cancer in 1982. Tony (real name, Bernie Lazar Hoffman) reportedly kept her on hand for months as he and his followers attempted to raise her from the dead. Unsuccessful, Tony remarried, and published reports say Tony is now on his fifth marriage.
- Arthur Blessitt, now divorced, continues to drag a huge wooden cross around the United States and overseas.
- Frederick K. Price founded, and continues to pastor, the Crenshaw Christian Center in Los Angeles. With more than 10,000 members, it is one of the largest black churches in the United States. He still preaches the prosperity doctrines of Kenneth Hagin.

- Hobart Freeman assured his followers that he would be around when Jesus returned, but he died of a heart attack in 1985. Prior to his death, and as a direct result of his teaching on divine healing, eighty-nine people in his Ohio church, Faith Assembly, died because they refused medical treatment for various illnesses.
- Don Basham broke away from his emphasis on demonology to become a leader in the controversial discipleship movement. He died in 1989 of a heart attack, following a long illness.
- Juan Carlos Ortiz is back in the United States, reportedly working with Reverend Robert Schuller at his opulent Crystal Cathedral in Garden Grove, California. The discipleship movement he introduced is still practiced within a number of groups. Discipleship, or shepherding, with its excesses, has destroyed many churches and families.
- Dr. James Dobson's book, *Dare to Discipline,* a Christian bestseller, is still widely available in Christian and secular book stores. The success of the book helped Dobson launch Focus on the Family, a $60-million-a-year ministry which employs 750 people.
- The Durfields—Ric is senior pastor of the San Gabriel Valley Christian Center, in Azusa, California. He and Renee founded and head an organization called "For Wedlock Only," to help young people preserve their virginity until marriage. Ric appeared on the April 1990 cover of Dr. Dobson's popular *Focus on the Family* magazine. Articles in the magazine promoted Ric and Renee's ministry.
- Marian Porteous, my mother, died of cancer in February 1985. She, too, sought joy and truth; and she loved God, in her own way, right up to the end. One day, a few days before her death, fully alert, she told me her long-time secret: "Fundamentalists are all crazy, and there isn't a word of truth in any of it. I've believed that for years," she said.

    Amen, Mom.

Reflections on Don Wildmon

In my observation and study of the Rev. Donald Wildmon, I noticed that he often used anti-Semitic innuendo. This seemed quite evident in his book, *The Home Invaders*. Also, in his monthly *AFA Journal* (previously, the *NFD Journal*), Wildmon frequently referred to a study of the television industry made by S. Robert Lichter, a professor of political science at George Washington University, and Stanley Rothman, a professor of government at Smith College. Wildmon's interpretation of the study indicated that he agreed with anti-Semitic stereotyping about Jews who supposedly control Hollywood.

Now, I'm sure I'm not as sensitive to anti-Semitism as I could be, probably because I'm not Jewish, but in relation to our work, I've studied the subject extensively. I showed the Wildmon material to several Jewish friends. Each of them felt the material was anti-Semitic.

Then, during an interview on Miami's WNWS, the conversation got around to Donald Wildmon, since the interview focused on censorship. I stated that, in my opinion, Rev. Wildmon is anti-Semitic, and based my statement on the observations mentioned above.

Several weeks later, I received a letter from Wildmon's staff attorney, Peggy Coleman. She said they reviewed a recording of the WNWS broadcast, and said that several statements I made were patently false. Specifically (she quoted me from the tape), "Most of the Jewish groups that we work with all agree that Rev. Wildmon is anti-Semitic, and if anyone would doubt that, all they would have to do would be to go to a Christian book store and pick up his book called *The Home Invaders* and read that. It is published by Victor Books and it would be very obvious. It slips through in most of his writings and speeches, especially some of the earlier speeches. . . . He feels that these people, Jews especially, want to eliminate Christianity."

Coleman asked me to make a public retraction of my statement, because, she said, "it is false and defamatory." She continued, however, that if I believed the statement to be true, to furnish a copy of all material which serves as the basis for such a statement." Furthermore, she asked me to "further refrain from making false and defamatory statements about Rev. Wildmon."

I ignored her letter, because I felt justified in what I said, and I wasn't going to dignify her threat with a reply. Instead, I decided to pursue the matter further, and gathered all the documentation I could find about Wildmon's apparent anti-Semitic bias. Incidentally, the Jewish groups I mentioned on WNWS included the Anti-Defamation League of B'nai Brith, and the Jewish Defense League, which had been in touch with us at the time.

Now, how to use this material became the question. I remembered how annoyed I was when, in 1986, the Attorney General's Commission on Pornography sent out a heavy-handed letter—on Department of Justice stationery—to the heads of convenience stores and other chains which sold magazines such as *Playboy* and *Penthouse*. The letter, signed by Alan Sears, the porn commission's executive director, said:

> The Attorney General's Commission on Pornography has held six hearings across the United States during the past seven months on issues related to pornography. During the hearing in Los Angeles, in October 1985, the Commission received testimony alleging that your company is involved in the sale or distribution of pornography. The Commission has determined that it would be appropriate to allow your company an opportunity to respond to the allegations prior to drafting its final report section on identified distributors.
>
> You will find a copy of the relevant testimony enclosed herewith. Please review the allegations and advise the Commission on or before March 3, 1986, if you disagree with the statements enclosed. Failure to respond will necessarily be accepted as an indication of no objection.
>
> Thank you for your assistance.

The "relevant testimony" mentioned in the letter was actually a report titled "Pornography in the Family Marketplace," prepared by Donald Wildmon. The report opened with: "Few people realize that 7-Eleven convenience stores are the leading retailers of porn magazines in America." It continued to say that if 7-Eleven discontinued the sale of porn, "*Playboy* and *Penthouse* would be seriously crippled financially."

Of course, Rev. Wildmon wasn't mentioned in the Justice Department letter, or the report enclosed with the letter. A letter of this type from the U.S. Department of Justice is certain to have a chilling effect on its recipients. And, indeed it did. Shortly afterward, the Southland Corporation, with 8,100 company-owned 7-Eleven convenience stores, announced that it was pulling the magazines. Other companies did likewise.

Several months earlier, I had spoken to an official at Southland who assured me that the company would not bow to these self-styled censors. Well, they bowed all right, after the U.S. Department of Justice played into the hands of the censors. What is ironic is that the two magazines mentioned in Wildmon's report are constitutionally protected. Even Wildmon agrees with that.

Alan Sears, by the way, eventually moved on to become the executive director of Charles H. Keating's organization, Citizen's for Decency through Law, in Phoenix, Arizona. As an apparent result of the Savings & Loan scandal, the group's name was changed to Children's Legal Foundation. (See Appendix B for the article "Righteous Keating Plays the Name Game.")

So, Sear's letter became the basis of my counter-attack on Wildmon. I put together a packet which included everything I had documenting Wildmon's apparent anti-Semitic statements. Then I compiled a mailing list from Wildmon's *Journal*. The list was based upon "223 top Christian leaders" whom the *Journal* claimed endorsed the National Federation for Decency.

Because we didn't have the funds to send the packet to all 223 Christian leaders, we randomly selected sixty of them. Here is the letter included with the packet. Notice the similarity to the Sear's letter. Our letter was printed on Simon, Porteous & Associates, Inc., stationery, not *Freedom Writer* letterhead.

For several years we have investigated activist organizations in America and their connection with anti-Semitism. We have received documentation which we believe establishes an anti-Semitic bias in the campaign of Rev. Donald E. Wildmon, head of the American Family Association, formerly known as the National Federation of Decency [NFD].

According to the *NFD Journal,* you have given the following endorsement to the NFD:

"Without necessarily agreeing with everything the National Federation for Decency does, we do endorse the organization's overall ministry and recommend the NFD to those who are concerned and want to do something about the problem of pornography in America."

As the head of a respected Christian organization, we are certain that you deplore any nuance of anti-Semitism by you or your colleagues. We have determined that it would be appropriate to allow you an opportunity to respond to the allegations prior to drafting a statement to the press concerning Rev. Wildmon's anti-Semitism, and listing those who endorse his efforts.

You will find a copy of the relevant documentation, including a three-page summary, enclosed herewith. Please review the evidence and advise us on or before March 6, 1989, whether you agree or disagree with the evidence enclosed. Failure to respond will necessarily be accepted as an indication of your continued support of Rev. Wildmon and his alleged anti-Semitism.

Thank you for your assistance.

As some very interesting responses came by return mail, we prepared our next issue of *The Freedom Writer*. The headline of the main article was titled "Religious Leaders Denounce Wildmon's Anti-Semitism." The article is reprinted in its entirety below:

In response to a *Freedom Writer* organization study, John L. May, president of the National Conference of Catholic Bishops, and other Christian leaders have denounced the tactics and tone of the Rev. Donald E. Wildmon's crusade to "promote the Biblical ethic of decency in American society." Wildmon heads the American Family Association (formerly known as the National Federation for Decency [NFD]) in Tupelo, Mississippi.

Since 1977, Wildmon has "declared war" on everything that fails to promote his version of a Christian America. While he advocates school prayer, a ban on abortion, and an end to sex education in public schools, most of Wildmon's efforts revolve around censorship. His campaign has created a chilling effect on the entertainment industry.

Wildmon recently scored several major successes in his assault on the broadcasting industry. NBC blames Wildmon for the loss of nearly $1 million in advertising revenue for its critically acclaimed made-for-TV movie, "Roe vs. Wade." Although Wildmon had not seen the film, he quoted a wire service story, out of context. Wildmon interpreted it to mean that NBC admitted that the movie "was pro-abortion." In fact, NBC went to great lengths to present a balanced view in "Roe vs. Wade," which was based upon the Supreme Court's 1973 decision to legalize abortion throughout the nation.

Another NBC program, "Saturday Night Live," which failed to comport with Wildmon's "Biblical ethic of decency" for America, lost millions in advertising revenue, after Wildmon convinced General Mills, Ralston-Purina, and Domino Pizza to cancel its advertising.

One month after Wildmon called for a boycott of Pepsi, Pepsico cancelled a $5 million contract with the pop singer Madonna. Wildmon was reacting to Madonna's video, "Like A Prayer," which he believed to be blasphemous. According to Wildmon, in this video, Madonna represents Christ, and is shown "suggesting that she has sex with a priest, obviously to free him from sexual repression."

Donald Wildmon has enjoyed some measure of success in his attempts at censoring the free press. In fact, he was largely responsible for the Southland Corporation's decision to drop the sale of *Penthouse* and *Playboy* from its company-owned 7-Eleven stores. This occurred shortly after a Wildmon-authored report on the effects of pornography accompanied a letter from the U.S. Department of Justice. The letter was mailed to companies, alleged by Wildmon, to be distributors of pornography. Certainly, the distribution and official sanction of Reverend Wildmon's religious opinion by the U.S. Government was a clear violation of church/state separation.

Wildmon creates tales to fuel his readers' desire to believe in the evils of "pornography." For example: the January 1987 issue of Wildmon's magazine, the *NFD Journal* (the *National Enquirer* of the religious right), ran an article with the sensational headline, "Murder Imitates Porn Magazine Layout." The article was about the tragic murder of an orphaned Chinese girl in North Carolina. Police arrested a George Fisher after the girl's body was found hanging from a tree. Subsequently, Fisher was convicted of kidnapping, attempted rape, and murder. The NFD article commented, "The location where she was found and the disposition of her body resembled a December 1984 *Penthouse* magazine feature showing Asian women bound with rope from neck to ankles, hanging from trees."

Police in North Carolina, however, dispute the NFD's contention that Fisher imitated a *Penthouse* photo. Police Lt. Arthur Summey of Chapel Hill, NC, who investigated the case, told *The Freedom Writer,* "We have no information that ties him to the photo in any way. The Lieutenant added, "As far as we know, he had never seen that photo or issue of *Penthouse.*"

The February 1986 *NFD Journal* had an article which described the woes of a Christian inmate, serving time in Leavenworth prison, who was supposedly leading an anti-porn campaign at the federal institution. The NFD claimed that due to the publicity he received through the *NFD Journal,* the prisoner, James Davenport, "has received so much mail that he is unable to answer all the letters." According to the *NFD Journal* story, the prisoner said, "The prison limits the number of stamps I can buy as a punishment for my stand against pornography."

When *The Freedom Writer* interviewed Karen Gray, a spokesperson for Leavenworth, she responded, "Everyone is allotted the same number of stamps each month." She added emphatically, "No one would be punished for taking a stand against pornography."

Due to their vagueness, many of Wildmon's stories are impossible to confirm. For example: the March 1986 issue of his magazine had the tale of a Christian teenage girl in Alberta, Canada, who was forced to shower with her stepfather as punishment for attending her fundamentalist church. As the *NFD Journal* told it, he demanded one shower for every sixth time she attended church. The stepfather, according to the NFD, was sentenced to prison. The article failed to name the stepfather, judge, attorney, or any other persons with whom we could corroborate the story.

An *NFD Journal* headline (March 1987) read, "Fort Lauderdale Free of Porn Videos." That story was based on a letter from Wildmon's friend, Bill Kelly, a former FBI agent. As reported in the *NFD Journal,* the letter stated: "As of today, there is not one videotape store in the city of Fort Lauderdale selling or renting X-rated video tapes."

A few days after that story was published, we happened to be in Fort Lauderdale. We sought out the nearest Fort Lauderdale video store and found an attractive, well-organized family-type video rental shop. After browsing through the Disney films and other "PG" fare, we asked if they rented X-rated movies. "Sure, they're in the side room," the clerk replied. A sign above the door indicated that the room was for adults only. We learned that other video stores in Fort Lauderdale also continued to rent adult tapes. These stories illustrate the fact that Wildmon, through his *NFD Journal,* makes claims which are not true.

Wildmon has claimed the support of religious leaders who say they never authorized him to use their names. Denver's Archbishop Stafford is listed as one of 223 Christian leaders who have endorsed the National Federation for Decency [now the American Family Association]. Yet, the Archdiocese of Denver told us in a letter that they were perplexed about allegations that the Archbishop had any relationship with Wildmon's organization, for they do not.

Detroit's Archbishop Edmund Szoka was also listed by Wildmon as a supporter. Yet, the Archbishop's office told the *Detroit Free Press* that in 1985 the Archbishop signed a general statement about television ethics, but "he has signed nothing else, nor does he endorse the organization" led by Wildmon.

The Freedom Writer successfully infiltrated Wildmon's organization in 1986. Our purpose was to obtain accurate, inside information. During a six-month period, the Great Barrington NFD was the darling of the Tupelo "home office." We corresponded personally with Wildmon, and conversed with him on the phone about our chapter's activities. We received chapter mailings and sent the "home office" reports of our activities. At the culmination of the project, Skipp Porteous visited Wildmon in Tupelo. After the first day, Wildmon realized that he'd been tricked. On the second day of the visit, Wildmon called in the police and local press. After the brief confrontation, Porteous left Tupelo.

According to a report in Tupelo's *Northeast Mississippi Daily Journal,* the police affirmed that Porteous had broken no laws. In the article, Wildmon accused Porteous of unsuccessfully attempting to infiltrate the NFD. He said this was not the first attempt to gain information under false pretenses, but may have been the first time someone tried to infiltrate the organization. For some reason, Wildmon couldn't bring himself to admit that the attempt was successful. So, instead, he lied to the press.

"Perhaps the most serious charge against Wildmon," according to the *Detroit Free Press* (5/21/89), "involves anti-Semitism."

Early this year, Simon, Porteous & Associates, Inc., publishers of this newsletter, documented the anti-Semitic position of Rev. Wildmon. This documentation was delivered to sixty national Christian leaders from whom Wildmon claims support.

The documentation includes evidence of Wildmon blaming Jews for objectionable TV programs and "anti-Christian" films. For years, Rev.

Wildmon has maintained that "Hollywood and the theater world is heavily influenced by Jewish people." And he has consistently expressed his belief that there is a conspiracy among television network executives and advertisers which amounts to "a genuine hostility towards Christians and the Christian faith." "This anti-Christian programming is," according to Wildmon, "intentional and by design."

Besides the religious leaders who denied any involvement with Wildmon, responses included that of James M. Lapp, Executive Secretary of the Mennonite Church: "I have reviewed the materials you have sent to us. I find the inferences and tone in these materials to be offensive. [We] do not wish to be on public record in support of any writings or programs with open or implied anti-Semitic biases. In summary, we support Mr. Wildmon in his concern for decency and positive values. We do not support some of his tactics, attitudes or biases against Jewish people."

John L. May, Archbishop of St. Louis, and head of The National Conference of Catholic Bishops, responded, "I certainly do not agree with the obvious anti-Semitic bias of Reverend Donald E. Wildmon." Other church leaders stated that they had objected to Wildmon's tactics. One, Robert M. Overgaard [who is listed as a member of Wildmon's Advisory Board], President of the Church of the Lutheran Brethren, said, "In so far as Wildmon equates MCA [which produced *The Last Temptation of Christ*] with the Jewish race, I find his tactics unacceptable." He continued, "I do not excuse Wildmon for his racial generalizations. I have objected to them."

Stuart Lewengrub, director of the Anti-Defamation League's Atlanta office, said of Rev. Wildmon, "He's encouraging his followers to believe that Jews are responsible for the kind of programming they dislike."

Much of Wildmon's trouble stems from his misuse of a 1982 study of television writers, producers, and executives. The independent study was done by S. Robert Lichter, a professor of political science at George Washington University, and Stanley Rothman, a professor of government at Smith College. Wildmon bases much of his anti-Semitic innuendo on his misrepresentation of their findings.

Lichter stated that his survey ". . . drew no conclusions about the nature of [TV] programming or the precise motivations of program directors." He added, "We naturally abhor any imputation of anti-Semitic inferences from our survey of television producers and executives."

Rothman went even further—he wrote directly to Wildmon. He said, "The inferences you draw from our data are not justified." In fact, Rothman told Wildmon that their findings presented "no evidence" to support any of Wildmon's allegations, and that a new study actually proved the contrary.

Wildmon now claims that his use of the Lichter/Rothman study is to point out that "these people are secular people who have spurned religion."

Lewengrub said the Anti-Defamation League has tried in a constructive way "to lean over backward to give him the benefit of the doubt."

If Wildmon's point is that Hollywood leaders are secular or atheists," Lewengrub said, "he can say so without alluding to their religious backgrounds. Nor does Wildmon need to note, as he often does, that the Jewish background of television executives '. . . contrasts dramatically with society as a whole, which is 2½ percent Jewish.' "

There is no doubt in my mind that Wildmon has engaged in anti-Semitism," Lewengrub said. "He didn't stop. He continued doing it."

Wildmon's platform consists of one concept, which we mentioned earlier in this article—to promote "the Biblical ethic of decency in American society." In order to achieve his goal, he wants to eradicate all ideas with which he disagrees. In his book *The Home Invaders,* Wildmon wrote, "The danger lies not in the vulgar and obscene pictures. . . . The danger is the philosophy behind those pictures. That philosophy is humanism." Wildmon insists that his philosophy is the correct one to be conveyed by the media. For example:

If a TV show had no scantily clad actors, nor the kind of language which Wildmon considers to be profane, such as "hell" and "damn," but, if its plot even hinted at the suggestion of sex outside of marriage, Wildmon would still be outraged. In his view, if television is to acceptably allude to sex, it must do so within the confines of a legal heterosexual marriage.

In the print media—if *Penthouse* and *Playboy* were to remove every photograph from their pages, Wildmon would still disapprove. Why? Because Wildmon disagrees with the editorial and philosophical viewpoint of these publications.

Wildmon has a constitutionally protected right to his beliefs. In his eyes, the "Biblical ethic of decency" must rule American society.

Soon after that issue of *The Freedom Writer* appeared, we distributed our documentation to various media and some other First Amendment organizations, including People For the American Way. Then, stories such as "Accusations of Bias Cost Minister Support" began to appear around the country.

It didn't take Wildmon long to figure out what was going on. He responded by sending out his own letter, which is reprinted below. For fairness, it is quoted in its entirety. My comments are found in brackets.

Recently, Charles R. Porteous of Simon, Porteous & Associates, Inc. has sent a letter accusing me of being anti-Semitic to approximately 200 Christian leaders. He threatens those to whom he writes that if they do not respond within a very short time, he will accept that no response as an endorsement of being anti-Semitic themselves and so identify them. Here is an explanation of the situation pertaining to Mr. Porteous.

Late in the fall of 1986 we received a call from a Massachusetts man who identified himself as Rev. Charles Porter who said he was a pastor of the Great Barrington Christian Fellowship. He said he was starting a local AFA chapter and was going to California to attend the wedding of his brother [actually I said I was performing the marriage ceremony of a "brother" meaning a Christian brother] and, would like to return via Tupelo to visit with us. He said his brother was paying for the trip. Of course we urged him to visit, although we thought it strange for one to return from a trip to Californian to Massachusetts via Tupelo.

We checked our records and found that a Rev. Charles Porter had, indeed earlier informed us that he was starting a local chapter in Great Barrington.

On the appointed day, he arrived at our office early and stayed the entire day. However, the kinds of questions he was asking were not those asked by someone interested in a local chapter but by a reporter. He even had a camera and took several pictures inside the office. He said that he wanted to return the next day and spend most of the day with us.

His questions and actions left us suspicious, so after he left late in the afternoon we started contacting people in Great Barrington to try to learn something about him. Rev. Edward Vergara of Calvary Christian Chapel Assembly of God told us that Porter was not Rev. Charles Porter, but rather Charles Porteous and that he was on some sort of "crusade against what he calls the extreme right." Neither could we find any listing for a "Great Barrington Christian Fellowship."

The next morning, we confronted "Rev. Porter" in a meeting in front of a reporter from the *Jackson (MS) Clarion Ledger,* the *Northeast Mississippi Daily Journal* and a detective from the Tupelo Police Department. When I confronted "Porter" with the information we had gained and asked for some explanation, he refused to explain, became extremely defensive and replied: "I guess our meeting is through," and immediately left the office. [Well, not quite. I left after giving into their demands for the film from my camera.]

The best we could piece together regarding the incident was that probably one of the porn (*Playboy* or *Penthouse*) magazines had offered Mr. Porteous a sizable sum of money if he could get an exclusive interview with me. The porn magazines have made several such attempts over the years. (Later Porteous told AFA that *Playboy* helps fund his organization.) [Wildmon said this because, on WNWS, I was asked if *Playboy* or *Penthouse* funded our organization. I replied that we received a $500 grant from the Playboy Foundation, and wished it was ten-times that amount.]

I later learned that Mr. Porteous was at one time a Christian minister. It is my understanding that he left the ministry, divorced and then remarried a woman who is Jewish and began his campaign against those who fight pornography and other social, moral issues such as those we deal with. The Simon partner in the "Simon, Porteous & Associates, Inc." which he uses on his letterhead is his wife. Porteous also operates under other names—i.e., *The Freedom Writer*.

Since the incident Mr. Porteous has made several attempts to discredit our work. The "anti-Semite" letter is only the latest.

As far as being anti-Semitic, I am not. I have a Jewish brother-in-law. Also, AFA has supported researcher Dr. Judith Reisman, who is Jewish, generously for over two years. And my Lord was a Jew.

In the letter Mr. Porteous sends out, his last paragraph indicates the way he works. [Remember where I learned it!] It implies that unless the person responds, then that person is also "anti-Semitic" and will be so identified.

It was my opinion when Mr. Porteous first began sending out his letter that he was fishing for some comment from some Christian leaders which he could then send to the media. I was correct in my opinion. Of the approximately 200 he has written, three of them have responded with comments he is currently sending to media people. [As I mentioned earlier, limited funds permitted us to send out only 60 letters.] One of the leaders I do not know. [That's strange, for the entire list of endorsements we obtained came from Wildmon's magazine.] Unfortunately, the other two responded without contacting me to discuss the situation prior to responding. They were afraid of being branded as anti-Semitic.

People For the American Way, the group Norman Lear founded, has picked up on Mr. Brannon's and Mr. Porteous' theme. [Robert Brannon was then a vice-president of Holiday Inn, and shared our concerns about Wildmon] PAW told the *Chicago Tribune* that since a majority of the television elite are Jewish, and since I document and complain about the sex, violence, profanity and anti-Christian bias in many of the television programs, that makes me anti-Semitic. That argument could be used to say if one opposes the politics of Rev. Jesse Jackson, that person is a racist because Rev. Jackson is black.

The religion or race of the people responsible for the trash on television, including the anti-Christian bias, is of no importance to me. But on the other hand, I refuse to stop fighting the sex, violence, profanity and anti-Christian stereotyping simply because some of those involved happen to be of a particular race or religion. Research has shown that the overwhelming majority of people responsible for television programs are thoroughly secular and would like to see religion have very little influence on our society. Therein lies the problem. And that is the problem we are addressing.

As AFA becomes more effective, we expect our adversaries will try more and more extreme methods to discredit us. That simply goes with the territory and is to be expected.

I'm not anti-Semitic, and I do oppose pornography and the anti-Christian bias of television programming, and I intend to continue doing so.

As a result of *The Freedom Writer* project, Wildmon seldom refers to the Lichter/Rothman study. At most, he'll say the study affirms the secular nature of those who run the television industry. Rev. Wildmon claims he's not anti-Semitic, so, so be it. His misuse of the Lichter/Rothman study certainly caused many to wonder. And, it may have even encouraged some Christians who *are* anti-Semitic to support Wildmon. At least in the future he'll take another tack.

Appendix A

Anatomy of a Small-town Crusader

The following article appeared in the Forum section of *Playboy* magazine (September, 1990). Cartoon caricatures of a furious and curious male letter-writer accompanied the story. It is reprinted by permission.

ANATOMY OF A SMALL-TOWN CRUSADER

Using his office as mayor, a born-again christian wages a religious campaign—with letters that get curiouser and curiouser.

City of Ravenna
(*city seal*)

April 1, 1988

Mr. Charles Nirenberg, Chairman
Dairy Mart, Inc.
Dear Mr. Nirenberg:

    On behalf of the City of Ravenna, I would like to welcome Dairy Mart to the Ravenna Community.

    I like your slogan, "the good people" store. I know that the people who are employed in the local Dairy Mart stores are good people. This is evident by the noticeable cleanliness of the stores both inside and out. Also, the courteousness extended to each customer is appreciated . . .

    However, there is one area of the Dairy Mart business that troubles me. That is the sale of pornographic magazines. Quite frankly, I am surprised that Dairy Mart chooses to sell pornography, being a "good people" business . . .

As Mayor and Safety Director for the City of Ravenna, I am concerned for the safety, health, and welfare of the Ravenna citizens and their families. After extensive personal research on the effects (physical and emotional) that obscene materials have on individuals, [I believe] without any doubt in my mind, that obscene material, which includes pornography, does not promote the safety, health, and welfare of the Ravenna citizen. In fact, pornography promotes just the opposite; the proper and perverted view of human sexuality—which has an immoral, debilitating, and destructive effect on individuals and their families. God designed human sexuality to be good and wholesome between husband and wife only. Sexual intimacy in a marriage is just one of many beautiful ways of expressing the love the married couple have for each other. Pornography transforms human sexuality from love to lust . . .

Sincerely,

Donald J. Kainrad, Mayor

Dairy Mart (*logo*)

April 8, 1988

Dear Mayor Kainrad,

I appreciate the time you took to write me about the "good people" of Dairy Mart and our stores in Portage County, Ohio. We work hard to make them clean, neat, full and friendly, and it's great to know people like you value our efforts.

Clearly, too, you have also voiced concerns about our stores' selling adult-oriented magazines. . . . Assume for an instant that the reasons you so eloquently state for not selling adult magazines are heeded and acted upon by every possible outlet for these magazines. Where do we draw the line? Where do we stop dictating values? Shouldn't cigarettes be removed from sale to avoid societal harm, or alcohol, or even milk (high cholesterol), for that matter?

If we remove ourselves from the rights of choice, then any governmental body or a committee of a select few can dictate what we read, eat, wear, or do for a living. I don't think you are a proponent of that form of government . . .

It was in this spirit of democracy, free speech, and the American way that we put the issues you brought up to a vote . . . to anyone who came to our stores, to our customers. In a well-publicized and certified election, people entering our stores all over Ohio were given the right to vote adult magazines in or out. Overwhelmingly, the vote indicated that the customers *want the right to choose* whether or not they buy adult magazines.

Mayor Kainrad, I am not trying to be combative with you; nor am I willing to engage in a running discourse on the subject. But I do respect your position. I hope you respect the position of all American consumers, of their right to decide for themselves what they want to purchase.

Very truly yours,

Charles Nirenberg,
Chairman of the Board and
Chief Executive Officer
DAIRY MART CONVENIENCE
STORES, INC.

City of Ravenna
(*seal*)

June 29, 1988

Dear Mr. Nirenberg:

The Citizens for Decency of Portage County, of which I am a cochairman, will not and cannot stand idly by while Dairy Mart continues to pander this filth and obscenity in our communities . . .

I am enclosing the first of many full-page newspaper advertisements calling for the boycott of Dairy Mart stores in Portage County. Also, random picketing will begin at some of the stores. We do not wish to take this type of action against Dairy Mart. But what choice have you given us?

Sincerely,

Donald J. Kainrad, Mayor

City of Ravenna
(*city seal*)

September 28, 1989

Dear Mr. Nirenberg:

I personally have a strong faith in the Lord, my God—Jesus! He is my source of joy, peace, strength, and wisdom in every area of my life. I rely on the spiritual wisdom and knowledge of God to direct my personal and professional life.

There is a Biblical principle that cannot be altered—"Be not deceived; God is not mocked; for whatsoever a man soweth, that shall he also reap." (Galatians 6:7)

Mr. Nirenberg, God is not mocked! Dairy Mart is sowing poison and destructive seeds in our society through the sale of pornography; and Dairy Mart will reap the bitter consequences. Dairy Mart has sowed to the wind "iniquity" and will reap the whirlwind of despair, confusion, and economic hardship.

God cannot and will not bless the Dairy Mart Corporation or any other business that willfully violates His Commandments. I am sure you have heard the Commandment of God "Thou shall not commit adultery." Pornography is sexual immorality and adultery. . . .

Mr. Nirenberg, do you feel that sexual immorality is normal and natural? God has said, "Woe unto them that call evil good and good evil; that put darkness for light, and light for darkness . . ." (Isaiah 5:20)

I respectfully request that you please give serious thought as to what has been revealed to you. If you truly care about the future of the Dairy Mart Corporation, and want the return of God's blessings, you must remove all forms of pornography from your stores. If there is any other business activity that you know in your heart is displeasing to God, you need to stop and redirect those activities in the light of God's Commandments.

I think it is important for you to know that for the past one and a half years, there has been an active boycott of the local Dairy Mart stores in Portage County. The Citizens for Decency of Portage County executive committee (of which I am a member) called for the county-wide boycott, and the boycott will continue until the pornography is removed.

Sincerely,

Donald J. Kainrad, Mayor

At this point, Nirenberg referred Kainrad's correspondence to Skipp Porteous, editor of *The Freedom Writer*, a national newsletter that defends the separation of church and state.

Porteous told Kainrad to stop his campaign against Dairy Mart, resign, or face legal action. The mayor agreed to stop using city resources to promote his religious views—but did not stick to his agreement. At last report, Kainrad was attacking Ohio attorney general Anthony J. Celebrezze, Jr. for his pro-choice stance, again writing letters on city stationery:

> There is no middle ground on this serious issue of life. You either acknowledge and support human life at conception as our Creator God has designed or you don't. I do not believe in the smokescreen fallacy of pro-choice. You are either pro-life or pro-death. God ordained and established human government. Those of us who are government officials are placed in these positions by God. Therefore, we are not only responsible to our constituents but primarily responsible to Him (our Heavenly Father). For the well-being of our country, we need to support and defend the moral laws of God. We should not, for the sake of political convenience and votes, set aside or deny the laws of God or the almighty God himself.

Kainrad, who told *The Freedom Writer*, "There is not a separation of church and state," obviously has missed the point of the First and Fourteenth Amendments.

In a recent editorial, *The Freedom Writer* said, "We respect Donald Kainrad's right to pursue his religious ideals, but as an elected representative of the city of Ravenna, he should not create the impression that the city of Ravenna endorses any religious view, for this action is violative of our Constitution."

If you don't understand that, Mayor Kainrad, you shouldn't be mayor.

Appendix B

Righteous Keating Plays the Name Game

The following article first appeared in the *Berkshire Eagle* on December 13, 1989. Then, almost simultaneously, in the November/December 1989 edition of *The Freedom Writer*.

Three months later I received a letter from Tad Ames, the *Berkshire Eagle's* Op–Ed page editor. He wrote, "I was particularly pleased, both for you and the *Eagle*, to see an article in *The New Republic* (April 2, 1990) on Charles Keating's anti-porn ways. I don't know if the writer was inspired by *The Freedom Writer* or not, but however it came about, you beat him to the punch by months."

RIGHTEOUS KEATING PLAYS THE NAME GAME
by Skipp Porteous

"For most, it's a question of money. For American Continental Corporation, it is a question of morals. Widely known for its support of anti-pornography issues, American Continental Corporation is the parent company of the Crescent Hotel Group, which opened the world's finest resort in Scottsdale, Arizona, on October 1 [1988]. The 605-room resort does not have porn movies in its rooms or porn magazines in the gift shops."

[The CDL Reporter, November 1988]

On November 16, 1989, more than sixty Federal agents and plainclothes police officers conducted a pre-dawn raid on the squeaky clean

Crescent Hotel. The agents seized the resort and secured the office of the president of the hotel, the long-time extreme Christian activist Charles H. Keating, Jr.

The feds' takeover of the porn-free Crescent Hotel was just another chapter in a scandal that will cost U.S. taxpayers billions of dollars. Keating has been the focus of criminal investigations by the Federal Bureau of Investigation, the Internal Revenue Service, the Justice Department, the Securities and Exchange Commission, and the House Banking Committee. The federal government has also filed a $1.1 billion suit against Keating and his associates. The suit arises from accusations of fraud and illegal loan activity by the Lincoln Savings and Loan Association, another Keating company.

Additionally, it was revealed that five U.S. senators who tried to stall regulatory actions against Keating had received $1.3 million in campaign contributions from him. Keating has openly admitted that he sought to buy congressional influence.

In 1957, Charles H. Keating, Jr. founded the non-profit organization, Citizens for Decency through Law [CDL]—a pro-censorship group. He has remained active with CDL for the past thirty-two years.

Earlier this year, I observed a subtle change in *The CDL Reporter*, the group's newsletter. Until that time, the words "Founded in 1957 by Charles H. Keating, Jr." appeared on the back of every issue. Suddenly, Keating's name was omitted. It wasn't that Keating withdrew his abundant financial support or his active involvement, but, perhaps, the group anticipated what lay ahead.

Then, in April, the government seized Keating's insolvent Lincoln Savings and Loan Association. [Keating is also chairman of the American Continental Corporation, Lincoln's parent company.] The government contends that American Continental took $95 million from Lincoln's depositors with bogus land investments. Some 23,000 uninsured customers lost their savings.

In July, CDL changed its name and became Children's Legal Foundation [CLF]. In its July/August newsletter, Executive Director, Alan Sears, attempted to explain the change. In doublespeak, he said the old name was "cumbersome and does not have the distinct message it originally carried." He added that their staff has "encountered increasing confusion about our name and mission." More likely, in light of the founder's deceitful activities, the old name had become an embarrassment.

Charles H. Keating, Jr. is to the savings and loan industry what Jim Bakker was to television evangelism. Both men, notable Christian crusaders, represent wealth attained through deceit and fraud.

Perhaps the Children's Legal Foundation will redeem its founder. It could come to the aid of the families who lost their Christmas club savings, and the families which put money aside for their children's education.

Citizens for Decency through Law, though, was not the first radical organization to change its name out of embarrassment.

The Moral Majority was chided about its name probably more than any organization in history. A popular bumper sticker proclaimed, "The Moral Majority Is Neither."

Then came a parade of disgraced TV evangelists—our keepers of morality. The scandals got so bad that the Rev. Falwell had to change his group's name to The Liberty Federation. At that time, I commented in *The Freedom Writer*, "The Liberty Federation will do no more for liberty than the Moral Majority did for morality." Since the January 1986 name change, The Liberty Federation has also become history.

Even before the advent of The Moral Majority, another moralist, the Rev. Donald Wildmon, founded The National Federation For Decency. His purpose was to "promote the biblical ethic of decency in American society." This "decent" fellow has recently been blasted over his use of anti-Semitic innuendo. Last year, the Rev. Wildmon announced that his group would henceforth be known as the American Family Association.

Radical religious zealots continue to be their own worst enemy. Decency and morality are more than a name. Unable to keep the standards implicit in their names, group after group has been forced to adopt new, "safe" names.

Index

Aberrant Christianity, 146
Abortion, 11, 12, 15, 19, 21, 22, 137, 214, 240, 255, 262, 263, 276
Abortionist(s), 12, 15, 230, 243, 248
Abraham, 31–32
ACLU, 22, 200. *See also* American Civil Liberties Union
ADL (Anti-Defamation League), 281
Adult movies, 192
Adulterers, 230, 252, 255, 256
Adultery, 11, 288
Advanced Metals Division (Whittaker Corporation), 87
AFA, 283, 284. *See also* American Family Association
AFA Journal, 273
Africa, 86, 173
African dialect, 81
African Methodist Episcopal (AME) Church, 80
Agape, 149
Agape Force, 150, 153
Agape House, 153–157
Agape Inn, 149–150, 153

AIDS, 178, 200
Akers, Doris, 80
Akers, Harley, 80–81, 86, 89–90
Alamo, Tony and Susan, 105, 270
Alcohol abuse, 58
Allen, A. A., 82, 270
Allen, Steve, 240, 242, 261
Altar, 29, 79, 81, 198
Altar call(s), 90, 114, 116
America Can Be Saved, 186
American Atheists, 225
American Christianity, 12, 231
American Christians, 12, 233
American Civil Liberties Union (ACLU), 22, 207
American Continental Corporation, 291–292
American Electric, 73, 74, 75, 87
American Family Association (AFA), 12, 189, 235, 276, 279, 293
American flag, 114
Americans United for the Separation of Church and State, 185, 187, 207
Ames, Tad, 291

295

Index

Amway, 130
Anaheim Stadium, 112–113
Angel(s), 31, 32, 82, 105, 149, 263
Angels of Light, 134
Angelus Temple, 89, 99, 123
Ansonia, 63, 66
Anti-Christian, 279, 284
Anti-Christian bias, 192
Anti-Defamation League of B'nai Brith, 274, 280
Anti-pornography, 197
Anti-Semite, 280, 283
Anti-Semitic, 131, 273, 274, 275, 276, 279, 280, 282, 283, 284, 293
Anti-Semitism, 222, 276, 279, 281
Apollo Theater, 61, 62, 78, 225, 227
Apostles, 242
Archbishop of St. Louis, 280
Archbishop Szoka, 279
Archdiocese of Denver, 279
Argentina, 144
Argentine, 144, 145
Armageddon, 10, 179, 184
Armstrong, Garner Ted, 80
Arrowhead Springs, 144
Assemblies of God, 23, 87, 195
A Street Car Named Desire, 170
Atheism, 267
Atheist(s), 267, 281
Atheistic, 250
Atheist Jew, 226
Attorney General's Commission on Pornography, 274
Australia, 211
Authorized King James Version, 158
Awake!, 73

Babylon, 243
Back sliding, 82, 117, 247
Bailey, Marie, 120–126

Bakker, Jim, 218, 219, 293
Baptism, The, 87–89
Baptism in the Holy Spirit, 81, 87, 88, 91, 105, 176
Baptist(s), 40, 41, 42, 45, 46, 48, 78, 105, 246
Bart, Teddy, 209
Basham, Don, 135, 271
Basic training/boot camps, 18
Bassett, Forrest and Barbara, 36
Battle For The Mind, The, 182
Bay Area Council of Pastors, 16
Being under conviction, 175
Bell South Mobility, 243
Berkshire Christian College, 183
Berkshire Eagle, The, 180, 182, 184, 207, 291
Berkshire Hills, 182
Bershefski, Joan, 197, 199, 200, 201, 202, 203
Bertram, Undersheriff Jim, 163, 164, 166–169
Between Christ and Satan, 134
"Beyond Reason," 209
Bible, 10, 11, 13, 15, 16, 23, 30, 31, 40, 41, 42, 45, 57, 62, 66, 81, 83, 87, 89, 92–94, 96, 98, 102, 103, 104, 108, 112, 117, 124, 125, 126, 129, 141, 151, 158, 177, 178, 196, 199, 200, 202, 203, 204, 220–222, 232, 239, 240, 242, 243, 247, 249, 258–261, 263, 265, 266
Bible-believing, 14
Bible-believing Christians, 232
Bible classes, 198
Bible clubs, 23
Bible distribution, 207
Bible-reading, 230, 265
Bible scholars, 178
Bible Speaks, The, 180, 183–184, 207

Bible study, 125, 126, 129, 132, 141, 142, 149, 153, 158
Biblical law, 252, 260
Big Apple, 182, 212
"Big house, the," 139
Bill of Rights, 25, 213, 232, 265
Billy Graham Crusade, 113
Billy Graham Evangelistic Association, 112–114, 117
Black, 82, 284
Black churches, 78
Black, Hugo, 205
Blacks, 57
Black theology, 107
Blessit, Arthur, 105, 270
Blue laws, 19
Board of education, 22
Boggs, Bill, 227
Bonnke, Reinhard, 10
Book Industry Study Group, 10
Book of Mormon, 93
Boone, Pat, 100, 151, 183, 202, 223
Born-again, 9, 12, 18, 21, 23, 25, 41, 57, 72, 82, 87, 139, 151, 158, 175, 202, 218, 222, 231
Born-againer(s), 42, 204
Botswana, 173
Brando, Marlon, 46
Branham, William, 82
Brannon, Robert, 270, 283
Brown, Dr. Robert K., 184
Buckingham, Jamie, 270
Bulimia, 137
Burch, Mrs., 30
Burns, George, 123

Caesar, Sid, 176
Cain, Paul, 9
Callahan, Henry, 61, 66
Calvary Christian Chapel Assembly of God, 282
Campbell, Laverne, 108, 150–152
Campbell, Luther, 21
Canada, 88, 134, 211, 230
Canadian, 134
Candidate(s), 13, 17, 22
Capital punishment, 15, 236, 258, 259, 262, 266
Carter, Jimmy, 151, 200, 202
Case Against Pornography, The, 190
Castro, Nestor, 56
Catholic Church, 238
Catholic(s), 36, 38, 63, 242, 246
Catholicism, 37
Catskill Game Farm, 64
CBN, 201, 202. See also Christian Broadcasting Network
CDL, 292. See also Citizens for Decency through Law
CDL Reporter, 291
CEE, 24, 25. See also Citizens for Excellence in Education
Celebrezze, Jr., Anthony J., 289
Celibacy, 34
Censor, 202, 213, 239
Censorship, 190, 198, 210, 277
Chalcedon Foundation, 12, 252
Chapel on the Strip, 105–107
Chappaquiddick, 219
Charisma & Christian Life, 23
Charismatic(s), 18, 88, 131, 135, 143, 145, 149, 152, 153, 177, 219
Checker, Chubby, 49
Checks and balances, 187
Chicago Tribune, 284
Chick, Jack, 112, 154
Chick Publications, 113
Child abuse, 139, 219, 222
Child evangelists, 227
Children's Legal Foundation (CLF),

21, 275, 292–293
China, 15
Chobe National Park, 173
Chosen People, 29
Christ, 247
Christian activism, 10, 12
Christian activists, 233
Christian America, 276
Christian and Missionary Alliance, 107
Christian Bible Clubs, 23
Christian book store(s), 149, 158, 231, 249, 271, 274
Christian Broadcasting Network, 201
Christian Coalition, 21, 22
Christian community, 22, 23
Christian conferences, 10
Christian contributions, 18
Christian denominations, 240
Christian fundamentalism, 205, 207
Christian heritage, 151
Christian missionaries, 9, 23
Christian nation, 151, 183, 190, 202, 211, 263
Christian political special interest groups, 20
Christian radio stations, 18, 80
Christian reconstruction, 12, 253, 258, 261, 264, 266, 267
Christian reconstructionist(s), 243, 257, 269
Christian right, 9, 20
Christian Science, 63
Christian Seders, 170
Christian sex manual, 249
Christian TV, 18
Christian view of man, 195–196
Christianity and Humanism, 195
Christianize America, 13
Christianize California, 16, 232, 265
Christmas, 58, 59, 87, 90, 91, 133, 134, 153, 185, 293
Christmas Eve, 270
Christmas tree(s), 90–91, 134
Church in the garage, 139
Church of God in Christ, 82, 141
Church of Jesus Christ of Latter-day Saints, 92
Church of the Lutheran Brethren, 280
Church of the Open Door, 80, 87
Church of What's Happening Now, 270
Church on the Way, 100, 151, 152, 270
Church/state, 183, 214
Church/state separation, 16, 185, 187, 189, 205, 206, 265, 277
Churcher, Sharon, 217, 218, 224
Citizen, 21
Citizens for Decency of Portage County, 287
Citizens for Decency through Law (CDL), 273, 292–293
Citizens for Excellence in Education (CEE), 23
City councils, 14, 22
City government, 14
City of God, The, 127
City of Ravenna, 285, 286–288
Clan of the Cave Bears, 24
Clarkson, Fred, 17, 269
Clifton's Cafeteria, 87–88
CNN (Cable News Network), 214
Coalition(s), 20, 21, 22
Coalition On Revival (COR), 12, 16, 231, 232, 235, 243, 245, 246, 255, 257, 261, 266, 269
Cohen, Dr. Edmund, 217–218, 224
Colclough, Mr., 56
Cole's, 262
Coleman, Peggy, 273, 274
College of St. Rose, 170

Columbia County Sheriff's Department. *See* Sheriff's Department
Columbia-Greene Community College, 161, 169, 171
Communist(s), 39, 40
Community Activities League (CAL), 55
"Completed Jew," 85
Concerned Women for America (CWA), 18, 19, 245, 248
Congress, U.S., 39, 40, 213, 219
Conn, Joe, 187
Connecticut General Statutes, 200
Conservative, 13, 22, 209
Conservative Christian, 20, 199
Conservative Digest, 193
Constitution (U.S.), 13, 151, 154, 155, 183, 203, 205, 213, 254, 265, 289
Control Q, 185
Cook, Janet, 220
Cooper, Ralph, 61
Copake Pharmacy, 163
Coppes, Leonard, 11, 231
COR, 12, 13, 14, 17, 20, 21, 23, 232, 237, 240, 248, 249, 256, 258. *See also* Coalition on Revival
COR-affiliates, 20
County council seats, 18
County government, 13, 15
County laws, 15
County supervisors, 14
Courage to Divorce, 159
Courts, 16
C. Porteous & Son, 27
Creationism, 19
Crenshaw Christian Center, 270
Crescent Hotel Group, 291–292
Crowell, Harold, 187
Crystal Cathedral, 271
"Cults and Isms," 93, 102

Cumberland Farms, 190, 194, 200

Dairy Mart Convenience Stores, Inc., 285–289
Dalton, B. (bookstore), 262
Damascus, 242, 247
D'Amato, Cus, 170
Dancing in the Spirit, 98
Daniels, Forrest Ann, 191
D'Antonio, Michael, 9
Dare to Discipline, 139, 271
Dark Continent, 173
Dart, John, 106
Davenport, James, 278
Day O'Connor, Sandra, 206
Death, 64, 65, 96, 271
Death penalty, 11, 15, 249, 251, 252, 257, 260–263
"Death Valley Days," 33
Debate Over Christian Reconstruction, The, 258
Decalogue (see Ten Commandments), 253
Decision, 117
DeMar, Gary, 255, 256, 261–262, 265
Democrats, 180
Demon influence, 136
Demon of chance, 135
Demon of greed, 135
Demon of lust, 135
Demon of violence, 135
Demon possessed, 134
Demon possession, 134, 190
Demon spirits, 135
Demonized, 135, 141
Demonology, 135, 271
Demons, 134–137, 141, 149, 176
Denver, John, 123
Denver University, 24
Department of Justice, U.S., 274

Department of Water and Power, Los Angeles, 120, 122–125, 129, 132, 142
DeRuzzio, Investigator Bobby, 163, 164, 166, 168, 169
Detroit Free Press, 279
Devil, 35, 42, 158, 190, 196, 204, 220, 225
Dewey, Thomas E., 50, 124
Disciples, 144, 145
Discipleship, 144, 145, 149, 271
Disney, 45, 100, 151, 202, 278
Divine healing, 177
Divine revelation, 34
Dobson, Dr. James, 19, 20, 22, 139, 214, 271
Dodds, Agnes, 27
Domino Pizza, 277
"Donahue," 217
Donahue, Phil, 223
"Don Wildmon Report," 189
Downey, Jr., Morton, 217, 218, 226, 227
Drug(s), 101, 105, 160, 161, 167, 171, 234
Drug abuse, 58
Duchardt, John, 40
Ducille, Cecil, 131, 133
Durfield, Kimberli, 140
Durfield, Renee, 139, 271
Durfield, Richard (Ric), 80, 145, 155, 270, 271
Durfields, the, 119, 134, 139, 173

Eagle Rock Assembly, 132
Easter, 208
Eastern religions, 102
Education, 11, 14, 21
Educational institutions, 15
Educational involvement, 13
Edwards, Mrs., 111

Elim Bible Institute, 152
Elim Fellowship, 152, 155, 157
Elvis, 46–47, 57
Embassy Hotel, 83
End-time, 134, 179
End-time message, 131
End-time preacher, 131
End-time prophets, 134
End-timers, 172
England, 27, 182, 237
Episcopalians, 246
Equal Access Act, 23
Erotic, 200, 249
Erotica, 194, 203
Europe, 181
Evangelical(s), 12, 18, 83, 95, 219, 223
Evangelism, 207
Evangelist, 41, 98, 100, 107, 111, 112, 114, 218, 221, 270
Evangelistic, 83, 98, 111
Evangelists, 66, 82, 177, 178, 222
Evangelize, 23, 207
Everson v. Board of Education (1947), 205
Evil spirits, 135. *See also* Demons
Evolution, 24, 194
Exorcism(s), 134–137, 219
Exorcists, 136

FBI agent, 278
Fairpark Coliseum, 133
Faith, 23, 31, 45, 179, 244
Faith Assembly, 271
Faith Center, 125
Faith healer(s), 82, 270
Fall From Grace—The Failed Crusade of the Christian Right, 9
False religions, 137
Falwell, Jerry, 9, 17, 25, 91, 182, 185–187, 193, 212, 217–225, 293

Family (Manson), 104, 124
"Family News in Focus," 214
Family Planning, 201
Farber, Barry, 211, 212
Fasting, 176, 220
Father, 36, 83, 179
Father of Reconstructionism, 12, 19, 231
Father, Son, and Holy Ghost, 226
Fear, 175
Federal agents, 291
Federal Bureau of Investigation, 292
Federal Communications Commission (FCC), 192
Federal Prison System, 192
Fife, Sam, 131, 133, 134, 172
"Fightin' fundy," 40
"Fingertips, Part II," 62
First Amendment, 203, 205–207, 254, 265, 267, 281, 289
First Amendment freedoms, 189, 206
First Amendment rights, 198
First Congressional District, 180
First Foursquare Church of Van Nuys, 100
First Hour Bible Studies, 23
Fisher, George, 277, 278
Fivefold ministry, 149
Flag-burning, 212, 213
Flame-retardant flag, 212
Flood, the, 243
Fluoridation, 184
Flynt, Larry, 220, 221
Focus on the Family, 18, 19–21, 271
Focus on the Family, 271
Folsom Prison, 104
Foot soldiers, 201
"Force," the, 150
Forceful Men, 10
Ford, Gerald, 125

Ford Motor Company, 69
Foreplay, 49
For Wedlock Only, 271
Founding Fathers, 13, 16
Foursquare church, 89, 97, 104, 108
Fourteenth Amendment, 205, 289
Fowler, Mark, 192
Franciscan nun, 36, 70
Freedom of religion, 246
Freedom of speech, 203, 236
Freedom of the press, 203
Freedom Writer, The, 188, 190, 198, 205–208, 212–214, 222, 229–233, 240, 246, 252, 256, 262, 268, 275–278, 281, 283, 284, 289, 291, 293
Freedom Writer, The (mailing address), 244
Free Inquiry, 176
Freeman, Hobart, 134, 271
Free press, 277
Free speech, 210, 286
Fromme, Lynette (Squeaky), 125
Fuller Brush Company, 111
Full Gospel Businessmen's Fellowship International, 80, 87, 88, 132, 270
Fundamental Christianity, 175, 207
Fundamentalism, 41, 157, 209, 221, 235
Fundamentalist(s), 17, 24, 25, 40–42, 49, 80, 87, 131, 150, 175, 176, 179, 182, 183, 185, 194, 199, 201, 209, 218, 220, 222–225, 245, 248, 261, 271, 278
Fundamentalist/Pentecostal Christians, 158

Gabler, Mel, 213
Gallup (pollster), 245
Gambling, 135
Garden Grove Community Church, 143

Gardner, Martin, 176
Gateway, The, 28, 37, 64
Gay, 19
Gay rights, 15
Gays, 58, 119, 186, 231, 232, 237
Geer, Michael, 20, 21
General Mills, 277
Genesis, 19, 220
"Gentleman's Y," 56
George Washington University, 273, 280
"Geraldo," 217
German, 12, 176
German evangelist, 10
Germany, 12, 267
Gideons, 207
"Gifts of the Spirit," 176
Glad Tidings (Vancouver), 119
Glad Tidings Tabernacle (Los Angeles), 108, 109, 119, 120, 125
Global education, 24
Glossolalia, 176
Glossolate, 176
"God and Country," 151, 202, 183
God in Government, 262
"God language," 183
God the Father, 187
God the Holy Spirit, 187
God the Son, 187
"God's anointing," 200
God's Commandments, 288
God's kingdom, 12
God's law, 11, 151, 155, 196
God's mind, 16
God's Word, 95
"Going down under the power," 83
Golden Gloves, 42
Golden Rule, 253
"Golden Swan," 167, 168, 169
Golden Tablets, 93

Gonzales, Paul, 229, 233, 241
Good Friday, 208
"Good people," 285, 286
Good, Sandra, 104
Gospel(s), 92, 93, 178, 179, 194, 220
Gospel concerts, 153
Gospel musical, 151
Gospel of John, 45
Gospel radio station, 189
Gospel singing, 77
Gospel songs, 75, 97
Governor of New York, 50
Graham, Billy, 40, 41, 46, 106, 111ff., 125, 149, 269
Grand Central Station, 56
Grange Hall (Madison, Connecticut), 197, 198
Grant, Bob, 211
Gray, Karen, 278
Great Barrington NFD, 190, 279
Great Britain, 182
Greyhound, 134, 156
Grimes, Albert, 131
Grimstead, Jay, 12–14, 16, 236, 240, 248, 249, 252, 257–259, 261, 265, 266
Guilt, 39, 58, 100, 175
Guyana, South America, 171

Hackett, Maxx, 211
Hagin, Kenneth, 107, 270
Hall of Justice (Los Angeles), 124
Harbor Freeway, 121
Harvest Fields Missionary and Evangelistic Association, 108, 109
Hayford, Jack, 95–97, 100, 108, 151, 270
Healing(s), 149, 207
Healing evangelist(s), 80, 98, 177, 178, 270

Healing meetings, 83, 177
Hearst, William Randolph, 111
Heaven, 34, 57, 64, 65, 103, 111, 154, 200, 201, 270
Heavyweight champ of the world, 170
Hebrew Republic, The, 187
Hell, 41, 49, 65, 103, 136, 154, 203, 281
"Helter Skelter," 125
Herald Express, 112
Heterosexual(s), 254, 281
High-school ministry, 23
Hillsdale Library, 27, 57
Hillsdale Methodist Church, 28
Hippie, 101
Hitler, Adolf, 71, 234, 240, 267
Hodgkins, State Representative Christopher, 184
Hoffman, Bernie Lazar (Tony Alamo), 270
Holiday Inn, 192, 283
Hollywood, 72, 100–107, 227, 273, 280, 281
Hollywood Freeway, 83, 90, 91
Hollywood Hills, 105
Holy Bible, 31, 93
Holy Communion, 36
Holy Ghost, 36, 83, 120, 201
"Holy Ghost SWAT teams," 23
Holy Roller, 98, 197, 238
Holy Spirit, 13, 81, 87, 90, 91, 95, 97–100, 102, 120, 124, 152, 198, 263
Home Invaders, The, 195, 273, 274, 281
Homosexual(s), 11, 12, 15, 58, 202, 119, 200, 220, 230–235, 241, 243, 247–249, 251–264
Homosexuality, 11, 15, 58, 119, 231, 240, 252, 254, 258–261, 264
Hong Kong Crusade (Billy Graham), 269

Horoscope, 136
"Hound Dog," 47
House Banking Committee, 292
How to Elect Christians to Public Office, 25
Hudson Bible classes, 150
Humanism, 24, 182, 195, 196, 253, 281
Humanist(s), 182, 195
Humanistic, 178, 200, 243, 250
Humanistic society, 11
Hussein, Saddam, 71
Hustler, 210, 221
Hymns, 29, 97

Idols, 36
If My People, 151, 152, 202
"I love Jesus" Bible, 57
"In God We Trust," 40
Independent, The, 149, 154, 157, 171
India, 132, 146
Indian(s), 92, 132
Inglis, Bob, 56
Inman, Charlie, 167
Innes, Roy, 226
Institute for First Amendment Studies, Inc., 25, 206
Intermountain Express, 171
Internal Revenue Service, 292
International Dateline, 211
International relations (global education), 24
Iran, 234
Iran-Contra, 219
Iraq, 234
Isaac, 31, 32
Isaiah, 58, 199

Jackson, Jesse, 284
Jackson Clarion Ledger, 194, 282
James, Jesse, 35

304   Index

Japanese, 176
Jefferson, Thomas, 205
Jehovah's Witnesses, 73, 94, 107
Jenkins, Leroy, 83, 270
Jesus, 17, 23, 28-30, 36, 41, 42, 43, 45, 52, 62, 82, 84, 85, 92, 93, 95, 96, 98, 101-103, 105, 122, 124, 125, 155, 171, 178, 179, 227
Jesus Christ, 96, 114, 201, 203, 204, 219
Jesus Doesn't Live Here Anymore, 250
Jesus Seminar, 178
Jew(s), 29, 30, 63, 85, 135, 155, 179, 186, 234, 236, 237, 273, 274, 279, 283
Jewish, 29, 30, 131, 155, 170, 182, 218, 273, 280, 281, 283, 284
Jewish Defense League, 274
Jewish Orthodox, 41
Jewish Passover, 170
Johnson, Lyndon, 74
Johnson, Ron, 25
Jonah, 141
Jones, Dean, 100, 151, 152, 183, 202, 223
Jones, Isaiah ("Ike"), 80
Jones, Jim, 172
Jonestown, 171, 172
Jordan, Joe, 88, 89
Joseph and Mary, 155
Journal (Wildmon's), 275
Judaism, 170
Judaism Anonymous, 223
Judeo/Christian, 250, 251, 253
"Just As I Am," 116
Justice Department, 192, 275, 292. *See also* U.S. Department of Justice

Kainrad, Mayor Donald, 206, 286, 288, 289

KDSU, Fargo, North Dakota, 211
Keating, Charles H., 275, 291, 292, 293
Kelly, Bill, 278
Kennedy, D. James, 231, 232, 235, 236, 248, 261
Kennedy, John F., 72, 74
KGER, Long Beach, 80, 85
King, Renee, 82
KING, Seattle, 208
Kingdom of the Cults, 93
King James Bibles, 45
King James Version, 199
Knights of Malta, 237
KNUS, Denver, 208
Koch, Kurt, 134
Krushchev, Nikita, 40
Kuhlman, Kathryn, 80, 82, 98-100, 150, 270
Kuwait, 10

LaHaye, Beverly, 18, 19, 22, 245, 248, 249
LaHaye, Tim, 182, 213, 238
LaHayes, the, 231, 235, 236, 248, 249, 261, 266
Lapp, James M., 280
Last days, 131, 133
Last Judgment, 17
Last Temptation of Christ, The, 225-227, 280
Latter Rain, 88, 108, 119, 152
Laurel and Hardy, 199
Law, 14
Law courts, 14
Law of the land, 232, 254, 255
Law system, 11, 250
Layzell, Reg, 229
Leadership School, 22
Lear, Norman, 185, 283
Leavenworth, 278

Lebanon Valley Speedway, 51
Lee, A. Earl, 82
Legislation, 16
Lemon v. *Kurtzman* (1971), 206
Lenox Board of Health, 184
Lesbian(s), 60, 66, 119
"Let's Do the Twist," 49
Lewengrub, Stuart, 280, 281
Liardon, Roberts, 9
Liberal(s), 18, 194, 209
Liberal Christians, 158, 178
Liberty Baptist College, 187
Liberty Broadcasting System, 193
Liberty Federation, 293
Lichter, S. Robert, 273, 280
Lichter/Rothman study, 281, 284
LIFE Bible College, 89–91, 95, 97, 99, 100, 105, 106, 108, 150, 219, 222, 270
"Like A Prayer," 277
Lincoln Savings and Loan Association, 292
Living Bible, The, 201–204
Local government, 11, 15
Local level, 20, 22
Local sheriffs, 18
"Loony Bin," 210
Lord & Taylor, 56, 58, 60
Lord's Prayer, 40
Los Angeles County Sheriff's deputies, 101
Los Angeles Department of Water, 120, 123. *See also* Department of Water and Power
Los Angeles Harbor College, 85
Los Angeles Herald Examiner, 112
Los Angeles International Airport (LAX), 86
Los Angeles Times, 101, 103, 106
Lot, 202, 220, 222

Lovett, C. S., 95
Lutheran, 134, 146
Lynch v. *Donnelly* (1984), 206

Mabley, Mums, 62
Maddox, Robert, 187
Madison, James, 254
Madonna, 277
Mafia, 200
Magic eyeglasses, 93
Mahaiwe Theater, 46
"Man-in-the-trunk," 163
Manson, Charles, 103, 104, 124, 125
Manson Family, 104
"Manson girls" (listed), 124
Mars, 160
Martelli, John, 187
Martin, Walter, 93
Marx, Karl, 253
Marxism, 253
Mary, 36
Mary and Joseph, 263
Mass, 37
Massachusetts Moral Majority, 187
Masturbation, 38, 108, 194, 220
May, John L., 276, 280
Mayor Kainrad, 287
MCA, 227, 280
McCarthy, Senator Joseph, 39, 209
McGee, J. Vernon, 80, 87
McPherson, Aimee Semple, 89, 99, 219
Meese, Ed, 193
Melodyland (Christian Center), 98, 143
Menendez, Al, 187
Mennonite Church, 280
Messiah, 29
Methodist(s), 29, 194
Methodist church, 45, 66, 77, 80
Methodist Sunday School, 45
Metropolitan (Opera), 63

Index

Mexican ministry, 143
Mexico, 132
Michael Farris, 19
Mickey Mouse, 45
"Mid-day Magazine," 181
Militancy, 10
"Militant Church Conference," 10
Militia(s), 13, 15, 233
Mind-control, 207
Mind of the Bible Believer, The, 218
Minnery, Tom, 21
Miracle Valley, 82
Missionaries, 85, 86
Money, 18, 152, 239
Moon, Sun Myung, 17
Moonies, 219
Moorehouse, Ruth Ann (Ouisch), 125
Moral Majority, 9, 185–187, 223, 231, 293
Morality In Media, 193, 198
Mormon(s), 33, 34, 91, 92, 94, 159
Mormon crickets, 34
Mormon Elders, 93
Mormonism, 34
Moroni, 93
Mort! Mort! Mort!, 228
"Morton Downey, Jr. Show," 213, 217, 224–227
Mother Jones, 257
Mother of God, 36
Mother Superior, 36
Mumford, Bob, 126
Muslim, 63, 235
Musson, Fred, 146

NACE/CEE, 24
"Name it and claim it" evangelist, 107
Name of Jesus, 135, 136, 177
National Association of Christian Educators (NACE), 23
National Conference of Catholic Bishops, 276, 280
National Educational Association (NEA), 24
National Endowment for the Arts, 257
National Enquirer, 277
National Federation for Decency (NFD), 189, 198, 275, 276, 279, 293
National Guard, 121
National Organization for Women, 19
"National Police Week," 160
National politics, 10, 21
National Religious Broadcasters (NRB), 18
National Republican Convention (Dallas), 180, 181
Native Americans, 92
Nautilus (submarine), 39
Nazi, 236, 237
NBC, 20, 277
Neo-Pentecostalism, 88
New Age religions, 210
Newark International Airport, 182
"New creature," 41
New England, 31
New Look, 210
Newman, Anne, 24
"New Radical Religious Right, The," 229
New Republic, The, 291
New Testament, 29, 45, 81, 95–97, 102, 134, 178, 179, 202, 263
New World, 92, 93
New York State Thruway, 50
New York Times, The, 10, 182, 186, 208, 213
NFD, 190, 191, 193, 194, 276, 277–279. *See also* National Federation for Decency
NFD/AFA, 190

NFD Chapter Newsletter, 190
NFD Journal, 191, 195, 273, 276–279
"9BP" (Nine Broadcast Plaza), 213
Nirenberg, Charles, 285, 287, 288, 289
Noah, 243
"No Hope Street," 123
"Northeast Dateline," 181
Northeast Mississippi Daily Journal, 194, 279, 282
Northeastern New York Speech Center, 48
Northside school board, 24
North Vietnam, 72
North Vietnamese, 71
Nun(s), 37, 70, 36, 37

O'Hair, Madalyn Murray, 225
Occult, 137
Offering(s), 78
Oh, God!, 123
Oklahomans Against Pornography, 193
Old and New Testament, 45, 240
Old and New Worlds, 93
Old Ranger, 33
Old Testament, 179, 240, 247, 251, 256
Old World, 92, 93
"One Nation Under God," 183
"Onward, Christian Soldiers!", 201
Open Bible, The, 158
"Oprah," 217
Organized crime, 135
Orgasms, 176
Orlando Christian Center, 10
Orthodox Presbyterian church, 11, 232
Ortiz, Juan Carlos, 144, 145, 271
Ouija board, 136
Overgaard, Robert M., 280
Owens, Jimmy and Carol, 151, 152

Pacific Telephone, 85
Palm Sunday, 29
Pan America Art School, 56, 57, 60
"Panhandler of the Month," 224
Parham, Charles F., 88
"Pastor Porteous Shares," 157
Paul, Apostle, 85, 179, 240, 241, 242, 247
Penance, 37
Pennsylvania Family Institute, 20
Pennsylvanians Against Pornography, 21
Pentecostal(s), 17, 25, 82, 87, 88, 97, 105, 119, 129, 135, 146, 149, 150, 153, 155, 172, 176–178, 218, 219, 231, 247, 256, 258
Pentecostal/Charismatic, 176, 270
Pentecostalism, 88, 219
Penthouse, 15, 190, 192, 193, 195, 203, 204, 210, 218, 221, 274, 275, 277, 278, 281, 283
"People Are Talking," 185, 187, 213
People For the American Way, 185, 187, 281, 283, 284
People's Tabernacle of Faith, 76, 77, 80, 81, 89, 119, 121, 147
Pepsi, 277
Pepsico, 277
Personal Evangelism, 95
"Personal separation," 42
Pillionel, Jacques, 57
Playboy, 15, 98, 190, 192–195, 200, 203, 204, 210, 221, 235, 274, 275, 285
Playboy Club, 105
Playboy Foundation, 283
Pledge of Allegiance, 39
Podesta, Anthony, 187, 188
Polanski, Roman, 104
Political action, 24
Political action groups, 18

Political activism, 25
Political freedom, 246
Political involvement, 13
Political process, 202
Political training seminar, 18, 22
Politics, 154
Polygamy, 34
Porn Commission, 193
Pornographers, 11, 255
Pornographic, 195, 201, 202, 221, 222, 286
Pornographic Bible stories, 222
Pornography, 11, 15, 17, 115, 135, 190, 193, 196, 198–200, 221, 240, 255, 274, 276, 277, 278, 283, 284, 286
"Pornography in the Family Marketplace," 275
Port Authority, 182
Porteous, Charles Edward, 27
Porteous, Charles R., 282, 283
Porteous, Marian, 271
Porteous, Reverend Charles, 201
Porteous, Skipp, 207, 213, 218, 227, 230, 233, 237, 240, 244, 246, 251, 256–258, 261, 263–265, 279, 283, 289, 291
"Power in the Blood," 80, 81
Pray, 12, 19, 23, 24, 28, 42, 151, 190, 200
Prayed, 34, 36, 50, 81, 115, 129, 130, 144, 175
Prayer(s), 12, 19, 24, 28, 34, 40, 42, 71, 102, 108, 115, 129, 144, 175, 176, 199, 220, 265
Prayer in school, 230
Prayer meeting, 81, 153, 158, 176, 198, 204
Prayer of faith, 81, 177, 178
Presbyterian(s), 12, 187, 231, 246
President of the United States, 20, 179, 184, 254
Presley, Elvis, 46, 189
Price, Frederick K., 107, 270
Priests, 36
Prince, Derek, 135
Pro-censorship, 292
Proctor & Gamble, 130, 131
Prometheus, 240
Proper, Sheriff Paul, 160, 168–170, 172
Property taxes, 11
Prophecy, 10, 159, 179, 181, 202
Pro-slavery, 240
"Prosperity" evangelist, 107
Protestant religious right, 237
Protestantism, 36
Protocols of the Learned Elders of Zion, 131
Providence Church, 11
Public education, 23, 24
Public school(s), 23, 18, 23, 24, 186, 227, 276
"Puff Graham," 111
Pulitzer Prize, 220

Racist, 179
Radio Shack, 208
Rae, Dan, 187
Ralston-Purina, 277
Rantel, Al, 212
Rapture, 83, 84, 179
Reagan, Ronald, 20, 22, 179–181, 193
Reconstruction, 17, 241, 251, 261. *See also* Christian Reconstruction
Reconstructionism, 10, 11, 257
Reconstructionist(s), 10, 11, 13, 15, 230, 231, 233, 234, 237, 238, 245, 246, 251–257, 258, 260, 261, 263, 264, 266
Reduction of Christianity, The, 257, 262

Reed, Ralph, 21, 22
Reformed Church, 150, 152
"Reformed Hieroglyphics," 93
Regent University, 21
Reid, J. Filson, 72
Reincarnation, 102
Reisman, Dr. Judith, 283
Religion, 28, 30, 58, 62, 63, 130, 133, 147, 155, 175, 178, 179, 182, 199, 205, 206, 211, 265, 284
Religion, Apostle Paul's, 242
Religious, 83, 158, 183, 205, 207, 210, 224, 244, 250, 255, 265, 277, 281, 289
Religious addiction, 207
Religious books, 10
Religious broadcasting, 18
Religious displays, 19
Religious freedom, 139, 205, 238, 245, 246
Religious humanists, 182
"Religious liberty" cases, 19
Religious right, 9, 10, 12, 17, 18, 20, 21, 25, 184, 196, 206–208, 210, 213, 218, 225, 230, 231, 240, 277
Republican(s), 20, 172, 180, 183, 184
Republican Convention, 223
Republican National Convention, 182
Republican Party, 182
Resurrection of the dead, 17
Revelation, book of, 103
Revised Standard Version, 45
Rex Communications, 208
Reynolds v. *United States* (1878), 205
Rise and Fall of the Third Reich, The, 30
Robbins, Jodie, 22
Roberts, Oral, 82, 224
Robertson, Dede, 42, 201
Robertson, Pat, 11, 17, 21–23, 25, 42, 201, 202, 213, 214, 221, 222, 239
Rock and roll, 105
Rock Church, 198
Rockwell, Norman, 55, 153, 154
Roe Jan Diner, 49
"Roe v. Wade" (TV movie), 277
Roe v. *Wade*, 19
Rogers, Neil, 212
Roman Catholic(s), 223
Roman Catholic church, 185
Roman Catholicism, 36
Roman Catholics Anonymous, 223
Ronettes, the, 62
Rooney, Kevin, 170
Rosary, 38
Ross, Diana (and the Supremes), 62
Rothman, Stanley, 273, 280, 281
Ruler of the Nations, 262, 265
Running for office, 14
Rushdoony, Rousas John, 12, 19, 231, 252
Russia, 250
Russian spies, 39
Rutherford Institute, 19

Sabbath, 37, 41, 254
Sagan, Carl, 238
Saint(s), 36, 38
Saint Anthony, 38
Saint Augustine, 127
Saint Bridget's church, 37
Saks Fifth Avenue, 56, 60, 61, 62, 66, 72, 73
"Sally" (Jessy Raphael), 217
San Bernardino Freeway, 142
San Gabriel Valley Christian Center, 271
San Jose Mercury, 14
San Simeon, 111
Santa Claus, 82, 225

310   Index

Satan, 17, 30, 104, 158, 210, 247
Satanic, 130, 141
Satanism, 131
Satanist, 130
"Saturday Night Live," 277
Saudi Arabia, 234
Saul/Paul, 179
Savings and Loan scandal, 275
Sayonara, 46
Schaeffer, Franky, 231
"Schizoid tendencies," 42
Schmid, Gerhard, 180
Schmid, Lilliane, 180-184
Schneider, Abe, 85, 86, 102
School board(s), 22, 24, 154, 239
School board candidates, 239
School councils, 22
School districts, 24
School prayer, 19, 276
Schuller, Robert, 143, 271
Scofield Reference Bible, 83
Scorsese, Martin, 227
Scripture(s), 12, 30, 78, 83, 96, 97, 102, 139, 178, 187, 196, 219, 259, 263
Sears, Alan, 274, 275, 292
Second Coming, 28, 100, 158, 202
Secular, 206, 281, 284
Secular humanism, 182, 195, 196
Secular humanist, 182, 238, 246, 247, 261
Secular humanistic system, 141
Secular nation, 190, 196
Securities and Exchange Commission, 292
Separation of church and state, 154, 182, 183, 185, 205 (definition), 205-208, 211, 230, 233, 246, 252, 265, 266, 269, 289
Separation of powers, 20
Sequeira, Antonia (Tiny), 197, 199, 202

7-Eleven, 275, 277
"700 Club," 22, 214
Sex, 33, 38, 42, 48, 49, 70, 105, 195, 196, 220, 234, 277, 281, 284
Sex appeal, 115
Sex education, 18, 23, 201, 276
Sexism, 60
Sexist, 179
Sexual, 38, 39, 48, 69, 194, 201, 210, 263, 277, 286, 288
Sexual/gender orientation, 24
Sexuality, 38, 46, 48, 194, 286
Seymour, William J., 88
Shakarian, Demos, 80, 270
Shakers, 34
Shaklee, 130
Sharpton, Al, 226
"Sheep," 40
Shepherding, 145, 271
Sheriff's Department (Columbia County, New York), 161, 169
Sherman, Rob, 225, 226
Sherrill, John, 88
Shire, William L., 30
Shrine Auditorium, 98
Sienna College, 152
Sikh, 235
Silvernail, Linda, 72
Simon, Barbara, 170-173, 179, 181, 182, 186-188, 198-201, 203, 206, 212, 283
Simon, Porteous & Associates, Inc., 275, 279, 282, 283
Simon's Rock of Bard College, 183
Simonds, Kathi, 25
Simonds, Robert L., 23, 24, 25
Sin, 17, 102, 112, 114, 125, 154, 179, 196, 220, 252
Sinful, 196, 252
Sinner(s), 41, 102, 243, 252

Sins, 82, 92, 114, 179, 239
"Sin sells religion," 179
Sister Carmencita, 37, 38
Sister Mary Robert, 36, 37
Skinheads, 227
"Skipp's church," 132
Sky Pilot Choir, 80
"Slain in the Spirit," 83, 89, 150
Slater, Christian, 185
Slater, Mary Jo, 185, 186
Slavery, 242, 247
Slaves, 242
Smith, Joseph, 34, 93
Smith College, 273, 280
Sodomy, 259, 261
Soldiers," 41
Son, 83
Son of God, 103
Soul-winner(s), 41, 95
Soul-winning, 95, 100, 102
"Sound Off," 229
South Africa, 173
South America, 134, 172
South Vietnam, 72
Southern Baptist, 57
Southern Baptist Convention, 246
Southland Corporation, 193, 275, 277
Soviet Union, 39, 40
Spanish Armada, 48
Speaking in tongues, 81, 87–89, 176
Spencer, Carlton, 155
Spirit, 120
Spirit of lust, 135, 219
Spirit of witchcraft, 135
Spirits, testing, 203
Stafford, Archbishop, 279
Stag, 200
"Star-Spangled Banner," 63
Star Wars, 150
State capital, 20

State Elections Division, Boston, 184
State legislators, 19, 20
State legislatures, 22
State level, 20, 21
State Line bar, 168
State University of New York, 169
Steiner, Rudolf, 159
Steve Allen on the Bible, Religion, & Morality, 240
Strang, Stephen, 23
Strange language, 79, 81, 88, 89
Stratford Coalition Against Pornography, 197
Strip, the, 101, 103
Strode children, 227
Stuart-Bell, Derek, 61
Suicide, 58, 137
Summey, Lt. Arthur, 278
Sunday school, 29, 30, 32, 41, 104, 108, 221
Sunday school Bible, 30
Sunset Strip, 101, 104–106
Superior Court, Santa Monica, 80, 83
Supreme Court (U.S.), 19, 23, 212–214, 220, 260
Surviving College Successfully, 262
Swaggart, Jimmy, 214, 218, 219, 222, 224
Swahili, 81
Sweden, 105
Sword, 112
"Sword drills," 30
"Sword of the Lord," 30
Szoka, Edmund, 279

"Take It By Force" conference, 10
Tancredo, Thomas G., 24
Task Force '84, 180, 183
Tate, Sharon, 104
Tax-exemptions for churches, 19

Teen evangelism, 23
Teen marriages, 72
Teens, 23, 105
Televangelist scandals, 214
Television, 33, 39, 150, 273, 280, 281, 284
Television evangelism, 219, 293
Television evangelists. *See* TV evangelists
Ten Commandments, 250, 253
Terkel, Studs, 176
Theocracy, 232, 234
Theology, 32
"Theology of Christian Activism," 256
They Speak With Other Tongues, 88
Thomas Nelson (publishers), 158
Thompson, Jack, 21
Tilton, Robert, 11
Times Square, 66, 198, 203
Tithe(s), 42, 78
Tithers, 86
"To the Jew first," 85
Tongues, 88, 97, 135, 176
Toole, Thomas A., 180, 183, 184
"Topics of The Times," 213
Tract(s), 23, 87, 112, 131, 154
Traditional values, 13
Transamerica Corporation, 90
"Troops," 10, 23, 207
Truman, Harry S., 50
"Tupelo Ayatollah," 194
Tupelo Police Department, 194, 282
TV evangelism, 218
TV evangelists, 9, 158, 231, 293
2 Live Crew, 21
Tyson, Mike, 170

"Under God," 40
Unification Church, 17
United Methodist Church, 72, 189

"USA Confidential," 217
U.S. Attorneys, 21
U.S. Department of Education, 24
U.S. Department of Justice, 275, 277. *See also* Justice Department
U.S. Government, 277
U.S. Senators ("Keating Five"), 292
U.S. Supreme Court, 213. *See also* Supreme Court

Values clarification, 24
"Vast wasteland," 215
Vergara, Edward, 282
Victor Books, 274
Vienna Boys Choir, 47
Vietnam, 71, 73, 74, 91
Vietnam War, 71, 91
Viguerie, Richard, 192
Villagio Italia, 67, 69–72
Violence, 33, 195, 210
Virginity, 271
VITAL Ministries, Inc., 153
Vote, 13, 14
Voters, 22

WABC, New York, 211, 214
Waldenbooks, 262
Waldo, Dr. Irma, 146, 155
Waldorf School, 159
Walk Away, 207
Walk of Fame, 269
Walt Disney World, 10
WAMC, Albany, 181, 182, 207
Warhol, Andy, 212
Washington (D.C.), 20, 22
Washington Post, 207, 214, 220
Watchtower, 73
Watergate, 219
Watts, 121, 122
WBAL, Baltimore, 215

WBZ-TV, Boston, 185, 213
WCKY, Cincinnati, 208
"We Lift Our Voices Rejoicing," 270
West Copake (Dutch) Reformed Church, 146, 150, 153, 154
Western Massachusetts, 180
WGOW, Chattanooga, 211
Where Did I Come From?, 201
Whitehead, John, 19, 231, 252, 261
White House, 193, 219
Whittaker Corporation, 87, 90
Who's Who, 12
WHUC, Hudson, 133
Widmark, Don, 125, 133, 143
Wigglesworth, Carl, 209
Wildmon, Allen, 190–193, 194, 195
Wildmon, Donald E. (Rev.), 12, 22, 190, 191–195, 196, 198, 225, 227, 231, 236, 246, 257, 261, 266, 273, 274–284, 293
Wildmon, Tim, 194, 213
Wilkerson, Ralph, 98
Williams, Jerry, 214
Williams, Kathi, 19
"Win Your Campus to Christ," 23
WINZ, Miami, 212
Witch-hunt, 198
Witness, 42, 154
Witnesses (Jehovah's), 73
Witnessing, 85, 102
WLW, Cincinnati, 210
WNWS, Miami, 212, 273, 274, 283
WOAI, San Antonio, 209
Women's Aglow Fellowship, 201
Wonder, Little Stevie, 62

Word of Faith World Outreach Center, 11
Word of God, 13, 92, 95, 112, 141, 151, 152, 199
Word of Life Boxing Champ, 42, 170, 221
Word of Life Ranch, 41, 42, 45, 201, 221
World Christian Encyclopedia, 18
Worldwide Church of God, 80
World Wide Pictures, 112, 125
WRKO, Boston, 214
WSB, Atlanta, 229
WSBS, Great Barrington, 172
WSIX, Nashville, 209
WTNS, Coshocton, 208
WUPE/WUHN, Pittsfield, 172
WWCN, Albany, 207
WWOR, Secaucus, 217, 218, 225, 227
Wyatt, Thomas, 119
Wyrtsen, Jack, 41

X-rated movies, 278

Year 2000, 9, 10
YMCA, 56
"You Can't Take It With You," 170
Young, Brigham, 34
Young, Dale, 108, 119, 120
Young, Ryan, 198
Youth Alive, 23
Youth Invasion Ministries, 23
YWCA, 60

Zimbabwe, 173